D1592572

Conference Papers Series
No. 13

The International Legacy of Lehendakari Jose A. Agirre's Government

Edited by Xabier Irujo and Mari Jose Olaziregi

Center for Basque Studies Press
University of Nevada, Reno

This book was published with generous financial assistance from the Basque Government

Conference Papers Series, No. 13
Series Editor: Xabier Irujo
Center for Basque Studies
University of Nevada, Reno
Reno, Nevada 89557
http://basque.unr.edu

Copyright © 2017 by Center for Basque Studies
All rights reserved. Printed in the United States of America.
Cover photo: Jose Antonio Agirre Lekube's speech during Aberri Eguna, Day of the Basque Homeland, 1933 in Maitea Jai-Alai, Donostia-San Sebastián, Gipuzkoa, Basque Country.
Photo source: Wikimedia Commons, via Fondo Foto Car. Ricardo Martin
Book design: Daniel Montero

Library of Congress Cataloging-in-Publication Data
Names: Olaziregi, Mari Jose, editor of compilation. | Irujo Ametzaga, Xabier, editor of compilation.
Title: The international legacy of Lehendakari Jose A. Agirre's government / edited by Mari Jose Olaziregi and Xabier Irujo.
Description: Reno, NV : University of Nevada, Reno, [2017] | Series: Conference papers series ; no. 13 | Includes bibliographical references and index.
Identifiers: LCCN 2017019539 | ISBN 9781935709817 (pbk. : alk. paper)
Subjects: LCSH: Aguirre y Lecube, José Antonio de, 1904-1960--Exile. | País Vasco (Spain)--History--Autonomy and independence movements. | Spain--History--Civil War, 1936-1939--Governments in exile. | Nationalists--Spain--País Vasco--Biography. | Presidents--Spain--País Vasco--Biography. | Basques--Foreign countries--Biography. | Political refugees--Spain--Biography.
Classification: LCC DP302.B43 A4846 2017 | DDC 946/.6081092 [B] --dc23
LC record available at https://na01.safelinks.protection.outlook.com/?url=https%3A%2F%-2Flccn.loc.gov%2F2017019539&data=01%7C01%7Cdmontero%40unr.edu%-7C0a216fdff267407f2f6008d4c3ebe529%7C523b4bfc0ebd4c03b2b96f6a17fd31d8%7C1&s data=ysqv2SGOwlm9WzMAvcwon%2FVV9Gr%2Bv%2Fo3L6%2FQRz03XiE%3D&res-erved=0

Contents

The International Legacy of Lehendakari Agirre's Government

Juan J. Ibarretxe

Jose Antonio Agirre's first instruction to the newly formed Basque government back in 1936, right before a few months of work followed by years of exile, was to get to work: "*Todos al trabajo para completar la organización del país y construirlo en instrumento apto de lucha en el frente y ejemplo de civilidad en la retanguardia,*" meaning "Everyone get to work, in order to complete the country's organization and turn it into a tool for fighting on the front, whilst being an example of civility in the rearguard."

And, as we say in Basque, *katea ez da eten* (the chain is not broken). In fact, both Lehendakari Agirre and I spoke here at Columbia about the very same Basque Country, the country that was presented here in the United States as an example by President John Adams, when the United States Constitution was drafted in 1786:[1] "this extraordinary people [Basques] have preserved their ancient language, genius, laws, government, and manners, without innovation, longer than any other nation of Europe."

We are speaking indeed about people at the forefront of Europe. According to the latest European data in relation to the Gini Index in 2012, we occupied the second position after Sweden in the ranking, with an index of 25.3 at the time. Now, in 2016, it is over 27.8. And all of that taking into account that, at the end of the 1970s, the Basque Country was emerging from forty years of dictatorship in which any expression of Basque culture had been repressed.

---

1. John Adams, *A Defence of the Constitutions of Government of the United States of America* (Philadelphia: Printed for Hall and Sellers, 1787).

At the time, we were undergoing a serious economic crisis, with unemployment at around 30 percent and an international image connected with terrorist violence. Despite these circumstances, the Basque Country managed to transform its economy in in a supportive way, and is now ranked highly in healthcare, education, and income per capita.

The Human Factor

The history of the Basque Country within the last thirty years has indeed been a story of radical (and successful) transformation. However, the clearest example to understand this social, political, and economic conversion lies in the data relating to human capital: back in the 1980s over 80 percent of the population had only primary studies, and according to the data from the last few years, since 2013, 85 percent of the population has acquired secondary or university studies.

Human capital is essential to sustainable development, it is as simple as that. We must build all our efforts on this principle, especially in a world in which the rights and freedom of individuals are at stake, with the migrant crisis in Europe, wars, and shortages of medicines, with more than 70 percent of the world population without social protection and more than 40 percent without any kind of health protection. According to the latest data, 1 percent of the world population, the richest group, owns more wealth than the remaining 99 percent. As Pope Francis recently stated in the *Evangelii Gaudium*, human rights are not only violated due to the terrorist attacks, but inequality is today the most influential factor in generating structural human rights violations.

It is not only an economic and human disaster, but also an ethical disaster, because we currently face a cultural crisis behind the financial crisis. A recent linguistic study by Stanford University offers a clear example of this: by the end of the twenty-first century, only 500 out of the more than 5,000 languages that exist today will survive. I am at least convinced that the Basque language will be one of those. We speak about universal culture, but what is the real meaning of a universal culture if it is not understood as a collective expression of local cultures?

Roots and Wings

Whatever the case, we cannot start to solve any of these questions without some diagnosis. As the philosopher José Ortega y Gasset said, "we do not know what the matter is and that is precisely the matter." If a physician has no diagnosis for a patient it is very difficult to treat that patient, and that is the same rule applies for economic and political issues.

And this is, in fact, the target of Agirre Lehendakaria Center, a University of the Basque Country powered project created in 2013 in collaboration with Columbia University and aimed at providing a better understanding of what is happening, not only in the Basque Country but all around the world. Our work up to now has been focused on relating the economic agenda to the social, cultural, and environmental agendas, looking up at the world to see the Basque Country.

What we have learned in the last three years is that to be in a global society, to put our country on the map, you need a local approach. We speak about a polynomic, about this formula for the future: R + D + I + K (Research, development, identity, and culture – with a "k" from *kultura*, "culture" in Basque).

And this can be applied to different countries and nations worldwide, not only to the Basque Country. Each one has their own "key" of *kultura*, and if we do not act with our own "k" the polynomic does not work. Identity and innovation are roots and wings for sustainable human development. In our case, to understand the sociopolitical transformation of the Basque Country, we need to take into account the fact that the Basque identity, culture, and language are at the core of our sustainable human development model.

Our motto is thus "the K is the key," and this is not only the position of the Agirre Lehendakaria Center for the Basque Country; it has been also stated by United Nations, by the Administrator of the UN Development Program (UNDP) and former Prime Minister of New Zealand for ten years, Helen Clarke, who says that culture is a vital aspect of human development.

The central question is learning from our own past, roots, and traditions to build the future. And this is a truly important question in relation to Lehendakari Agirre's ideas, because we work not only for preserving his legacy, his myth, but also his ideas. In my opinion, if you only vindicate the myth, the symbol, and not the ideas, that means nothing.

Modern Ideas in an Old World

Jose Antonio Agirre is an essential figure, not only in the Basque Country but here at Columbia University as well, where he was Professor of the Contemporary History of Europe between 1942 and 1946.

He was really thankful because those years would offer him the opportunity to speak up on behalf of the Basque people. On September 25, 1941, he wrote in his diary, in relation to his decision to move to the US: "first thing in the morning, before 8:00 AM, we received a cable from Inchausti, fighter and friend, he has obtained my nomination as Professor at Columbia University." For him this was "incredible news."

After giving his first lesson as a professor at Columbia in 1942, he wrote: "I have started my first class, my first lesson in English. An Argentinian lady has been a great comfort, when she showed me the notes she had taken following my explanations. I very much doubted that they would understand me, but they did."

He was indeed glad to be able to open the Basque Country to the world. And we have the same objective in 2016 at the Agirre Lehendakaria Center. We must pass on what we have learned. In sum, both Agirre in the past and we now want to answer a simple question: "is another world possible?" You can construct the world from a position of power or choose to find a clear response in order to guarantee the right of individuals and peoples, which is the dilemma that must be dealt with today. And it was the same for Lehendakari Agirre.

Ahead of His Time

Consequently, we vindicate his vision and ideas today at our research center: first, ethical principles; then democratic principles; and finally sustainable human development; this is our whole intellectual base.

In 1950 President Agirre spoke in Caracas, Venezuela, about what is referred as the "Basque Habeas Corpus" (the Sixteenth Law, Fuero de Bizcaya): "according to our written documents, since the fourteenth century no one could be arrested without a warrant by a competent judge." And in regard to democratic principles, the idea that the ancient laws or *fueros* were the Constitution of the Basque Country: "I think they are, the only one that the Basque Country has ever had, its historical rights."

And he said it in the Spanish Parliament when he defended the new Statute of Autonomy, in regard to the Basque democracy: "I accept everything . . . What I can't accept is it being said that the fueros were not freedom, were not sovereignty, were not independence, and were not homeland, because that is an historical falsehood."

Not only that. In relationship with Sustainable Human Development, there was the regulations of his family business, Chocolates Bilbaínos, which spoke about a better society, a better world. Article 15 of these regulations concerned a family wage, profit sharing, taking into account the total amount of the wages, to apply the same part of the benefits among the stakeholders of the company, accident insurance, sickness, maternity leave, and so on. That is why we vindicate now in 2016 not only the myth of this one man, but also his ideas.

Now the world has changed completely and we have to move on from knowing to understanding. And to do that, we need two things. First, we need to be all in it together (or not at all). And second, we need culture, the "k" is the key.

I would like to finish with this quote from Agirre's diary describing his feeling about his first lecture at Columbia, in which his last words were *"ahora, adelante"* (now, carry on). *Katea ez da eten.*

— Juan Jose Ibarretxe Markuartu
New York, June 9, 2016

Introduction

1936–2016: The International Legacy of Lehendakari Jose A. Agirre's Government

Xabier Irujo and Mari Jose Olaziregi

In 2016, to commemorate the seventy-fifth anniversary of the escape into exile of Lehendakari Jose Antonio Agirre (1904–1960) after the fall of the Republican government, international academic and cultural organizations such as the Etxepare Basque Institute (Basque government), the Euskal Etxea (Basque Club) of Berlin, the Center for Basque Studies at the University of Nevada, the University of Leipzig, and Columbia University organized a complete commemorative program. Among other activities, an international conference took place between March and June of 2016 in Reno, Berlin, and New York; on the other hand, the Euskal Etxea of Berlin also organized several events from May 31 to June 2 in the German city (www.agirreinberlin.eus).

The papers included in this publication were presented at the academic conference entitled "The International Legacy of Lehendakari Jose Antonio Agirre's Government," co-organized by Mari Jose Olaziregi (Etxepare Basque Institute-University of the Basque Country), Carsten Sinner (Universität Leipzig), and Xabier Irujo (William A. Douglass Center for Basque Studies at the University of Nevada, Reno.) Other institutions from the University of the Basque Country, such as the Agirre Lehendakaria Center, the Mikel Laboa Chair, and the MHLI Research Group also contributed to finance and organize those academic events.

The conference program was an integrative approach to Jose Antonio Agirre's legacy, a modern reflection on the European and universal dimensions of the first democratically legitimized president of the Basque Country, his personal and institutional relationships as well as his political, social, and cultural convictions. We could say without any doubt that it was the most important academic conference ever held on the importance and the figure of Jose Antonio Agirre, and a high level event, not only because of the quality of the speakers, but also because of the variety of topics that were studied.

This book has been organized in three different sections. The first includes the foreword penned by Juan Jose Ibarretxe, lehendakari of the Basque government from 1999 to 2009. It offers a comprehensive and thought-provoking introduction to the topics covered by the contributors of the book: the international legacy of Jose Antonio Agirre's Basque government. The two subsequent sections include chapters by experts who analyze the international relations and projection of Agirre's Government (part 1), and contributions that aim to provide a reflection on the Agirre government's cultural or academic legacy (part 2). In the following lines we will try to resume briefly the content of each contribution.

Lehendakari Juan Jose Ibarretxe, Director of the Agirre Lehendakaria Center at the University of the Basque Country, begins his reflection by quoting his counterpart Jose Antonio Agirre when, back in 1936, he asked the newly formed Basque government to work hard, "in order to complete the country's organization and turn it into a tool for fighting on the front, whilst being an example of civility in the rearguard" (sic). As Ibarretxe says, that is precisely the situation of the Basque Country at present. According to the latest European data in relation to the Gini Index, Euskadi is at the forefront of Europe. The human factor has been, as Ibarretxe argues, crucial for the remarkable social, political, and economic conversion the Basque Country has experienced in recent decades. We are speaking about a community that continues to be highly rooted in its past and its traditions and that builds its future without forgetting the roots. In the end, as Ibarretxe states, Basque identity, culture, and language are at the core of our sustainable human development model. Ibarretxe declares his admiration for Agirre and underlines that the research center named after him, the Agirre Lehendakaria Center, vindicates his vision and ideas through its research activity, a vision that could be summarized in three basic ideas: first, the ethical principle, secondly, the democratic principle, and, finally, sustainable human development.

The chapter "The Dictatorship that Emerged out of the War" by Julian Casanova, from the University of Zaragoza, opens the first part of the book with an analysis of the strategies deployed by the winners of the Spanish Civil War to endure their control and leadership after the war. The army, the Falange, and the Church represented those winners and out of them came the high-ranking leaders, the system of local power, and the loyal servants of the public administration. The enduring and harsh repression that the winners exerted at the end of the war lasted for decades, thanks, among other things, to the laws that, as Casanova underlines, the special jurisdictional bodies maintained throughout the entire dictatorship. Tyranny and cruelty were the course of action of a government absolutely loyal to the Caudillo. Casanova also analyzes the international policy that Spain followed in the 1940s, after the fall of European fascism. This policy was based on the defense of Catholicism as a basic component in the history of Spain and it served as a front for the dictatorship in that crucial period for its survival. Although Spain did not play a central role in international politics during those years, the truth is that Franco always enjoyed global sympathy and support from widespread Catholic and conservative sectors.

"Repression against Loyalist Officers in the Basque Country" is the title of the chapter by Joan Villarroya Font, from the University of Barcelona. The author begins by highlighting how concerned the plotters were in the spring of 1936, particularly Brig. Gen. Emilio Mola Vidal, with the attitude of the officers who remained loyal to Spain's Republican government. Not only a clear warning to the loyalists was posted in the Court of Instruction no. 5, but also several officials were arrested and shot by firing squads during the months that followed the uprising of Franco's army. Villarroya offers a detailed account of the dramatic repression that many of those loyalist officers suffered in different parts of the Basque Country. Among the officers who were repressed and killed, Villarroya mentions the commander of the Guardia Civil, Juan Colina Guerra, along with Lt. Col. Juan Cueto of the Carabineers, Lt. Col. Gumersindo Azcárate of the Infantry, and the Guardia Civil Capts. Eugenio García Gunilla and José Bolaños López. All held important commands in the Basque Army and were shot and killed by the Francoists when taken prisoner. Other officials that are mentioned, such as, Col. Juan Cueto Ibáñez of the Carabineers or the officers who had served in the Basque Army since the first months of the war and had, in some cases, led major units in the Spanish Republican Army, such as, Andrés Fernández-Pinerúa and Juan Ibarrola, stood trial and were found guilty, but their lives were spared. Others, such as Eugenio García Gunilla and Joaquín Vidal Munárriz, were sentenced to death and shot. The article finishes by quoting the words written by infantry officers like Lt. Col. Daniel Irezabal Goiti (Goñi) and Lt. Col. Gumersindo Azcárate Gómez before they faced the firing squad.

Xabier Irujo, Director of the Center for Basque Studies at the University of Nevada, Reno, is the author of the chapter entitled "The International Dimension of the Basque Government's Politics in Exile," which analyzes the atrocities carried out by the Spanish, German, Italian, and the Vichy regimes on Basque soil between 1936 and 1945. The author stresses that these atrocities and the war itself internationalized the political action of the Government of Euskadi led by lehendakari Jose A. Agirre. This government also made a great effort to internationalize the Basque case by launching a militantly interventionist policy in the context of World War II. On the fundamental principles of the integral defense of human rights and the rights of peoples at the international level and the defense of the rights of Basque citizens, oppressed under the dictatorship of General Franco, the Basque government opted to participate actively in World War II by creating a dense network of counter-espionage at the service of the Allies that came to count on hundreds of agents in three continents and the creation of a battalion that fought in 1945 in the last battles for the Liberation of the European continent. From 1945 onward, the Basque government actively participated in the international arena, defending the creation of a European political space respectful of human rights, a political project that would later crystallize in the creation of the European Communities and much later in the European Union.

Nicholas Rankin offers in his "Agirre: A President Hunted by the Dictatorships" a personal and moving account of Agirre's escape to America through different European cities. As the author says, this essay-like article can be considered part of a work in progress: his book about the Basques and the Allies in World War II. Rankin's narration of Agirre's runaway begins with the description of the main protagonist of the story: Agirre, a man who is described as an almost child-like optimist, an energetic and vigorous mayor of Getxo, and the charismatic young leader who modernized the PNV and who led Euzkadi in its fight before being overwhelmed in the summer of 1937 by Franco's forces, heavily supported by Hitler and Mussolini. Agirre and his family took refuge in France, where their second son, Joseba Andoni was born. Years later, World War II broke out in September 1939, and the Basque government-in-exile committed to the French and British Allies. But things were going to change radically for Agirre's family when they decided to go on vacation to Belgium and shortly after Adolf Hitler launched *Fall Gelb*, Operation Yellow, the German attack on Western Europe. The end of the story, Agirre's escape to Berlin with a Panamanian passport in the name of Dr. José Andrés Alvarez Lastra, is well known. Only on May 14, 1941, was Agirre joined in Berlin by his wife and children and on July 31, 1941 they could definitively leave Sweden on their way to America. An incredible odyssey told by Jose Antonio Agirre himself in his well-known book *Escape via Berlin*, published in English in 1945.

The chapter that follows, "Agirre in Berlin and How He Was Able to Escape the Gestapo" by historian Ingo Niebel, offers an interesting analysis of Jose Antonio Agirre's hidden days in Berlin. Niebel also contributed to the program of activities that the Euskal Etxea of Berlin organized to commemorate the seventy-fifth anniversary of Agirre's successful escape through the German heartland by translating some excerpts of Agirre's diary into German and by collecting the essential information for two historical maps that show the most important places Agirre frequented when he was in Berlin. Both the diary-excerpts and the maps can still be accessed on the website AgirreInBerlin.eus. All the details provided by Niebel show that the Gestapo could have had sufficient material and eyewitnesses, who had dealt with Agirre, for opening a file on him. If it did not happen it was because the Sipo/SD had other priorities in 1940–41. As Niebel stresses, for a German observer it seemed obvious that Jose Antonio Agirre made, under the name of José Andrés Álvarez Lastra, a normal life in Berlin and that he was close to diplomats whose countries were still not opposed to the Reich, such as Panama and Venezuela. In Niebel's opinion, the successful escape of Agirre from Berlin was possible, mainly, for two reasons. First, because he did not act as was expected and did not use the traditional escape routes, but dared to enter Hitler's Grand German Reich. Second, he could pose as a Latin American lawyer thanks to the financial and logistical support he received from both the diplomats and his Basque friends in the United States.

For his part, the topic of the relations between the Vatican and Euskadi during the conflict is analyzed by the great expert on the role of the Catholic church during the civil war, Hilari

Raguer i Suñer, from the Abbey of Montserrat. The starting point for his analysis is made up, inevitably, by establishing the human drama of a questioning of their Catholic faith that was implied for many Basques because they were fighting on the Republican side. As Raguer notes, authors like Josep M. Tarragó and François Mauriac testified to this devastating and cruel attitude toward the collective of Basque clerics and Church members in the Basque army. Raguer's reflection is based on the premise of the excellence of the diocese of Vitoria-Gasteiz prior to the conflict, and on the use of the Vatican by the rebel side to repress nationalisms like those of the Catalans and Basques by means of appointing outside bishops in their territories. The drama of Bishop Múgica of Vitoria-Gasteiz, the Castelgandolfo Speech by Pope Pius XI in 1936, and the telegram sent by the Vatican to Agirre to negotiate the surrender of Bilbao, a telegram that the lehendakari never received, all culminated in the harsh repression suffered by the Basque church following the war, a repression encouraged by the winning side until the arrival of John XXIII in the Vatican allowed, thanks to the Second Council, the beginning of a recovery as regards the justice infringed.

"How the British Administration kept Franco Neutral in World War II" by Angel Viñas, reflects on the reasons Franco had to remain in a state of neutrality/non-belligerence/neutrality during World War II. Viñas offers two reasons in his analysis. The first has to do with the economy, and especially with the state of economic prostration Spain was experiencing and the minimal interest that Hitler took in a possible Spanish entry into the war. Second, the Allies helped maintain Spain on this course. To do so, political and diplomatic action went hand in hand with economic and commercial pressure. Furthermore, there was the bribery operation: The British government gave bribes to Spanish military members who were close to Franco with the goal of influencing the dictator to keep Spain neutral. The article mentions that among the beneficiaries there were two ministers and three generals. In Viñas's opinion, the bribes were the central operation in the effort to keep Franco neutral, and he supports his argument with data on the origins of the bribes, as well as on their implementation and economic significance. With regard to the origins of the bribes, the chapter mentions the Embassy's Naval Attaché, Captain Allan Hillgarth, who transmitted to Sir Samuel Hoare, British Ambassador to Spain from 1940 to 1944, the idea of the bribery, and the important cooperation of a Spanish banker, Juan March. With regard to the economic significance of the bribes, the chapter mentions 6.5 million pounds, a really considerable amount of money.

After stating that nationalism is probably one of the most complex and intricate concepts, Ludger Mees, from the University of the Basque Country, suggests in his "Transnational Nationalism: The Basque Exile: Barcelona-Paris-New York (1936–1946)" a transnational approach to the analysis of Basque nationalism. With that aim, he focuses on the Basque nationalist exile after the defeat in the Spanish Civil War and reflects about Jose Antonio Agirre's government's transnational or even cosmopolitan strategy between 1937 (the conquest of the Basque Country by the Francoist troops) and 1946 (the settlement of the Basque government in Paris). In the end, Agirre's government's strategy aimed at building a transnational network of cooperation and at supporting the struggle against Franco and for Basque self-government, once the dictatorship had been abolished. The map of the Basque government-in-exile shows three important metropolises: Barcelona, Paris, and New York City, cities that hosted the government-in-exile and that exerted an important influence on its politics. Nevertheless, although Agirre and his colleagues were successful in building up an important transnational network, they failed, in Mees's opinion, to make any tangible political capital out of it. Be that as it may, the author concludes that, despite failure, the history of Basque nationalist cosmopolitanism in exile has a clear projection into the globalized world of the twenty-first century, in which traditional concepts and notions like sovereignty, nation, and state have been questioned.

Leyre Arrieta, from the University of Deusto, Spain, is the author of the chapter entitled "Agirre's Government and Europe's Political Construction," which analyzes the Europeanist policy of the Basque government led by José Antonio Agirre during the exile years (1945–1975). As Arrieta says, the victory of the World War II Allies and the establishment of Western liberal democracies boded well for the Basque Country and the PNV, its major party. Both fully supported a united Europe and were very active participants in its sundry forums. As Arrieta points out, the Basque government's Europeanist policy was based on what was latterly termed the Agirre Doctrine, which called for a free Euskadi in a federal and united Europe of nations. Under the leadership of Lehendakari Agirre at 11, Avenue Marceau, the Basque government's headquarters in Paris, a generation of young politicians designed a Europeanist discourse and engaged actively with pro-European figures, parties, and organizations.

The chapter that completes the first part of this book has been authored by Miren Arzalluz from the University of Deusto and the current director of the Etxepare Basque Institute. Under the title "Basque Fashion in Exile: Creativity and Innovation, from Balenciaga to Rabanne," her chapter aims to explore the way in which war and exile impacted the work of two of the most influential fashion designers of the twentieth century, the Basques Cristobal Balenciaga (1895–1972) and Paco Rabanne (1934). Forced by the Spanish Civil War to leave their native Basque Country, and compelled to confront further hardships and uncertainties during the World War II in France, they overcame adversity and stood out in the challenging scene of Paris fashion through unprecedented creativity, rigor, and innovation. Resourcefulness, adaptability, resilience, and rebelliousness forged in hardship and struggle were at the heart of some of the most iconic creations in the history of fashion design.

The second part of the book opens with the chapter "Agirre at the Crossroads" by Joseba Zulaika, from the William Douglass Center for Basque Studies at the University of Nevada, Reno. It provides a suggestive essay on the centrality of Jose Antonio Agirre's political and human role during his life. As Zulaika reveals, Agirre was at the most important crossroads of his time, crossroads that speak about opposite concepts such as nationalism/internationalism, particularism/universalism, democracy/fascism, and separatism/federalism, and which help to depict a portrait of Agirre's ideology and beliefs. Mauriac's words serve as a starting point for Zulaika to describe Agirre's times as those in which modernity ended and with it any belief in God, Democracy, Liberty, or Justice. The author refers to many politicians and influential people in his chapter, such as Areilza, Prieto, Arrupe, Madariaga, as well as to the dramatic events that marked the twentieth century: the bombing of Gernika, the Holocaust, and the bombing of Hiroshima and Nagasaki. As Zulaika stresses, Agirre was the most charismatic Basque leader ever, a free man who claimed freedom for his country and who foresaw the violent era that would follow the dictatorship of Franco. A leader who faced Fascism and became a Basque exile, whose international agenda pursued the right of a small country to be heard and taken into consideration in postwar Europe.

Mari Jose Olaziregi, from the University of the Basque Country/MHLI Research Group, focuses in "Literature and Political Conflicts: The Basque Case" on the debates and controversy that Basque political conflicts, namely the Spanish Civil War and the terrorism of ETA, have generated in the Basque literary field. As Olaziregi contends, although institutionalized discourses have come to censure the word "conflict" in recent decades, Basque writers have had an active engagement with our conflictive past through amazing narratives, mainly from the 1990s on. Transformed into storytellers who narrate and reflect on the Basque convulsive reality, the desire and obligation to relate/understand what has happened determines the reflexive metafictional tone of texts that seek an ethical and moral debate around questions such as legitimacy, justice, and blame. Moreover, Olaziregi highlights that the dynamics of memory that are being produced in Basque narrative are different when the writers are men or women. Men's novels demonstrate metafictional structures that serve to represent the active role that the Basque (male) writer seeks to take in the conflict, while women's narratives relate the Basque conflict as an element that conditions their role as wife, girlfriend, or mother in current Basque society. Olaziregi ends by stating that the interpretation offered in her chapter from the prism of gender will have to discern if the dynamics of memory that are being produced in Basque narrative will perpetuate or not the role divisions on which the patriarchal logic is based.

The main focus of the contribution by Andrea Bartoli and Borislava Manojlovic, from Seton Hall University, is the international academic legacy of Lehendakari Agirre's government. Their chapter, entitled "The Growth of the International Legacy of Lehendakari Jose A. Agirre's Government through Academic Cooperation," explores the genesis of the cooperative agreement between Columbia University in the City of New York and the Agirre Lehendakaria Center, at the University of the Basque Country, in Leioa, the Basque Country. The authors go back to the days when the Lehendakari Jose A. Agirre, while in exile from the Basque Country, was given an academic appointment at Columbia University, an appointment that was ultimately very productive and fruitful, and that marked his future work for the independence of his people. Decades later, this initial contact with academic institutions in the United States was crucial in the establishment of a joint cultural venture involving several academic institutions across continents such as the abovementioned Columbia University and the Agirrre Lehendakaria Center.

Finally, Amaia Agirre Muñoa, Senior Fellow at the Agirre Lehendakaria Center and granddaughter of president Agirre, is the author of the contribution that completes the book. She presents a really emotive and suggestive chapter under the title "Reflections on a Grandfather I Never Met." Dr. Agirre depicts, thanks to the reading of her grandfather's writings and to family memories, a personal narration of the main ideas and values that president Agirre defended during his intense life. She underlines the constant presence of the image and legacy of the lehendakari in successive generations of the family and describes him as a passionate and very family-oriented man with clearly marked values, ideas, and goals, such as his strong patriotism and strong Basque identity, deep Catholic faith, strong sense of individual and collective freedom, social consciousness, and so on, attributes that make Agirre an incredibly charismatic leader with a clear European sense and who believed in the power of words and diplomacy to reach agreements.

Part 1

On the International Dimension of Agirre's Government, 1936–1960

1

The Dictatorship that Emerged
out of the War

Julián Casanova

An interminable postwar era, an omnipresent victory, an almost forty-year-old dictatorship. The military uprising of July 1936 and the civil war it triggered became key events in Franco's dictatorship, in its excluding, ultranationalist, and repressive culture.

Those that had caused the war, who had won it, and who oversaw the victory from the new state established the idea, impossible to contend, that the republicans were responsible for all the disasters and crimes that had taken place in Spain since 1931. Projecting the blame exclusively on the defeated republicans exonerated the winners from even the most minimum suspicion. The supposed collective suffering gave way for the punishment of just one side. Francisco Franco often recalled this in the religious language that the Catholic Church served him on a platter: "The suffering of a nation at a specific point in its history is no whim; it is spiritual punishment, the punishment that God imposes on a crooked life, on an unclean history."

Victory

"The red army captured and disarmed," the war ended on April 1, 1939 with the complete triumph of Franco's "national" troops.

---

* This work was published originally in Spanish in Julián Casanova, ed., *Cuarenta años con Franco* (Barcelona: Crítica, 2015). I wish to thank Cameron Watson for the translation.

The same day the capital was "liberated," Leopoldo Eijo y Garay, bishop of the diocese of Madrid, published his pastoral letter "La hora presente" (The present time): "Beneath the blessed yellow and red [Spanish flag], which our fathers bequeathed us, and the protection of our heroic soldiers and volunteer militias, enjoy peace now, which, with such longing, with such intense yearning, we have wished for you and we have asked God for you."

The war had been necessary and inevitable because Spain could not save itself "by ordinary means" and "the present time" was, nothing more, nothing less, all over the world but "especially" in Spain, "the time to settle all humanity's accounts with the political philosophy of the French Revolution."

These were times of celebration, Te Deums, the resurrection of Spain, and pride in the martyrs of the Crusade. A few hours after announcing that the red army had been captured and disarmed, the Generalissimo received a telegram from Pius XII, formerly Cardinal Eugenio Pacelli, who had been elected Pope on March 2 that same year following the death of Pius XI on February 10. Nor did Cardinal Isidro Gomá miss this occasion, from Pamplona, to remind Franco on April 3 of "the great interest with which I joined in your efforts from the beginning; how I collaborated with my humble powers and within my attributes as church prelate to the great undertaking."

The great undertaking was the total regeneration of a new nation forged through the fight against evil, the parliamentary system, the secular Republic, and revolutionary atheism, all the demons buried by Franco's armed victory under divine protection. It was a question of achieving a Catholic confessional state, "the despotism of soldiers and clerics" as it was termed by Barcala, one of the characters in Manuel Azaña's *La velada de Benicarló* (Evening at Benicarló). Cities and towns were chock-full of parades, demonstrations of victory, the symbolic return of virgins to their sacred sites, acts of atonement, and processions.

Franco and his comrades-in-arms had come to the rescue of the fatherland, which legitimized the coup d'état and the bloody civil war. In reality, that goal of redeeming Spain was the common denominator among the political and social forces that joined together in that "great undertaking," who were identified more by what they sought to destroy—the Republic, liberalism, communism—than by any agreement on defining the new regime. Victory had to be savored, expressed in a symbolic framework, as Zira Box captures so well, of rites, festivals, monuments and mementos, and homage to the martyrs.

The images we can see in photos and documentaries do not lie. People went out into the streets to celebrate victory with the fascist Roman salute, institutionalized as the official salute in Franco's Spain following the unification of political forces in April 1937, and singing the Falangist "Cara al Sol," the official anthem, together with the Movement's Carlist anthem, "Oriamendi." The blend of fascist and religious symbols led for some time to the fascisization of the sacred and the consecration of fascist policies until, with the defeat of the Axis powers in World War II, the Church and its National Catholic discourse ultimately ended up prevailing.

April 1, 1939 was Passion Saturday, the day before Palm Sunday, and Holy Week was a special occasion to reinstate, in certain cities like Madrid, Valencia, or Barcelona, the liturgy of such momentous dates as "the triumph of the City of God and the Resurrection of Spain." It was the beginning of a new Baroque politico-religious liturgy, full of gestures, beliefs, and fervor, with a crucified Christ coming out of churches to join processions and crowds receiving him with the fascist salute.

No facet of political or social life lay outside that symbolic construction of the dictatorship. The calendar of festivals, established officially by order of Ramón Serrano Suñer on March 9, 1940, although some of them had already begun to be held since the start of the civil war in territory occupied by the military rebels, summed up the commemorative will and universe of the winners. In the first place, religious festivals abolished by the Republic, from Epiphany to Christmas, were reinstated. Besides religious festivals, those of a traditional nature associated with the true Spain were highlighted—May 2 and October 12. Yet those that defined that new symbolic universe of the dictatorship were those created to celebrate the new ideas and values established with the coup d'état and the war: April 1, "Día de la Victoria" (Victory Day); July 18, "Día del Alzamiento" (Uprising Day); October 1, "Día del Caudillo" (Leader's Day); and November 20, to remember the execution of the Falangist leader José Antonio Primo de Rivera.

In order to remember forever its victory in the war, so that nobody would forget its origins, Franco's dictatorship filled up Spanish soil with sites of memory, with an obsessive cult of remembrance for the fallen, which was a cult of nation, of fatherland, of the true Spain as opposed to that of the anti-Spain, a way of uniting through blood ties the families and friends of martyrs in contrast to the hidden memory of the defeated, whose remains were abandoned in ditches, cemeteries, and common graves.

"Martyrs of the Crusade" were from the outset, and they appear thus in documented sources and newspaper features, the combatants of the Francoist army who had died in battle, the priests who fell at the front "praising God and acclaiming Spain," Catholics and right-wingers and, especially, the almost seven thousand members of the murdered clergy, all of those, ultimately, whose "martyrdom" signified "religious hatred and persecution of the Church."

The ravages caused by anticlerical persecution, the confirmation of sacrileges, and murders of the clergy by "reds" multiplied the emotional impact that underlay the constant remembrance of the martyrs. The ritual and mythology amassed around them provided the Church with still more power and an increased presence among the winners of the war, cancelled out any trace of feeling for the defeated, and encouraged the violent revenge that persisted for years.

Remembrance began already prior to the end of the war, when a state decree of November 16, 1938 proclaimed November 20 a "day of national mourning" in memory of José Antonio Primo de Rivera, and stated, "by means of agreement with the church authorities," that "on the walls of each parish an inscription will appear that contains the names of the Fallen, already during the present Crusade, already victims of the Marxist revolution."

That was the beginning of putting up commemorative plaques and inscriptions to those "fallen for God and Fatherland" in churches, mounted on or carved into the old stonework of singular artistic monuments. And although it did not appear in the decree, most of those inscriptions ended up being headed by the name of José Antonio, a sacred fusion of the dead for political and religious reasons, which at times caused tension among soldiers, priests, and Falangists.

Streets, squares, schools, and hospitals in hundreds of towns and cities took on, from that moment on, the names of those involved in the military coup, fascist leaders, and Catholic politicians. Quintanilla de Abajo, in the province of Valladolid, became Quintanilla de Onésimo, in honor of one of the founders of the Juntas de Ofensiva Nacional Sindicalista (National Syndicalist Offensive Committees, JONS) who had died in combat in the Guadarrama Mountains on July 24, 1936, right at the outbreak of hostilities and without any time to consolidate his marginal fascist leadership. In Madrid, as was the case in all the cities that fell into the hands of Francoist troops at the end of the war, the city council proposed, that same month as the victory, cleaning the city "of all the symbols and names" associated with the Republic, "a corrupt and disastrous political regime for the Fatherland." So disastrous and odious that a town in Toledo named Azaña, which had nothing to with the main republican leader, changed its name to Numancia de la Sagra.

Spaces that had been desecrated by the "reds" became symbols of Catholic moral resurgence. The soil of many cemeteries and outlying areas, on which priests had been killed, was fenced in, as in the town of Barbastro in Huesca, "due to it being ground consecrated and bathed in martyrs' blood." Those pieces of land would serve to remind coming generations of the cruel persecution and the "profound lesson that whoever moves away from the Catholic Church ultimately falls into betraying God and the Fatherland."

For a long time, in cathedrals and churches bishops and priests celebrated religious acts and held funeral ceremonies in memory of the martyrs. During those "shining days" of Franco's peace, their remains were exhumed and transported in processions that traversed with great solemnity towns and cities, from the cemeteries and martyr sites to the chapels and churches selected for the eternal rest of their remains. In Málaga, martyrs' remains were transported in a funeral procession that proceeded through its streets with ninety-nine coffins. The "Día de los Caídos" (Day of the Fallen) was celebrated in every city, during both the postwar era and in the later years of development, with masses, floral tributes, and parades. They were signs of victory, still present in the early 1960s, a symbolic compensation for the dead of one side that was never extended to the other.

According to some martyrologies, many faithful attended those exhumation acts with the aim of "bagging some piece of those [religious] spoils," a relic to preserve devotedly. The fame of those martyrs demonstrated the justice of the cause for which they had fought, reminded people of the division between winners and losers, that the Church had won the war and the peace, and that their blood had not been spilled in vain.

Soldiers, Falangists, Carlists, and the Church contributed their symbols to the new Spain, although National Catholic discourse would end up, from 1945 on, dominating. Everyone did, however, agree on the cult paying homage to General Franco. From October 1936 on, bishops, priests, and members of religious orders began to treat Franco as someone sent by God to bring order to the "earthly city." Once the war had ended, the "distinguished, victorious, and beloved Caudillo" was surrounded by a heroic-messianic aura that put him on the same level as the greatest saints in history. Statues, busts, poetry, prints, and hagiographies appeared all over the place. Franco's image as a redeeming savior warrior was carefully dealt with and idealized in the *Noticiario Español* (Spanish Newsreel, NO-DO). For almost the entire forty years of the dictatorship his portrait presided over classrooms, offices, and public establishments, and was repeated on stamps, coins, and bills. And as no legitimacy could be greater than that originating in divine authority, Franco was "Caudillo of Spain thanks to the grace of God." On the occasion of his visit to Sabadell in 1942, the president of the Manufacturers' Guild in that city, Manuel Gorina, recalled that "after God it is Generalissimo Franco and his courageous Army to whom we owe the ending of our captivity and the preservation of our homes and the recovery of our industrial heritage."

The winners were winning a lasting peace, constructing a new state and a new Spain in which things were returning to normal, to that time before 1931, and at the same time history was beginning anew. Apparently, as Manuel Azaña had written in his notes on October 6, 1937, what was emerging in Francoist Spain was all "sabers, chasubles, military parades, and homages to the Virgin Pilar." Yet beyond the appearances, rhetoric, and ceremonies, the idea that everything may be returning to normal and beginning anew, anti-Spain, those who may still be living there and in its symbols and ideas, had to be eliminated by means of violence, without any concession to forgiveness or reconciliation.

Policies of Punishment and Plundering

The collapse of the republican army in the spring of 1939 led 200,000 soldiers to prisons and improvised concentration camps. At the end of that year and through 1940 official sources recorded over 270,000 prisoners, a figure that fell constantly in the years that followed due to numerous executions and the thousands who died as a result of illness and malnutrition. The demographic cost of the war and of the immediate postwar period numbered around 600,000 people, to which one must add 200,000 more who, after the great "retreat" during the first three months of 1939—when close to half a million men, women, and children crossed the French border—never returned to Spain.

At least 50,000 people were executed in the decade after the end of the war, most of them in the last provinces conquered by Franco's army. There were, among the thousands of those executed, illustrious figures detained in France from a list drawn up by José Félix Lequerica and handed over to the Francoist authorities by the Gestapo. These included Lluís Companys, president of the Generalitat (Catalan government) as well as ministers of the Republic during the war, the socialist Julián Zugazagoitia, and the anarchist Joan Peiró. Ricardo Zabalza, the main leader of the Federación Nacional de Trabajadores de la Tierra (National Federation of Land Workers), was tortured, tried on February 2, 1940, and executed on the morning of February 24. As he wrote to his parents, already "awaiting execution," "when you read these lines I will already be no more than a memory. Men who call themselves Christian have wanted it that way . . . You in your religious simplicity would not understand how a man who committed no crime— the district attorney himself acknowledged this in his report—and about whom nor is there an accusation of any shameful act, can suffer the death that awaits him."

The death sentence for Lluís Companys, whose trial lasted less than one hour, was signed by Captain General of the 4th Military Region, Luis Orgaz. He was executed by a Guardia Civil (Civil Guard) firing squad at 6:30 am on the morning of October 15, 1940. In the initial postwar months, all death sentences required Franco's approval, but from January 1940 on, in order to cope with the high number prisoners on the waiting list, the process was speeded up by canceling this procedure. And it was decided, as Paul Preston reminds us, that in cases of high-ranking political leaders of the Republic there would be no recourse to clemency. Besides them, the most sought after people were the political commissars of the republican army and journalists.

Franco's dictatorship, having emerged out of the war and consolidated its power during the years of World War II, situated Spain on the same trail of death and crimes followed by the majority of countries in Europe. People were needed to plan that violence and intellectuals, politicians, and priests who justified it. In reality, the long Spanish postwar era anticipated some of the purges and punishments that would take place elsewhere after 1945. Destruction of opponents in war gave way to the centralizing and control of violence on the part of the military authorities, an institutionalized terror protected by the laws of the new state. That political culture of violence, the divide between winners and losers, "patriots and traitors," or "nationals and reds," prevailed in Spanish society for at least two decades after the end of the civil war.

This was special justice, set up to repress retroactively activities that were legal when they took place, like resisting the military rebellion and being loyal to the Spanish Republic during the civil war. Because the main feature of that violence is that it was organized from above, based on military jurisdiction, which practically replaced the army. Although the explosion of revenge in the last cities captured was still accompanied by "*paseos*" (journeys toward executions) and summary executions, the new state's monopoly on violence was soon in force, and it set up extraordinary mechanisms of terror sanctioned and legitimized by laws. The war councils, which tens of thousands of people passed through between 1939 and 1945, were juridically a mere farce in which nothing had to be proved because it had already been established at the outset that the accused were reds and, therefore, guilty. The rebels punished those who had remained loyal to their constitutional government with the charge of "rebellion," the "reverse justice" that Ramón Serrano Suñer referred to.

The peace of Franco, who maintained a state of war until April 1948, transformed society, destroyed whole families, breaking the basic networks of social solidarity, and imbued everyday life with fear, coercive practices, and punishment. The threat of being persecuted, humiliated, the need to have some form of protection at one's disposal and good information to survive, could affect anyone who could not certify unswerving membership of the Movement or a past clean of any republican sin.

The first violent avenging assault on which Francoism was based began on February 9, 1939 with the Political Responsibilities Law, which continued the economic repression set up in January 1937 by the provincial confiscation commissions in areas controlled by the military rebels during the war. The law declared "the political responsibility of persons, both legal and natural," who, since October 1, 1934 "contributed to creating or aggravating the subversion of all order of which Spain was a victim" and from July 18, 1936 "have opposed or may oppose the National Movement through specific acts or serious passivity."

From that moment on tens of thousands of cases were opened to "deal with the guilt" of those who contributed "to forging red subversion." According to Manuel Álvaro Dueñas, the eighteen regional courts charged with passing sentence processed 229,549 cases to September 1941, of which only 36,018 had been resolved, 88,618 were still under consideration, and 104,913 pending. The force of that justice affected 9.5 percent of all Spaniards. Given the impossibility of getting through all those piles of cases, the law was partially modified in 1942 and abolished on April 13, 1945.

In accordance with the law, the investigating judge would have to ask "the mayor, the local chief of the Falange Española Tradicionalista y de las JONS [Traditionalist Spanish Falange and the National Syndicalist Offensive Committees], the parish priest, and the commanding officer of the Civil Guard in the town in which he resides or was his last residence" about the alleged person in question. The law thus marked out the circle of powerful omnipresent authorities, possessing unlimited coercive and intimidating power, which was going to control people's assets and lives during the long years of Franco's peace.

The sanctions that the law envisaged were extremely harsh and could be, according article 8, of three types: "restrictive of activity," with special and total disqualification from practicing careers and professions, which in turn opened up an extensive and selective process of purging; "limiting freedom of residence," which entailed banishment, "deportation to our African possessions," confinement, or exile; and "economic," with the complete or partial loss of certain specific assets and the payment of fines.

Most cases, as recent research confirms, initially involved the working classes and rural poor with few economic resources, but also the republican middle classes with higher incomes. Fines of 100 million pesetas were imposed on the most well-known politicians of the Republic, from Manuel Azaña to Indalecio Prieto, by way of Diego Martínez Barrio. Almost two thousand books considered subversive were seized belonging to the historian and archivist from Zaragoza, José Ignacio Mantecón, appointed governor general of Aragón by Juan Negrín in August 1937. And the judge advocate in the case, Ramiro Fernández de la Mora, fined him ten million pesetas, a figure higher than that imposed on Niceto Alcalá Zamora and equivalent to that of the socialist leader Margarita Nelken or the republican ambassador to London, Pablo de Azcárate.

And although the prototypical accused was a middle-aged man affiliated to left-wing organizations, many women, between 4 and 8 percent of all those affected, were victims of the law. Indeed, as Ángela Cenarro points out, "the sentence imposed on their fathers or husbands was often applied to them," which in turn forced them to "get by in conditions of extreme adversity."

In any event, it would affect rich and poor people, men and women. The setting in motion of that repressive, confiscating mechanism ruined the lives of losers and reds, paving the way for an open season made up of arbitrary extrajudicial persecution that in everyday life resulted very often in looting and pillage. Falling under the weight of that law meant, in the words of Marc Carrillo, "civil death." Those affected, condemned by the courts and pointed out by their neighbors, sank demoralized into abject misery. In many cases, sentences were imposed on people who had already been executed.

The first president of the National Court for Political Responsibilities was Enrique Suñer, professor of Pediatric Medicine at the University of Madrid, who, as vice-president of the Commission for Education and Culture of the Technical Council of State, and already during the war, began an obsessive persecution of teachers, professors, and intellectuals. In his book *Los intelectuales y la tragedia española* (Intellectuals and the Spanish Tragedy, 1937) he considered them, as children of the Institución Libre de Enseñanza (Free Educational Institution, ILE), "those primarily responsible for so much suffering and so much misfortune," the perpetrators of an "infernal antipatriotic effort that sought to eradicate from the Spanish soul Christ's faith and love for our glorious *nacionales*."

Nor did his replacement, Wenceslao González Oliveros, professor of the Philosophy of Law at the University of Salamanca, in charge of the General Directorate for Higher and Secondary Education during the dictatorship of Primo de Rivera, and the first civil governor of Barcelona following the arrival of Franco's troops, like the ILE, "the mocking vixen." And although González Oliveros demonstrated open sympathy for the Nazi cause, he believed that Spanish fascism did not need to import any foreign traditions, because the war and peace had been won by a new "Hispanic Imperial Falange." With men like him, "the future of the Fatherland" was assured. As well as being President of the Court for Political Responsibilities, he was appointed vice-president of the Court for Repression of Masonry and Communism and, later, until 1962, he added to his resume the presidency of the National Education Council.

Most of those who had not won a place in that "Hispanic Imperial Falange" ended up confined in prisons, concentration camps, prison detachments, and forced labor camps, the backbone of the repressive system imposed by the dictatorship. According to the *Anuario Estadístico de España* (Statistical Yearbook of Spain), which only took into account the "prison population," the greatest number of prisoners were held in late 1939 and early 1940, 270,719—of which 23,232 were women—to whom one should add 92,000 people interned in different types of concentration camps.

The size of those figures, 363,000 deprived of their freedom, can only be understood by setting it against the fact that prisons during the Republic were capable of holding barely 20,000 people and in those years, with the exception of the months following the October 1934 revolt, there were an average of 10,000 inmates. In 1943 there were still 125,000—11,688 of them women—and close to 16,000 people were completing their sentences in the 121 penal detachments that, scattered all over Spain, employed prisoners for general rebuilding work as well as work on roads and reservoirs. The need for a workforce, the threat of administrative collapse, and the evolution of World War II toward the defeat of the fascist countries all led to a sharp decrease, through a policy of prison releases and pardons, of what the *Anuario* had termed the "prison population." Even so, those released received a supervised probation card and when they went up before Sentence Examination Commissions, created on January 25, 1940, they required favorable reports from the political, military, and religious authorities.

The Francoist concentration camps, examined in detail by Javier Rodrigo, were not extermination centers, but were instead used to classify, reeducate, keep an eye on, and "break" prisoners of war. The model was based on that of the war, "purgatories of the Republic," and when it was created there were still no such thing in Europe as the direct massive system of extermination that the Nazis started operating in the summer of 1941 with Operation Barbarossa to invade the Soviet Union. One thing was a police state, like that of the Nazis before World War II or that constructed by the Franco dictatorship, and another genocide. Nor were the Soviet camps, through which passed close to seven million people between 1943 and 1947, designed or used, despite the deaths they caused, as extermination camps.

That culture of cruelty and indifference toward whoever was considered the enemy became a badge of identity for dictatorships across Europe in the 1930s and 1940s. The magnitude of the problem of confining millions of men and women transformed into victims by state policies was resolved in the Third Reich, in the Soviet Union, and, during the early years of Franco's Spain, through concentration and work camps that moreover became indispensable for their economies at a time when, for different reasons, the labor market did not offer a sufficient workforce to sustain them. Those camps were the offspring of ideological warfare and not just a product of circumstances or the logic of terror. The 275,000 Spanish republicans interned in French camps that existed in March 1939 gradually declined in number until there were only a few thousand one year later, at the moment France was invaded by Nazi troops.

From that date on, some 40,000 Spanish republicans were forcibly transported to Germany to work in war industries and many of them ended up in concentration camps, above all in Mauthausen, where 5,000 out of 7,000 interned there died. In Vichy France, Germany, and Algeria, Spanish republicans were treated during World War II as "reds" that had no right to life. It was the prolongation of murders, persecutions, and humiliations for the defeated, for their children, and for their children's children. "Here only death grants freedom," Major Caboche told them when he received Spanish survivors of the Durruti Column in in the Algerian camp of Djelfa (where the writer Max Aub was held from November 1941 to October 1942). It was the prolongation of murders, persecutions, and humiliations for the defeated that took place in Spain.

But maintaining so many inmates in prison for so long, torturing them and allowing them to die of hunger and epidemics, was not, like the harsh postwar repression in general, something inevitable. It was the necessary punishment for defeated reds. Catholics, Falangists, and soldiers admired during those years, although they had to hide it later, the moral and political cleansing carried out by Hitler in Germany. Vicente Gay y Forner, professor of Economics at the University of Valladolid and Franco's press and propaganda officer following the 1936 uprising, expressed his fervent admiration for Nazi Germany and considered Dachau "a true educational establishment," a "sanitized village," ideal for prisoners.

The system of reducing sentences in return for work, whose main inspiration, the Jesuit José Antonio Pérez del Pulgar, attributed to a new "extremely Christian" conception of the prison system backed by the Caudillo, was also an excellent means of supplying a cheap workforce to many companies and the state itself. In Asturias new prisons were built around the coal mines in order to be able to exploit prisoners. Numerous prisoners were used in the mercury mines of Almadén and in the coal mines of León and the Basque Country and hundreds of them worked on the construction of the Bajo Guadalquivir Canal ("the Prisoners' Canal"). Some dams and reservoirs, which Franco inaugurated from the 1950s on, such as those of the Pyrenees in Huesca and that of Yesa in Zaragoza, were built with forced labor, as was the reconstruction of towns and cities managed by the Council for Devastated Regions. That was also how the symbolic new town of Belchite, inaugurated in 1954, was constructed.

In the two decades it took to build the Valle de los Caídos (Valley of the Fallen), that grandiose site constructed in order to challenge "time and oblivion" and an homage to the sacrifice of the "heroes and martyrs of the Crusade" inaugurated on April 1, 1959, some twenty thousand men, many of them, especially up to 1950, "reds" captured in war and political prisoners, exploited by the companies that were awarded the different construction contracts, Banús, Agromán, and Huarte. The prison and the factory, blessed by the same religion, blended together during those early years of Francoism and formed part of the same repressive system. Political prisoners were given work and "free" workers were disciplined with patriotic propaganda and religion.

That whole machinery of organized terror from above required, however, widespread "popular" participation, by informants, sources, and accusers, among whom one came across not just the natural beneficiaries of the victory, the Church, the military, the Falange, and the traditional right. The purge was, of course, both social and political and powerful members of the community, the people of order, the authorities, made the most of the opportunity to get rid of "undesirables," "animals," and troublemakers. But what that minority wanted was approved by many more, who thought it politically necessary to punish their neighbors, whom they accused or did not defend if others accused them.

They were times of personal hatreds, of accusations, and of silence. In Valencia, where, after falling into Francoist hands, the Policy and Order Column of Occupation under the leadership of Colonel Antonio Aymar began a bloody punishment campaign, the authorities established from day one complaints centers, whose doors were besieged by long lines of people who were looking for revenge or who wanted to avoid any of the repression coming their way, instructed by the warnings that were issued by the military government: "Any person who may know of the commission of a crime carried out during the red-dominated era, is obliged to report the fact . . . with the aim of carrying out in an appropriate manner the spirit of justice that inspires our caudillo."

Collaborating by means of denunciation meant also getting involved in the beginning of a wide range of indictment processes deployed by the winners. For that reason there was such insistence on active participation and apathy was persecuted and sanctioned. The terror also demanded breaking ties of friendship and social solidarity, preventing any seed of resistance. Because reporting "crimes," pointing out "delinquents" was something "good patriots" did, people who were forging the "New Spain." Accusation thus became the first link in Franco's justice, a state-sponsored means of being able to jump over the barrier constructed between reds and winners.

Hatred, revenge, and resentment nourished the desire for the violent theft of thousands of positions that the murdered and the victims of reprisals had left vacant in the public administration, in town councils, and provincial and local institutions. A law of February 10, 1939 institutionalized the purge of civil servants, a process that the military rebels had started without any need for laws in the summer of 1936. Behind that law, and in general all processes of purging, there was a dual objective: depriving those "hostile to the regime" of their jobs and their means of living, an exemplary punishment that condemned those accused to social alienation; and, in second place, assuring positions were filled by all those who had served the national cause during the civil war and demonstrated their loyalty to the Movement. There lies one of the lasting bases of support for Franco's dictatorship, the "unswerving support" of all those who had benefited from the victory.

A year after the war had ended the dictatorship created and put into force a system of legal accusation, a state instrument to stimulate allegations. The "general complaint informing about criminal acts and other aspects of life in the red zone from July 18, 1936 to the liberation" was created by decree of the Ministry of Justice on April 26, 1940, with the aim of "investigating matters concerning the crime, its causes and effects, procedures employed in its execution, attribution of responsibilities, identification of victims, and specification of damage inflicted."

In practice, the "general complaint," which compiled heaps of documents, achieved several targets. It aired publicly and marked in the memory of many people the different manifestations of "red terror" during the civil war. It compensated the families of victims of that violence, confirming the social division between winners and losers. And above all it became the instrument of accusing and persecuting people who had nothing to do with the events in question. Research carried out on this topic reveals the social support that Francoism enjoyed from the beginning. In the words of Conxita Mir, it was a society "watched over, silenced, transformed almost into a spy itself, in which . . . collaboration was essential in order to guarantee the efficient replacement of mass politics by submissiveness to power."

All those reports by the security forces, priests, Falangists, and "ordinary" people, the necessary endorsements and safe-conduct passes to get by, testify to the level of involvement by the general public in that system of terror. And that means, in short, that Francoism did not just live off violence and terror, nor was it sustained solely by repression.

Without that citizen participation, the terror would have been reduced to force and coercion. Once the bloodiest years were over, what showed up in reality was a police and self-surveillance system in which there was nothing appealing about disobedience and, less still, opposition or resistance. The losers who were able to carry on living had to adapt to the forms of coexistence imposed by the winners. Many lost their jobs; others, especially in the rural world, were forced to move to different cities or towns. Hounded and denounced, members of political organizations and labor unions on the republican side bore the major brunt of all this. As regards the less involved, many of them illiterate, Francoism imposed a silence on them so that they may survive, forcing them to choke back their own identity.

There were those who got involved in armed resistance against the dictatorship, the so-called *maquis* or guerrillas. Their origins lay in those who had "fled," those who, in order to escape the repression of the military rebels had taken refuge at different times during the civil war in the mountains of Andalucía, Asturias, León, or Galicia, knowing that they could not return if they wanted to save their lives. The initial resistance of those who fled, and all those who did not accept giving in to the winners, gradually led to a more organized armed struggle that copied antifascist resistance models tried out in France against the Nazis. While many socialists and anarchists fought with the guerrillas, only the PCE (the Spanish Communist Party) openly supported the armed approach. In that decade of the 1940s, some seven thousand *maquis* participated in armed activities in different Spanish mountain ranges and some sixty thousand go-betweens or collaborators ended up in prison for helping them. If we believe Civil Guard sources, 2,173 guerrillas and three hundred members of the armed forces died in confrontations.

Until the end of World War II, people still dreamed of overthrowing the dictatorship. Moreover, many old combatants from the republican side, defeated and exiled, enlisted in the French resistance against Nazism, thinking that it was still their war, one that would overthrow all tyrannies, and Franco was the greatest of them all, allowing them to return to their homes, jobs, and birthplaces. The most important operation during those World War II years was the invasion of the Arán Valley, in which between 3,500 and 4,000 men occupied several Pyrenean towns and villages between October 14 and 28, 1944, until Vicente López Tovar, the military head of operations, had to order the retreat, leaving an outcome of sixty dead and eight hundred prisoners.

Hitler and Mussolini died, the Axis powers were defeated, and Franco continued. With the passage of time, violence and repression went through a change of face, the dictatorship evolved, it "softened" its methods, and, with no external harassment, it could relax, offer a more amiable face. Yet the dictatorship never renounced the civil war as a foundational act, which was remembered time and time again in order to preserve the unity of that wide-ranging coalition or winners and in order to carry on humiliating the losers. Repression was a useful investment that Franco knew how to administer until the end, "a social policy of 'cleansing' and 'purging' enemies and adversaries," in the words of Enrique Moradiellos, "enormously productive for the Franco dictatorship, without which its consolidation and survival for so many years and in such different international contexts is not fully comprehensible."

Some months after the end of the civil war, an attack by the German army on Poland in September 1939 started another war in Europe, the second major conflict of the twentieth century, which would become global with the Japanese bombing of the US naval base in Pearl Harbor on December 7, 1941. It was a worldwide war, six years of destruction and death, which Franco and his dictatorship were able to avoid, although thousands of Spaniards also participated in the battle, against fascism or against communism, a second act in the tragedy that they had just left behind in their own country. And it is precisely during those years of the Spanish postwar era and world war that Franco constructed his peace, saved his Fatherland, and presided over the construction of his new Spain.

The New Spain

In that new Spain, from April 1, 1939 on Franco and his army ruled and together they remained, with barely any splits, for almost forty years. In the first government appointed by Franco after the war, on August 9, 1939, soldiers occupied five of the fourteen positions, among them, and as was going to be typical throughout the dictatorship, the then created Ministries of the Army, Navy, and Air Force. During the initial years of the postwar period, until the defeat of the Axis powers in 1945, the military enjoyed a significant presence in ministerial posts and in the public administration.

Although a state of war was maintained until April 1948, the army was by that time no longer the principal body in charge of public order, as had traditionally been the case in contemporary Spain, because new armed forces had been created with powerful mechanisms of repression. In the first place, in March 1940 the Civil Guard was reorganized with the expulsion of five thousand guards due to their support for the Republic or their lukewarm adherence to the Movement and the incorporation of hundreds of guards who had stood out in the war as provisional junior officers. Led between 1943 and 1955 by General Camilo Alonso Vega, a veteran of the African War and close friend of Franco, the Civil Guard became a rigidly disciplined and militarized body that took charge, in those difficult years of the 1940s, of combatting the guerrillas.

The Cuerpo de Seguridad y Asalto (Security and Attack Force), created by the Republic and which had been led in its early years by General Agustín Muñoz Grandes, was dissolved and a law of March 8, 1941 created the Policía Gubernativa (Government Police), made up of the Cuerpo General de Policía (General Police Force) and the Policía Armada y de Tráfico (Armed and Traffic Police). Ex-combatants selected "from among the best in the war of liberation" and very loyal to the Caudillo, Falangists, and Requetés

(Carlist militiamen), were initially drafted into that Armed Police. The General Police Force, to which the Brigada Social (Social Brigade) was accountable, and the Armed Police were, together with the Civil Guard, responsible for watching out for and repressing any dissidence and maintaining the new order that, according to that law, "in totalitarian states" was achieved "thanks to a precise combination of perfect technique and loyalty."

During the early years that police state, which defined itself unapologetically then as totalitarian, had in its favor the fascist winds that were blowing through Europe at the time, originating in Nazi Germany and Mussolini's Italy, whose intervention and aid had been decisive for the triumph of Franco's troops against the Republic. And even though Francoist foreign policy aligned itself clearly with the fascist powers, Spain did not participate officially in World War II because of its disastrous economic and military situation and because the costs of any such intervention would have been too high for Germany and Italy. This was revealed in the talks that Franco held with Hitler in Hendaye, on October 23, 1940, and Mussolini, in Bordighera, in February the following year. The main European fascist leaders always considered Franco the dictator of a weak country that scarcely counted in international relations.

Enthusiasm for Franco and, from the most fascist sector in his dictatorship, for the Nazi cause and against communism manifested itself, despite official Spanish neutrality, in the creation of the División Azul (Blue Division). When Operation Barbarossa began in June 1941 and German troops invaded the Soviet Union, Ramón Serrano Suñer, the Minister of Foreign Affairs, suggested to his brother-in-law, General Francisco Franco, forming a volunteers' unit to fight alongside the Germans "against the common enemy": Bolsheviks, Freemasons, and Jews. It was called the Blue Division, a name proposed by José Luis Arrese, but in reality it was the 250th Division of the Wehrmacht, made up of Spaniards who swore an oath of loyalty to the Führer. Until the dissolving of its last remains in March 1944, close to forty-seven thousand combatants passed through its ranks on the North Russian Front and in the siege of Leningrad. They earned the wages of a German soldier, as well as a subsidy received by their families, and they were promised work on their return, although five thousand of them died in combat on that eastern front.

One third of the eighteen thousand who left with the first draft in July 1941 were university students, members of the SEU

(Sindicato Español Universitario, Spanish Students' Union), Falangists who wanted "to pay two debts of blood," take revenge on communists who had fought in the Spanish Civil War and return the favor to Germans for their generous and decisive contribution to Franco's victory. There were from the outset a lot of soldiers in search of adventure, glory, and promotion; soldiers who went in order to atone for the sin of having fought on the wrong side during the war between Spaniards; and later, new volunteers got involved, blue-collar workers, day laborers, and peasants with few resources, motivated by a good salary in times of hunger, repression, and misery, and by that additional family subsidy.

Distinguished people who were already by that time well situated in political spectrum of the winners joined the Blue Division, such as the Falangists Dionisio Ridruejo and Agustín Aznar, and the professor of Law Fernando Castiella, later Minister of Foreign Affairs between 1957 and 1969, as well as the crème de la crème of fascism, militarism, and the far right of that era, headed by its chief, the Falangist General Agustín Muñoz Grandes.

The calamitous economic situation of Spain had conditioned Franco's decision in his negotiations with Hitler and it shaped the lives of millions of people for more than a decade. Data on the economic and social costs of that long postwar period are conclusive. Salaries remained below the prewar level throughout the 1940s. Prices rose, in line with inflationary rises, from an average of 13 percent in the early years to 23 percent in the two-year period 1950–1951. Per capita income barely rose up to 1950 and maximum prewar productivity in the industrial sector did not recover until 1952.

In that Spain of poverty, hunger, fear, ration books, the black market, and high mortality rates due to illnesses, militarization, order, and discipline took control of the workplace. A law of September 29, 1939 gave the Falange the assets of the "old Marxist and anarchist labor unions." Members of the workers' movement, collectivists, revolutionaries, and reds lost their jobs and had to get down on their knees to beg to be taken on again. The prohibition of the right to free association and strike forced what little remained of those labor unions underground. They no longer had leaders, dead or imprisoned as they were, or any premises in which to meet or any space in which to protest.

Totalitarian winds also blew during those years across the domestic policy of the dictatorship, which experienced its most fascistic period that had already begun in the civil war with German and Italian intervention. It was also the time of maximum power and glory for Ramón Serrano Suñer, Minister of the Interior since January 1938, a post that he did not leave until May 1941, head of the Political Council of the then influential Falange, and Minister of Foreign Affairs from October 16, 1940 until September 3, 1942, when he was dismissed after a confrontation in the Virgin of Begoña Sanctuary in Bizkaia between Carlists and a group of Falangists.

The defeat and persecution of the workers' movement paved the way for the creation of the Organización Sindical Española (Spanish Labor Union Organization, OSE), an "instrument to frame and control workers, to dissuade them from potential positions of protest or claims, and repressive if the deterrent function failed." The Francoist labor union framework, as Carme Molinero and Pere Ysás have demonstrated, was an essential piece of the dictatorship that, in trying to subjugate the working classes and eliminate the class struggle, "coincided in character and function with the labor union apparatuses of other European fascisms." The OSE was made up of twenty-eight labor corporations or *sindicatos verticales* (vertical syndicates) that included workers and businessmen by branch of production, controlled by the Falangist bureaucracy. The vertical syndicate was, moreover, charged with mobilizing the masses in order to demonstrate the passionate support for Franco and the authorities during official acts and activities.

In those early years of the fascization of the dictatorship, Serrano Suñer sketched out a plan for indoctrination, propaganda, and social mobilization, which Franco supported while the military successes of the Axis powers lasted. This desire to control public opinion was apparent in the setting up of an extensive chain of Movement press outlets, a network of radio broadcasters, and the NO-DO, the projection of which was obligatory in all movie theaters. The Press Law of April 22, 1938, which was in force until the law of 1966, transformed the media, as it stated in its preamble, into decisive organs "in the formation of popular culture and above all in the creation of the collective consciousness."

The single party Falange Española Tradicionalista y de las JONS, also termed the National Movement, grew from 240,000 members in 1937 to almost half a million in 1942. Its leaders, together with military personnel, occupied the senior positions in central government and many civil governors, mayors, and councilmen were also Falangists. The main sections of the organization that, prior to the civil war, and like the party in general, had barely any members, were transformed into state institutions. The SEU was the instrument for controlling university students, who were obliged since 1943 to join this union. The Frente de Juventudes (Youth Front) took charge of the political and paramilitary education of thousands of young people. And the Sección Femenina (Womens' Section), led by Pilar Primo de Rivera, sister of the Falange founder, trained Spanish women in submission and subordination to men. Millions of these women undertook a minimum six-month period of social service, which supplied a free workforce to different social institutions.

When the fate of World War II began to swing clearly in favor of the Allied powers, dictatorship propaganda started to present Franco as a neutral and impartial statesman who had known how to liberate Spain from the disaster of the global conflict. There was a need to get rid of any fascist appearances and highlight the Catholic basis of the regime, the essential identification between Catholicism and the Spanish tradition. The regime that had emerged out of the civil war had nothing to do with fascism, declared Franco in an interview with United Press on November 7, 1944, because fascism did not include Catholicism as a basic principle. What there was in Spain was a Catholic and "organic democracy."

Catholicism, which had drawn together the different forces of the rebel side during the civil war, fulfilled in the victory a similar function. Isidro Gomá, cardinal of Toledo and primate of Spain, one of the architects of transforming the civil war into a crusade, friend of Franco and diehard defender of his authority, died on August 22, 1940. His replacement, Enrique Plá y Deniel, bishop of Salamanca and ideologue of the crusade, kept the Spanish Catholic Church in "amicable harmony," as he termed it, with the new state. He was convinced, and he expressed it in such terms on numerous occasions, that the Spanish Civil War had been armed plebiscite, that the postwar repression was a "surgical operation on the social body of Spain," and that, with the fascist powers defeated, there was nothing to reexamine because the Spanish Church was enjoying the fruits and peak of its powers that the consecration of war and its identification with the Franco dictatorship had conferred upon it.

Already during the civil war, but above all after the victory, the church hierarchy considered very seriously the idea of re-Catholicizing Spain through education. They were supported in this by fascistic Catholic intellectuals, to whom Franco handed over the Ministry of Education. In his first government, appointed on January 30, 1938, the post went to Sainz Rodríguez, an extreme right-wing Alphonsine university professor. Once the war was over, when Franco formed his second government on August 9, 1939, José Ibáñez Martín was chosen. He stayed at the head of the ministry until 1951, twelve years in which he had time to finish up purging the teaching profession, Catholicizing schools, and favoring church schools with generous subsidies.

Ibáñez Martín maintained Tiburcio Romualdo de Toledo and José Permatín, two ultra-Catholics from the Sainz Rodríguez era, as the principal people in charge within his ministry; and he also incorporated some "old hands" from the Falange, yet another example of that blend of fascism and Catholicism that dominated Spanish postwar society. Between them, they kicked thousands of teachers out of their jobs and converted Spanish schools into plunder divided up among Catholic, Falangist, and ex-combatant families. Disqualification and sanctions also affected university professors, whose posts were distributed out, under the watchful eye of Ibáñez Martín, among Catholic propagandists and Opus Dei.

The Church was the soul of the new state, brought back to life after the death it had been put to by anticlericalism. The Church and the Catholic religion swamped everything: teaching, habits, public administration, and the centers of power. Liturgical rites and displays, processions and open-air masses filled the streets of towns and cities, side-by-side the Roman salute, termed "national" instead of fascist, the singing of "Cara al Sol," and the cult of the Leader, whose face adorned coins with the legend "Caudillo of Spain by the Grace of God."

Bishops attacked "dishonest debauchery" and urged women to dress in an "explosion of Spanishness." Women were also relegated to the "chores of their sex," deprived of any legal, financial, or cultural autonomy, and condemned to obedience and sacrifice. That was how Spain was re-Catholicized, with rosaries, popular missions, morality campaigns against blasphemy, short courses on Christianity, and spiritual exercises. And the Church was happy with that "Catholic apotheosis," with that "religious pride," with "flamboyant acts of aggressive Catholicism," as Cardinal Francesc Vidal i Barraquer termed them from his particular exile in Rome.

That symbiosis between fatherland and religion, National Catholicism, was cemented after the July 1936 military uprising as a binding agent of the heterogeneous groups within the rebel side and emerged out of the war, in the words of Alfonso Botti, "as the unifying hegemonic ideology" of that reactionary coalition that concentrated around the authority of General Franco. National Catholicism, as the perfect antidote to the secular Republic, separatism, and revolutionary ideologies, had a special meaning for the bourgeoisie and landowners, for military personnel, and for a widespread sector of small rural landowners and the urban middle classes. It turned out to be an efficient ideology to mobilize all those groups that resolved to eradicate social conflicts and give them a surgical solution.

The army, the Falange, and the Church represented, in short, those winners and out of them came the high-ranking leaders, the system of local power, and the loyal servants of the public administration. Those three bureaucracies competed among themselves to increase their power bases, rivalries that recent research has detailed in many cities and towns in Spain. The share-out was difficult and the rivalry between those who had always exercised power and the upstart members of the Falange created tensions aired publicly by the Catholic and Falangist media and registered in numerous documents. It seems clear that in Franco's Spain power did not reside in the party, but in the traditional state apparatus, beginning with the armed forces, in the Catholic Church, in landowners, many of them converted to Falangism, and of course, in Francisco Franco, the Generalissimo, Caudillo, and Saint.

After the fall of European fascism, the defense of Catholicism as a basic component in the history of Spain served as a front for the dictatorship in that crucial period for its survival. National Catholicism ended up prevailing in a country converted into a kingdom without a king in 1947, although it did have the Caudillo, and in which the only party ceased to have any allies in Europe after 1945.

Fascism fell and Franco carried on, although the dictatorship had to live through some years of international ostracism. On June 19, 1945 the foundational conference of the United Nations Organization (UNO), held in San Francisco, passed a Mexican motion that expressly vetoed admitting Spain to the new body. That veto was followed by different condemnations, the closure of the French border, and the withdrawal of ambassadors, but what many republicans in exile as well as in Spain itself were waiting for never arrived: that the democratic powers would expel Franco for being a bloody dictator, brought to power with the aid of arms from Nazi Germany and Fascist Italy.

In reality, Franco's Spain never played, nor could it play, a central role in international politics during those years. And according to Enrique Moradiellos, "the democratic powers, faced with the alternative of putting up with a harmless Franco or provoking in Spain a political destabilization of uncertain outcome, resolved to put up with his presence as the inevitable lesser of two evils." Furthermore, however democratic those nations were, Franco always enjoyed global sympathy and support from widespread Catholic and conservative sectors. Luis Carrero Blanco, Presidency undersecretary, was convinced that the great western capitalist powers would take no energetic measures, whether military or economic, against a Catholic anticommunist Spain. He told Franco so in one of the reports he sent frequently at that difficult time: "the only formula for us can only be: *order, unity, and endure*."

And they endured, administering the returns from that lasting investment that was repression, with laws that the special jurisdictional bodies maintained throughout the entire dictatorship, with an army that, united around Franco, presented no cracks, with the mask the Church provided the Caudillo as a refuge from his tyranny and cruelty, and with the support of widespread social sectors, from landowners and industrial leaders to poorer rural landowners. The major challenges stemming from socioeconomic changes and restructuring the state and public administration would arrive later, but the apparatus of political power in the dictatorship was preserved intact, order and unity guaranteed. Just as Carrero Blanco had predicted.

Bibliography

Álvaro Dueñas, Manuel. *"Por ministerio de la ley y voluntad del Caudillo". La Jurisdicción Especial de Responsabilidades Políticas (1939–1945)*. Madrid: Centro de Estudios Políticos y Constitucionales, 2006.

Aróstegui, Julio, coord. *Franco: la represión como sistema*. Barcelona: Flor del Viento Ediciones, 2012.

Box, Zira. *España, año cero. La construcción simbólica del franquismo*. Madrid: Alianza Ed., 2010.

Casanova, Julián, coord. *Morir, matar, sobrevivir. La violencia en la dictadura de Franco.* Barcelona: Crítica, 2002.

De Riquer, Borja. *La dictadura de Franco.* Barcelona: Crítica, 2010.

Moradiellos, Enrique. *La España de Franco (1939–1975). Política y sociedad.* Madrid: Síntesis, 2000.

Nicolás Martín, Encarna. *La libertad encadenada. España en la dictadura franquista, 1939–1975.* Madrid: Alianza Ed., 2005.

Prada Rodríguez, Julio. *La España masacrada. La represión franquista de guerra y posguerra.* Madrid: Alianza Ed., 2010.

Preston, Paul. *El holocausto español: Odio y exterminio en la guerra civil y después.* Translated by Catalina Martínez Muñoz and Eugenia Vázquez Nacarino. Barcelona: Debate, 2011. English edition: *The Spanish Holocaust: Inquisition and Extermination in Twentieth-century Spain.* London: harper Press, 2012.

Rodrigo, Javier. *Cautivos. Campos de concentración en la España franquista, 1936–1947.* Barcelona: Crítica, 2005.

2

Repression against Loyalist Officers in the Basque Country

Joan Villarroya Font

One of the aspects of greatest concern to the plotters in the spring of 1936, particularly to Brig. Gen. Emilio Mola Vidal (known as "the Director" because he acted as the chief planner behind the coup), was the attitude of the officers who remained loyal to Spain's Republican government.[1] This concern arose out of Mola's personal view that they were the ones best able to foil the coup.

This concern became so great that a clear warning to the loyalists was posted in the Court of Instruction no. 5: "The timid and hesitant are advised that he who is not with us is against us and shall be treated as an enemy. For comrades who are not comrades, the triumphant Movimiento shall be inexorable."

Indeed, one of the officers loyal to the government was Brig. Gen. Mola's immediate superior, Maj. Gen. Domènec Batet i

---

1. In recent years, a series of books and articles have appeared within the historiography of the Spanish Civil War studying and analyzing the actions of military officers who remained loyal to the Republican government and its institutions. Noteworthy examples include: José Luis Cervero, *Los rojos de la Guardia Civil. Su lealtad a la República les costó la vida* (Madrid: La esfera de los libros, 2006); Javier García Fernández (coord.), *25 militares de la República* (Madrid: Ministerio de Defensa, 2011); Juan Barba Lagomazzini, *Hombres de armas de la República: Guerra civil Española 1936-1939. Biografías de militares de la República* (Madrid: Ministerio de Defensa, 2015); Joan Villarroya i Font, "Militars contra el cop d'estat de juliol de 1936", *Segle XX* 2 (2009), 83–106; and Iñaki Egaña, *Los crímenes de Franco en Euskal Herria 1936-1940* (Tafalla: Txalaparta; Altaffaylla, 2009). A chapter in Egaña's book (228–33) addresses the actions of officers loyal to democracy.

Mestres,[2] commander of the 6th Organic Division. Amid persistent rumors that Mola was embroiled in a plot against the regime, Batet is known to have met with his subordinate in the Monastery of Irache[3] and asked him whether or not the rumors were true. Mola flatly denied them and gave Batet his word of honor that he was not engaged in any plotting. History, however, tells a different story. Mola broke his word and Batet was shot by firing squad in Burgos on February 18, 1937.

In July 1936, the provinces of Bizkaia, Gipuzkoa, Araba (Álava), and Navarre were the responsibility of the 6th Organic Division, which was precisely where the mutiny was being planned, because Brig. Gen. Mola was commander of the 12th Infantry Brigade stationed in Pamplona (Iruñea). Indeed, Pamplona is where Mola revolted on July 18 and rapidly sent orders for the uprising to commence in Bilbao, Donostia-San Sebastián, and Vitoria-Gasteiz in line with the plans developed by the plotters. Apart from Pamplona, however, the coup met with success only in Vitoria-Gasteiz.[4] In Donostia-San Sebastián, the coup leaders' hesitancy resulted in their being surrounded in their barracks and ultimately, after violent clashes, forced to capitulate. In Bilbao, where the only military garrison was the Garellano 6th Mountain Battalion, the decisive attitude of the civil governor José Echevarría Novoa and of the various commanders of the military and police corps managed to

---

2. Hilari Raguer, *El general Batet. Franco contra Batet: crónica de una venganza* (Barcelona: Península, 1996).

3. See the foreword to Luis Romero, *Tres días de julio. (18, 19 y 20 de 1936)* (Barcelona: Ariel, 1994), xxxi. Romero recounts that Mola's adjutant, Emiliano Fernández Cordón, provided extremely valuable documents for the first edition of his book in 1967. When Romero published the article "Mola frente a Batet" in the journal *Historia y Vida*, he concluded with the following remarks: "Both men died as victims of decisions taken in accordance with what they believed to be their duty and as their conscience dictated." Fernández Cordón's response was impertinent; he frowned on "comparing a 'deeply honorable military man' with a 'Marxist', freemason, and I cannot recall what further descriptor, but one just as inexact as it was pejorative on his scale of values. . . . He refused to rectify a single adjective; one of the most frequently used was to label as "Cossacks" the Republican officers whom he considered without exception to be Stalinists."

4. Germán Ruiz Llano, "Los compañeros que no son compañeros. Represión, disciplina y consenso en la guarnición vitoriana durante la guerra." Research seminar, Departamento de Historia Contemporánea, Universidad Complutense de Madrid, November 26, 2013. At https://www.ucm.es/data/cont/media/www/pag-13888/textogerman.pdf.

thwart the coup, though not without some tensions and despite the fact that most of the senior and junior officers in the Mountain Battalion backed the coup. Echevarría called the military leaders and the commanders of the Guardia Civil, the Carabineers, the Assault Guard, and the provincial police (known as the Miñones) into his office and informed all present that, given the circumstances, he was taking command of all forces in Bizkaia. The commander of the Guardia Civil, Juan Colina Guerra, was the first to pledge his allegiance to the government of the Republic, after which the other men in attendance followed suit.[5]

Given the doubts raised by the attitude of the Mountain Battalion, the garrison commanders from the army and police corps headed to the barracks as soon as the meeting finished. Following an exchange of words, Lt. Col. Juan Colina warned that he and his guardsmen, with the backing of the people, would open fire on the battalion's forces if they were to join the uprising. Colina, through the forcefulness of his threat, succeeded in garnering the support of the other senior officers present, including the commanders of the Assault Guard and the Miñones. But his words would remain etched in the minds of the rebels and ultimately play a crucial role in his later death sentence and execution in April 1939. Some authors, like Vicente Talón, locate this meeting in the office of Col. Andrés Fernández-Piñerúa Iraola, without specifying whether it was in the barracks of the Mountain Battalion, while the accounts given after the war by officers in attendance point to the meeting having taken place in the barracks.

Talón[6] does mention an incident in which Lt. Col. Vidal Munárriz, having returned to the barracks, came upon First Lieutenant del Oso haranguing a group of soldiers. When Vidal tried to stop him, del Oso slapped him, so Vidal drew his pistol and ordered del Oso's arrest. His request, however, was met with indifference by the officers who supported the coup.

Of the officers present in the meetings at which the fate of Bilbao was decided, two would be executed at the end of the war, basically because of their attitude in the above meeting. They were Infantry Col. Joaquín Vidal and Lt. Col. Juan Colina of the Guardia Civil. The other officers present were "more fortunate,"

---

5. Vicente Talón, *Memoria de la guerra de Euzkadi de 1936* (Esplugues de Llobregat: Plaza y Janés, 1988), vol. 1, 94.
6. Ibid.

in that they were only arrested and sentenced to prison. Infantry Col. Andrés Fernández-Piñerúa Iraola, for example, stood trial on September 27, 1940 and was sentenced to thirty years in prison. His health was not good, however, and he died behind bars.

In Pamplona the only serious opposition to the coup was put up by the chief of the Guardia Civil José Rodríguez Medel and some of his officers. Rodríguez Medel was the first of the military and Guardia Civil commanders to pay for his loyalty to the government with his life. Maj. José Rodríguez Medel Briones, deployed to Pamplona only a few months earlier, was killed by some of his own guardsmen when he refused to take part in the coup, rejecting a personal appeal directly from Brig. Gen. Mola, and instead tried to move the Guardia Civil south of the Ebro River to block the advance of the rebels out of Navarre. There is no doubt that the plotters had foreseen the attitude and resistance of Maj. Rodríguez Medel and so organized his murder.[7] According to the account of José Antonio Balduz, a group of guardsmen came out of their headquarters and treacherously shot their commander.[8]

Rodríguez Medel would not be the only senior or junior officer in the Guardia Civil to lose his life in defense of Republican legality in Navarre. Maj. José Martínez Friera and Capt. Ricardo Fresno Urzay were also shot and killed. Ricardo Fresno was seen as a hero for his defense of Nador in the Spanish protectorate in Morocco in July 1936. On August 26, both men were taken from Fort San Cristóbal, where they were being held on Mola's orders, and shot by firing squad.

Before the close of July 1936, another official of the Guardia Civil would be killed by rebel forces. This was Capt. Alejo Beñaran Garín, chief of the Guardia Civil in Eibar, Gipuzkoa, and a Basque born in Legutio (Villarreal), Araba,[9] who organized a column with his guardsmen and a large group of militia forces and hurried to the front to prevent the entry of Carlist militias into Beasain, Gipuzkoa. After heavy fighting, the rebels occupied

---

7. For additional information on this major in the Guardia Civil, see Gonzalo Jar Couselo, "La Guardia Civil en Navarra (18/07/1936)," *Príncipe de Viana* 192 (January–June 1991), 281–323. See also Cervero, *Los Rojos de la Guardia Civil*.
8. A testimony that appears in a documentary shown by the television channel ETB-2 on April 16, 2009, entitled *Rodríguez Medel. El primero de la lista* (Rodríguez Medel: First on the list).
9. Cervero, *Los Rojos de la Guardia Civil*, 343.

Beasain and Beñaran was taken prisoner. That very night, July 27, he was executed by firing squad in the cemetery. Eight members of the Guardia Civil and numerous militiamen were also shot that night. According to some sources, Capt. Beñaran's eyes had been gouged out before he was shot and his body appeared to have been torn to pieces.[10] The harshness of this repression, which marked a turning point in the civil war in Gipuzkoa, was a result, among other things, of the staunch resistance put up by the Republicans and of a plan to spread terror among the inhabitants and defenders of other localities.[11]

On July 28 in Bilbao, a lieutenant in the Assault Guard, Justo Rodríguez Rivas, was buried.[12] Rodríguez had marched from Bilbao at the head of a column of guardsmen and militiamen to assist in putting down the rebellion in Donostia-San Sebastián. Rodríguez, who was seriously wounded in the fighting, died hours later.

Lack of space does not permit a detailed account of the evolution of military organization in the Basque Country,[13] but it is necessary to offer some comments on the subject to keep track of the officers who held various commands from July 1936 to the end of the northern campaign. Not all of the officers who served in the Basque Army were deployed in the territory covered by the 6th Organic Division in July 1936 and some arrived in the Basque Country from Madrid in October and November of that year. This was the case of Lt. Col. Juan Cueto of the Carabineers, Lt. Col. Gumersindo Azcárate of the Infantry, and the Guardia Civil Captains Eugenio García Gunilla and José Bolaños López. All held important commands in the Basque Army and were shot and killed by the Francoists when taken prisoner.

A cursory look at the military organization shows how it developed from some initial columns into a military structure organized into battalions, and then, in parallel with the Spanish Republican Army, into brigades and divisions. This military structure reported

---

10. Jesús Gutiérrez Arosa, *La guerra civil en Eibar y Elget* (Eibar: Eibarko Udala-Ayuntamiento de Eibar, 2007), 30.
11. Pedro Barruso Barés, *Violencia política y represión en Guipúzcoa durante la guerra civil y el primer franquismo (1936–1945)* (Donostia: Hiria, 2005), 114–15.
12. José Antonio Urgoitia Badiola, *Crónica de la guerra civil 1936-1937 en la Euzkadi peninsular* (Oihartzun: Sendoa, 2001), vol. 1, 262.
13. Carlos A. Pérez, "Aproximación a la génesis y formación del 'Ejército de Euzkadi', julio 1936–mayo 1937," online paper, at http://www.belliludi.com/historia_aproximacion.html.

to a general staff, created in embryonic form by the Basque regional president Jose Antonio Agirre in November 1936 and made up of a core of professional soldiers. Notable among them was Maj. Alberto de Montaud y Noguerol, who served as chief of staff until May 1937 when he stepped down and Agirre himself took over.

Jumping ahead to late April 1937, we find a document in which the general staff of the brigades of Navarre adds in its operations communique of April 29 to the General of the 6th Army Corps and General Franco that, "we have captured Cavalry Col. Arturo Llarch who commanded an enemy Division that was defending Guernica [Gernika] together with Two Captains and a Lieutenant of his staff who were killed as they tried to lead a counterattack against our forces." A copy of this telegram is found in the documentation of the summary court-martial[14] of Col. Arturo Llarch Castresana. This is the colonel who had been vacationing in Villasana de Mena, Burgos, in July 1936 and would lead various military units in Santander and Asturias until the Basque Army corps was reorganized into four divisions in late April 1937, at which point he was named chief of the first division that was defending Gernika on the same April 29 that he was taken prisoner. The other three divisions were led by Col. Joaquín Vidal Munárriz, the Guardia Civil Maj. Juan Ibarrola, and Col. Daniel Irezabal. With the exception of Ibarrola, who was pardoned, the other three all met their deaths before a firing squad. According to Ramón Salas Larrazábal: "On that same day of April 29, after the occupation of Guernica, which the Basque corps had fought doggedly to defend, the first division launched a counterattack during which the division commander, Col. Llarch, was taken prisoner, along with two of his staff captains and a lieutenant; all four were shot and killed by Gen. Solchaga in Ajangiz that same day."[15]

Upon capture, Col. Llarch was transferred to the cavalry barracks where the Numancia 6th regiment was headquartered. At 6 pm that same day, April 29, he was called to testify before the investigating judge. After he testified, his indictment was handed

---

14. Ferrol Intermediate Military Archive (AMIF), Court-martial (unnumbered) of Cavalry Col. Arturo Llarch Castresana for the crime of military rebellion. The court documents are numbered: there are twenty-one in total and an unnumbered copy of the death certificate. From the order to initiate proceedings to the execution of the sentence, less than twelve hours elapsed.

15. Ramon Salas Larrazábal, *Historia del Ejército Popular de la República* (Madrid: Editora Nacional, 1973), vol. 2, 1392.

down and he was informed of his right to a defense counsel. Statements were taken and the case proceeded to trial. The prosecutor
and the defense counsel were given an hour to prepare. At 8 pm,
a court-martial of general officers was convened in the courtroom
of the barracks. A few minutes later, the verdict was read out. The
minutes of the court-martial and the sentence, which was death,
take up less than two sheets of paper. Llarch was informed of the
sentence, which had been approved by the judge advocate, at which
point his life was put in the hands of the chief of staff, who approved
the sentences a few hours later and gave the green light for the execution to proceed. With unusual speed, before midnight on April
30, the military commander Col. Luis Campos Guereta-Martínez[16]
gave the order to carry out the execution in front of the wall of
the cemetery of Santa Isabel in the part corresponding to the Hip-
podrome. The prisoner entered the chapel at 3 am and at 6 am a
firing squad made up of soldiers from the Numancia regiment was
dispatched to carry out the sentence.

Barely ten days after Bilbao fell to Franco's troops, Col. Juan
Cueto Ibáñez[17] of the Carabineers faced the firing squad in the
early morning of June 29, 1937. A resident of Araba and a friend
of the philosopher Miguel de Unamuno, Cueto had been born in
Legutio on January 20, 1881 and had graduated as a second lieutenant in the Carabineers. This had marked the start of a long and
eventful career in the military.

Cueto, who was a hugely cultured man, wrote two books
between 1916 and 1918. The first was a broad reflection on Don
Quixote entitled *La vida y la raza a través del Quijote*, while the
second explored his thinking as a democrat and an officer, entitled

---

16. In July 1936, Campos was in command of the Numancia 6th Cavalry Regiment. By July 1938, he commanded the 50th division at the Ebro front. When
his unit was overwhelmed by the Republican offensive launched on July 25, he
was discharged from the army and arraigned. See the *Boletín Oficial del Estado*
(BOE), 1/08/1938, 497: "Cavalry Col. Luís Campos Guereta Martínez has been
discharged from the Army and retired from active service, without prejudice to
any responsibilities that may arise from the judicial proceedings to which he is
subject."

17. Germán Ruiz Llano, "Juan Cueto Ibáñez, un alavés defensor de la República," *Revista Sancho el Sabio* 34 (2011), 159–78. The reference to the proceedings that appears in the article is: Ferrol Intermediate Military Archive (AMIF),
Courts and Tribunals of the Province of Bizkaia, Urgent summary trial no. 15,
box 4, sheet 7.

De mi ideario: Divagaciones de un militar demócrata alrededor de varios temas de actualidad. A staunch supporter of the Allied Powers in World War I, he was a man of democratic and leftist ideas, and a champion of the Basque language and of his homeland, but not a proponent of Basque nationalism.[18] Between 1920 and 1922 Cueto was a lecturer in Spanish at Columbia University in New York City. On his return, he was deployed to Pamplona and Bera (Vera de Bidasoa) in Navarre, now as captain of a company of carabineers. Cueto stood opposed to the dictatorship and the monarchy, had a lively character, and liked to speak the simple unvarnished truth. Soon he was prosecuted by the sitting judge major of the Pamplona post on the charge of insulting a superior officer in an official document, and also by the military judge of Oviedo, in 1926, on the charge of publishing and distributing clandestine papers. It was at that time that he entered the freemasons with the name "Indarra" and became a member of lodge "Helenes 7" in the city of Pontevedra, Galicia, and then, from 1931, of lodge "Ibérica 1" in Madrid.[19] By the time the Republic was proclaimed, Juan Cueto held the rank of major and was stationed in the Military Chamber of the Presidency of the Republic, occupying the post of military adjutant to Presidents Niceto Alcalá Zamora[20] and Manuel Azaña. He was promoted to Lieutenant Colonel in February 1935. With the outbreak of the civil war, he left the post of military adjutant and in October 1936 proceeded to Bilbao to lead the Azaña-Vizcaya Battalion of the Republican Left. In the offensive launched on November 30 to take back Vitoria-Gasteiz, he was in command of one of the four columns in the attack. The president of the Republic, Manuel Azaña, took a dim view of the fact that military units were being led by officers of advanced years without military experience: "When I found out they had put [Cueto] in command of frontline troops I was not pleased (either for him and for what the case revealed), because a senior office of the Carabineers, already late in his life and professionally distant from all

18. See the Juan Cueto Ibáñez de Zuazo website at https://leopoldocueto.word-press.com/biografia/. Consulted on April 13, 2016.
19. Manuel de Paz Sánchez, *Militares masones de España. Diccionario biográfico del siglo XX* (Valencia: Biblioteca Historia Social, 2004), 129.
20. In Niceto Alcalá Zamora's view, Juan Cueto was "a deeply cultured and very honorable man" who was well-known for his strokes of wit and whose "iniquitous execution after the surrender of Bilbao" was a source of genuine sorrow. Niceto Alcalá Zamora, *Memorias* (Barcelona: Planeta, 1977), 364.

battlefield training, did not seem the person best suited for the case." Cueto was then deployed in the rearguard until a few days before Franco's troops entered Bilbao. On June 14, 1937, he was put in charge of defending a sector of Bilbao. Probably because of health issues, he remained in the city. On June 23, he was arrested after having sent two letters to the new military governor in which he expressed that his "failure to report was due to the fact that he esteemed the separatist Reds as loyal and legitimate forces with whom he was absolutely identified in his soul, given that he could not be with them in body."[21]

His biographer, Germán Ruiz Llano, sums up the life and career of Juan Cueto Ibáñez writing that he was a soldier and a committed defender of democracy; this is why he did not waver in the civil war to align himself with the government that he believed legitimate and legal, a decision that ultimately cost him his life.

In late August, shortly after the unsuccessful Santoña Agreement, Cueto was taken prisoner by Franco's army, along with numerous professional senior and junior officers in the Basque Army who had served since the early months of the war. The result for many of them would be devastating. By early September, a large number of them had already been brought before the investigating judge to testify. The court-martial[22] was convened in Santoña, Cantabria, on the premises of the prison colony of Dueso and the defendants numbered eleven senior and junior officers serving in the Basque Army.

On September 5, 1937, the same date that appears on the defendants' witness statements, the court-martial delivered its sentence, including the following statement: "As members of the armed forces who, serving the Marxist cause, also served in some regions of Spain and, among these, in the Basque provinces of Gipuzkoa and Bizkaia, they fought in a secessionist cause on behalf of the territorial disintegration of the *Patria* with the aim of forming an independent state under the guise of the revolt, ending ultimately in the grotesquerie of the Basque Country."

The sentence also specified the posts that the convicted men had held in the Republican army. First on the list was Lt. Col. Daniel Irezabal Goiti (Goñi) of the infantry, who had been in charge of the recruiting office in Bilbao in July 1936 and later commanded a division. Second on the list was Lt. Col. Gumersindo

---

21. Paz Sánchez, *Militares masones de España*, 129.
22. AMIF, Case no. 1/1937.

Azcárate Gómez of the infantry, who had commanded the Alcalá de Henares Bicycle Battalion and been seriously injured by one of his officers. Later he held the post of inspector in the Basque Army. Third came Capt. Salvador Gómez Bullón of the engineers, who had led the signal battalion in the Ondarroa sector, among other duties. Fourth was Capt. José Bolaños López of the Guardia Civil, who had been transferred to the north from Madrid and held various posts at the front and later in the officer school for militias, in Bilbao. Fifth on the list was 2nd Lt. Joaquin Barba del Barrio of the infantry, who eventually commanded the 115 and 135 battalions on campaign. The sixth man on the list was José Duarte Ansorena. Duarte, who had been on leave in Santander, was later to lead various battalions. The sentence also emphasizes that all of the defendants had received immediate promotions because of their loyalty and allegiance to the Popular Front government. In addition, the sentence mentions Capt. Ernesto de la Fuente Torres, who had served as interim chief of staff for the Basque Army among other posts, and Capt. Ángel Lamas Arroyo,[23] who had graduated from the staff college and served on the frontline in Madrid and in Extremadura before being sent to the north, where he served on the general staff of the Basque Army until he reported to the Nationalist forces in Santoña. Two other officers to be convicted were 1st Lt. Emilio Rodríguez Arce and 2nd Lt. Eduardo Rogina Pulpello, both of the infantry. The military court also made exceptions in two cases, ruling that "as special circumstances modifying the responsibility of this Court, we find for Gumersindo Azcárate the aggravating factor of social and political danger, and for Ernesto de la Fuente Torres the significance of the duties performed."

Death sentences were handed down to Lt. Col. Daniel Irezabal[24] of the infantry (his name on the sentence appears as Irazabal), Lt. Col. Gumersindo Azcárate Gómez of the infantry, Capt. Salvador Gómez Bullón of the engineers, Guardia Civil Capt. José Bolaños López, 2nd Lt. Joaquín Barba del Barrio of the infantry, 2nd Lt. José Duarte Ansorena of the infantry, and general staff Capt. Ernesto de la Fuente Torres. Capt. Ángel Lamas was sentenced to life imprisonment, 1st Lt. Rodríguez Arce and 2nd Lt. Rogina were

---

23. Lamas penned a memoir in which no mention of the court-martial appears. Ángel Lamas, *Unos… y… otros* (Barcelona: Luis de Caralt, 1972).

24. These are the ranks held by the officers in July 1936, because the rebel forces did not accept promotions that the officers had obtained over the course of the civil war.

given twelve years and a day in prison, and Lt. Col. Antonio Gudín received a prison sentence of six months and a day.

The judge advocate gave his assent to the sentences on September 8, leaving them unchanged in their entirety. The Chief of Staff's approval, which was addressed to the office of the judge advocate in Santander, arrived from Salamanca on October 9, 1937. The officers sentenced to death were removed to the prison in Bilbao and put before a firing squad on the morning of December 18, 1937 in the cemetery of the Bizkaian capital. The executed men were Col. Gumersindo Azcárate Gómez, Maj. Ernesto de la Fuente Torres, Maj. José Bolaños López, and Col. Daniel Irazabal Goti.[25]

Some of the other officials who were also taken prisoner in late August, such as Maj. José Gállego Arangües, later promoted to lieutenant colonel, stood trial twice in Santander and were sentenced to death on both occasions, but the judge advocate quashed the first sentence because Maj. Gállego was supposed to be judged by a summary court-martial of general officers, which did not occur the first time. The second court-martial was convened in Santander on January 10, 1938 and the verdict was the same: death. The sentence was carried out on the morning of May 28, 1938 within the walls of the Vista Alegre cemetery, in Bilbao.[26] Gállego, when taken prisoner, had been chief of staff of the Basque Army in Santander.

On the very day that the civil war ended militarily, April 1, 1939, Lt. Col. Juan Colina Guerras of the Guardia Civil was shot by firing squad in the Barcelona neighborhood of Camp de la Bota.[27] Colina had been commander of the Guardia Civil in the province of Bizkaia in July 1936 and we do not know the reason that he was not transferred to Bilbao, because most of the servicemen who remained loyal to the Republic and were detained during the war or in April 1939 stood trial in the cities in which they had resided in July 1936. The case of Lt. Col. Colina is all the stranger because the main charge against him was based on his activity between July 18 and 22, 1936 in the city of Bilbao.

---

25. This is what appears on the notification of his execution. His name was Daniel Irezabai Goti or according to other sources Goñi.

26. José Gállego is discussed by Marcelino Laruelo Roa, *Muertes paralelas. El destino trágico de los prohombres de la República* (Gijón: Gráficas Apel, 2004), 189–201.

27. Third Territorial Military Tribunal, Barcelona (ATMTT). Ordinary summary proceedings no. 28 against Juan Colina. I am grateful to Professor Manuel Risques Corbella for the information on these proceedings.

In early 1939, Juan Colina was in Barcelona, serving eight years in prison for collaborating with a ring of spies and members of the Fifth Column operating inside the Republican National Guard. Despite these circumstances, however, he was put under arrest when he reported to the new authorities on February 2, 1939. In the file of his pretrial proceedings, there are two voluntary statements of denunciation. The first was made on February 21, 1939 by Capt. Juan Zamora Moll, who had been the captain of the Garellano 6th Mountain Battalion in July 1936. The second was made by Lt. Col. Guillermo Vizcaíno Sagaseta of the infantry on February 24, 1939.

Both statements put particular emphasis on Colina's attitude in the meeting held in the Garellano barracks on July 19, 1936 and accuse him of being the main culprit behind the failure of the coup in Bilbao. All of the other facts were of secondary importance, including Colina's two detentions, the first in Bilbao from which he was exonerated and the second in Barcelona where he was found guilty. Colina always denied having made the remark that was attributed to him and he downplayed its importance in a statement made on March 14, 1939. According to him, Lt. Col. Vidal had already left at the head of a column advancing toward Otxandio and the man actually calling the shots in the meeting had been Col. Fernández-Pinerúa. An additional voluntary statement, given by Infantry Capt. Mario de Hormaechea y Ganime when he learned of the case being mounted against Colina, further aggravated Colina's situation. Capt. de Hormaechea had served under Colina in October 1934. He described Colina personally as an outspoken republican and leftist and said that he, acting as a liaison in the plotting of the military revolt, knew that Colina would not support the Movimiento. In fact, he recalled that Colina became known throughout Bizkaia as the primary cause for the coup's failure, given that the Guardia Civil had more troops than the Mountain Battalion. In the end, a court-martial was convened on March 23 and the verdict was, as the record shows, the death penalty. By coincidence, the judge in charge of overseeing the carrying out of the execution was Col. Guillermo Vizcaíno Saraseta, one of the men who had given testimony against Colina and was on duty in Bilbao in July 1936. At five in the morning[28] on April 1, the sentence was carried out.

---

28. The time of execution was related to the hour of sunrise. As a result, it varied by time of year.

At the close of hostilities, a number of officers who had served in the Basque Army since the first months of the war and had, in some cases, led major units in the Spanish Republican Army, were detained in various Mediterranean localities. Because it is impossible to mention all of them, I will address the case of a number whose actions throughout the war were particularly distinguished. Two examples are offered by Andrés Fernández-Pinerúa and Juan Ibarrola, who stood trial and were found guilty, but whose lives were spared. Others, such as Eugenio García Gunilla and Joaquín Vidal Munárriz, were sentenced to death and shot. In the case of Capt. García Gunilla, who had held numerous military posts after his transfer to the north and was detained in Alicante at the war's close, he was court-martialed in that city on November 14, 1939 and shot by firing squad in 1940. García Gunilla had been in Madrid in July 1936 and then transferred to the north in late September with the rank of captain. He rapidly took control of the Lekeitio sector and subsequently commanded the 2nd brigade of the 1st division led by Col. Llarch. After the fall of Bilbao, he commanded the 2nd brigade of the 3rd division led by Lt. Col. Ibarrola. He succeeded in reaching the central zone and fought in the province of Badajoz until the end of the war.

Two of the servicemen who were deployed in the Basque Country in July 1936, Lt. Col. Joaquín Vidal Munárriz of the infantry and Guardia Civil Capt. Juan Ibarrola, would ultimately command their army corps. Juan Ibarrola Orueta held the rank of captain in the Guardia Civil barracks in La Salve, in Bilbao. Born in Laudio, Araba, in 1900, he had served as infantry lieutenant in Morocco before joining the Guardia Civil. In July 1936, he was placed in charge of the Otxandio sector as a major. In November of that year, he led a column in the unsuccessful operation against Vitoria-Gasteiz and later commanded the 3rd division of the Basque Army. After the fall of Bilbao, he went on to lead various units until the final defeat in Asturias. Transferred to the Teruel front, he commanded the 22nd Army Corps, which had Enrique Líster Forjan and his legendary 11th division. He led the 22nd Army Corps in the Levante campaign and, in January 1939, took part in the offensive against Peñarroya, on the front in Andalusia, which after heavy fighting was unsuccessful. Ibarrola was detained in Alicante, escaped, and was then recaptured. Court-martialed in Alicante on November 11, 1939, he was sentenced to death but received a pardon. When he was released from prison in 1943, he moved to Bilbao and made his living as a representative for a perfume company. He died in August 1976 in the Bizkaian capital. His actions during the war earned him high praise from the men who served under his command and from the historians who have studied his military career. The judgment of José Luis Cervero[29] about Ibarrola is emphatic. He called Ibarrola, who would rise to command one of the army corps, the most brilliant Guardia Civil officer to serve in the Basque Army throughout the entire campaign.

The last officer discussed her is Lt. Col. Joaquín Vidal Munárriz, who was commander of the Garellano 6th Mountain Battalion in Bilbao in July 1936 and in the following months served in the Basque Army at the head of some of its principal units. When the northern campaign ended, he succeeded in reaching the central zone and was put in charge of the 19th Army Corps in the Levante area, a command which he held until the end of the war. For his distinguished actions in the war, he was decorated with the Medal of Valor in June 1938, at which time he held the rank of colonel. The end of the war caught him in Valencia where he was detained on April 5 and taken to Mont-Olivet prison. After his initial statements before the investigating judge between April 11 and 15, he was arraigned for trial. However, at the request of the judge advocate of the 6th military region, he was transferred to Bilbao on April 30 and held in the provincial prison. In their statements,[30] most of the officers in the Mountain Battalion confirmed the loyalty of Vidal Munárriz and his efforts to stop the unit from joining the military revolt. From the lengthy statements, some conclusions can be drawn as to what happened in Bilbao between July 18 and 21. A particularly damaging factor for Vidal was the accusation of his participation in cases against senior and junior officers in the Mountain Battalion brought before the popular tribunals. Some of those in attendance had considered his testimony to vary in tone between ironic and coarse. The prosecutor took the view that Vidal's appearance as a witness had, to a great extent, been the cause of the death sentence being handed down to some of the senior and junior officers who had supported the revolt, and he considered that these facts, together with the duties he had performed for the "Red" army, amounted to treason. Finally, on July 12, a court-martial of general officers was convened and its

---

29. Cervero, *Los rojos de la Guardia Civil*, 341–42.
30. AMIF, Ordinary summary proceedings 10, 221.

proceedings are summarized for history in little more than a single page. The sentence was death for the crime of supporting rebellion. The sentence was carried out on the morning of August 4 in the cemetery of Vista Alegre.

To sum up the trajectory of these senior and junior officers, I turn to words written by a few of them shortly before they faced the firing squad.[31] Col. Daniel de Irezabal Goti wrote: "[I] die having always done [my] duty and feeling great affection for [my] dear homeland Euzkadi." Maj. Ernesto de la Torre wrote: "Please receive a warm embrace from your good friend[32] who goes to his death with the satisfaction of having done his duty." And finally, Gumersindo Azcárate, considered by the prosecutor to be a man who was both socially and politically dangerous, wrote in a letter to his wife: "The generous Republic for which I die will take care of you and our children. I give everything that I am. If I had a hundred lives, I would offer them all to the Republic. It will be able to reward you. That is all, I die loyal to the Basque Government, I have done my duty, you will be taken care of."

Bibliography

Alcalá Zamora, Niceto. *Memorias*. Barcelona: Planeta, 1977.

Barba Lagomazzini, Juan. *Hombres de armas de la República: Guerra civil Española 1936–1939. Biografías de militares de la República*. Madrid: Ministerio de Defensa, 2015.

Barruso Barés, Pedro. *Violencia política y represión en Guipúzcoa durante la guerra civil y el primer franquismo (1936–1945)*. Donostia: Hiria, 2005

Cervero, José Luis. *Los rojos de la Guardia Civil. Su lealtad a la República les costó la vida*. Madrid: La esfera de los libros, 2006.

Egaña, Iñaki. Los crímenes de Franco en Euskal Herria 1936–1940. Tafalla: Txalaparta; Altaffaylla, 2009.

Eusko Jaurlaritza, Justizia, Lan eta Gizarte Segurantza Saila-Gobierno Vasco, Departamento de Justicia, Empleo y

---

31. These texts are taken from Eusko Jaurlaritza, Justizia, Lan eta Gizarte Segurantza Saila-Gobierno Vasco, Departamento de Justicia, Empleo y Seguridad Social, *Cómo mueren los vascos: Testimonios póstumos de fusilados en Euzkadi por los invasores franquistas (confidencial), marzo de 1938* (Vitoria-Gasteiz: Eusko Jaurlaritzaren Argitalpen Zerbitzu Nagusia-Servicio Central de Publicaciones del Gobierno Vasco, 2009).

32. The letter was addressed to Juan Ajuriaguerra.

Seguridad Social. *Cómo mueren los vascos: Testimonios póstumos de fusilados en Euzkadi por los invasores franquistas (confidencial), marzo de 1938*. Vitoria-Gasteiz: Eusko Jaurlaritzaren Argitalpen Zerbitzu Nagusia-Servicio Central de Publicaciones del Gobierno Vasco, 2009.

García Fernández, Javier, coord. *25 militares de la República*. Madrid: Ministerio de Defensa, 2011.

Gutiérrez Arosa, Jesús. *La guerra civil en Eibar y Elgeta*. Eibar: Eibarko Udala-Ayuntamiento de Eibar, 2007.

Jar Couselo, Gonzalo. "La Guardia Civil en Navarra (18/07/1936)." *Príncipe de Viana* 192 (January–June 1991): 281–323.

Lamas, Ángel. *Unos... y... otros*. Barcelona: Luis de Caralt, 1972.

Laruelo Roa, Marcelino. *Muertes paralelas. El destino trágico de los prohombres de la República*. Gijón: Gráficas Apel, 2004.

Paz Sánchez, Manuel de. *Militares masones de España. Diccionario biográfico del siglo XX*. Valencia: Biblioteca Historia Social, 2004.

Pérez, Carlos A. "Aproximación a la génesis y formación del 'Ejército de Euzkadi', julio 1936–mayo 1937." Online paper (2001). At http://www.belliludi.com/historia_aproximacion. html.

Raguer, Hilari. *El general Batet. Franco contra Batet: crónica de una venganza*. Barcelona: Península, 1996.

Romero, Luis. *Tres días de julio. (18, 19 y 20 de 1936)*. Barcelona: Ariel, 1994.

Ruiz Llano, Germán. "Juan Cueto Ibáñez, un alavés defensor de la República." *Revista Sancho el Sabio* 34 (2011): 159–78.

———. "Los compañeros que no son compañeros. Represión, disciplina y consenso en la guarnición vitoriana durante la guerra." Research seminar, Departamento de Historia Contemporánea, Universidad Complutense de Madrid, November 26, 2013. At https://www.ucm.es/data/cont/media/www/pag-13888/textogerman.pdf.

Salas Larrazábal, Ramón. *Historia del Ejército Popular de la República*. 5 vols. Madrid: Editora Nacional, 1973.

Talón, Vicente. *Memoria de la guerra de Euzkadi de 1936*. 3 vols. Esplugues de Llobregat: Plaza y Janés, 1988.

Urgoitia Badiola, José Antonio. *Crónica de la guerra civil 1936-1937 en la Euzkadi peninsular*. 5 vols. Oihartzun: Sendoa, 2001.

Villarroya i Font, Joan. "Militars contra el cop d'estat de juliol de 1936." *Segle XX* 2 (2009): 83–106.

3

Nature, Significance, and Scope of the International Dimension of the Program of the Basque Government-in-Exile, 1937–1960

Xabier Irujo

In September 1939, the Basque government-in-exile in Paris was already at war with Nazi Germany, Fascist Italy, and Falangist Spain. This was the understanding of the ministers of that Basque government-in-exile and of their prime minister, all of whom understood that the so-called Spanish Civil War was merely a prologue to World War II. Interventionism was consequently one of the guiding principles and the principal focus for action of that Basque government, which decided to participate in the international conflict both militarily and politically, as a Basque government and as a representative of the Basque people. Along the same lines, on January 24, 1939, *lehendakari* (prime minister) Jose A. Agirre wrote in his official capacity to the prime minister of the French state, Édouard Daladier, informing him that when the global conflict broke out, the government of Euzkadi would position itself in opposition to the totalitarian forces and on the side of the democracies. The Basque government's foreign policy foresaw no other option. Neither morally, nor ideologically, nor politically, nor strategically, nor even from the perspective of so-called political realism, the frequent object of criticism in the correspondence between Agirre and Manuel Irujo, former justice minister of the Spanish Republic, was there any other solution than intervening on the side of the democracies, in opposition to the totalitarian powers.[1]

---

1. Iñaki Goiogana, Josu Legarreta, and Xabier Irujo, *Un nuevo 31: Ideología y estrategia del Gobierno de Euzkadi durante la Segunda Guerra Mundial a través*

As a consequence, following the declaration of war in September 1939, the government of Euzkadi, in a public statement issued by the International League of Friends of the Basques (Liga Internacional de Amigos de los Vascos, LIAB)[2] and in another one issued and signed by the *lehendakari,* publically and officially announced its intervention in the conflict on the side of the Allies. Moreover, on September 3 itself, *Euzko Deya* of Paris, one of the Basque government-in-exile's periodicals, published a long article that included the following note:

> The international crisis of last September has had a recurrence that no one could have prevented, in view of the fact that it was announced for a set date by those in a position to make predictions of this kind, that is, precisely by those who have provoked the gravity of the current situation. We are therefore essentially facing the same crisis as a year ago, even if it is true that the incidental circumstances are different and more serious. Our position, consequently, is likewise the same as the one we took in view of September's dramatic situation. The Basques' attitude was given official expression at that time. It is enough to reproduce it in full. This is the note sent to Prime Minister Daladier on September 27: The representatives of the Catalan and Basque governments have the honor of renewing to Your Excellency, in the current circumstances and in all eventualities, the assurance of the loyal friendship of their peoples and of their attachment to the noble and just cause defended by France and England. In the event that the Burgos administration might wish to involve the part of Spain within its power in acts of war against France and England (contrary to the policy of benevolent neutrality implemented by Spain with regard to the Allies of 1914–18), the position of Catalonia and of the Basque Country would be naturally and decidedly at the side of France and England.[3]

---

de la correspondencia de José Antonio Agirre y Manuel Irujo (Bilbao: Fundación Sabino Arana, 2007), 10–55.

2. Organization created by the Basque government and made up of prominent French politicians and cultural figures, for the purpose of advising and assisting the Basque government-in-exile in its relations with the government and other institutions of the French republic.

3. "Les Basques devant la crise: Aux côtes de la Liberté et de la Démocratie avec le Droit et la Justice," *Euzko Deya* (Paris) 176 (September 3, 1939).

In line with this declaration and in order to underline its reality and practicality, around three thousand Basque refugees in France who were fit for military service signed the following statement: "Mr. ...., of Basque nationality, declares that he is ready to assume all the consequences of the commitment signed by the International League of Friends of the Basques to aid France and its government."[4]

This position rejecting neutrality crystalized in the foreign policy guidelines of the "Draft Program for the Government of Euzkadi" (Proyecto de programa para el Gobierno de Euzkadi) signed in Paris on April 12, 1940, two months before the occupation of the city:

> The Basque government ratifies its commitment made in Gernika on October 7, 1936, according to which Euzkadi will strengthen the ties that unite it to the peoples who maintain democratic forms of government and particularly with those others among whom important Basque communities reside. European war having been declared, these norms should be developed and put into practice as follows: a) The Basque government rejects spiritual neutrality in a conflict in which the freedom of men and of peoples is being defended against tyranny and force. Its position is one of spiritual belligerency and maximum material support in favor of the democratic nations in their struggle against the totalitarian dictatorships. b) The Basque government condemns the German-Russian pact and as many acts or manifestations of this nature as have occurred or may occur in opposition to the freedom of peoples. c) The Basque government ratifies the protest published on the occasion of General Franco's signing of the Anti-Comintern Pact, denying to the current government of Spain any representation of or jurisdiction over the Basques.[5]

For the members of the Basque government-in-exile, intervention meant a position of open hostility to any form of totalitarian government and the necessity of offering maximum material support to the democratic nations in their struggle against the dictatorships.[6] Agirre understood that the global conflict was a clash

---

4. Report by Jose A. Agirre on the international situation in relation to the Basques, Paris, September 11, 1939. Document included in Agirre's letter to Joxe M. Lasarte, Paris, September 11, 1939.
5. Draft program for the government of Euzkadi, Paris, April 12, 1940.
6. Ibid.

between two antagonistic civilizations. "It is a matter of a struggle between civilizations and between entirely distinct conceptions. If totalitarianism were to triumph, freedom would suffer a
long eclipse, since the methods of force would impose their brutal
methods even against the will of the peoples. The triumph of the
democracies, naturally, would change the face of the world's more
or less totalitarian systems, and their fall will be inevitable."[7]

The Euzkadi government maintained a series of principles of
action with respect to its participation in World War II. First of
all, the position taken by the Basque government in the conflict
was decided and implemented independently of the position that
might be adopted by Franco's government in the conflict or, for
their part, the policies that the French, British, and United States
governments chose to hold in the dictator's regard.[8] At the same
time, the strategic positioning of Agirre's government was also
not limited by the attitude that might be adopted by the Spanish republican government-in-exile. That is, the Basque government coordinated its actions with those of the Spanish republican
government-in-exile, but in a completely independent and autonomous way. It intervened in the global conflict as a political and
military subject, as in 1936, in the name of the Basque government, as a representative of the Basque people, and with its own
troops under Basque command.[9]

These principles were upheld in practice. The Gernika Battalion's participation in the war of liberation in May 1945 is one
example of this, as is the Basque government's collaboration with
President Franklin D. Roosevelt's administration on counterintelligence matters starting in 1942, working with the OSS (Office of
Strategic Services). As a consequence of a May 1942 agreement,
hundreds of Basque agents collaborated with the OSS on counterintelligence missions in South America and the Philippines.
Other agencies and intelligence and resistance networks inside
Spain likewise collaborated with the Allied effort, but in all these

---

7. Report by Jose A. Agirre on the international situation in relation to the
Basques, Paris, September 11, 1939. Document included in Agirre's letter to Joxe
M. Lasarte, Paris, September 11, 1939.

8. Instructions by Jose A. Agirre for communications with the Basque Country,
Paris, September 11, 1939.

9. Report by Jose A. Agirre on the international situation in relation to the
Basques, Paris, September 11, 1939. Document included in Agirre's letter to Joxe
M. Lasarte, Paris, September 11, 1939.

cases, the Basque agents worked solely for and reported exclusively to the members of Agirre's government, who subsequently passed the information on to the OSS's American agents or to British intelligence, as appropriate. The Basque agents acted under direct Basque military command and under the authority of *Lehendakari* Agirre and the political officers designated by the Basque executive for this task.

From the time of the Euzkadi government's establishment in October 1936, certain factors influenced the internationalization of the Basque case and consequently motivated the government's own international policy. Some of the factors that had the earliest repercussions along these lines were the internationalization of the 1936 war by the intervention of German and Italian contingents in aid of Franco and, at the same time, the participation of the Western powers in the context of the so-called Non-Intervention Committee.[10] The exile of 150,000 Basques abroad and the children's exile, which entailed the evacuation of 32,000 Basque children between May and August 1937 in order to protect them from the indiscriminate bombing carried out by the German and Italian air forces on Franco's behalf, likewise gave rise to unavoidable international contacts, which put the Basque government in contact with the British Labour Party and through it with the British government itself, with the French government, and with the administrations of at least ten other European and Western Hemisphere countries. The waves of tens of thousands of Basque refugees who sought shelter in France after the fall of Irun in September 1936, after the collapse of the Basque front in June 1937, and after the fall of Barcelona in March 1939, similarly led to countless political and diplomatic negotiations. Nonetheless, it would not be until the declaration of war in September 1939 that the Basque government effectively initiated an international policy, signing political, diplomatic, and cultural treaties with European and Western Hemisphere governments.

With the start of World War II at the beginning of September 1939, the Euzkadi government's political activity took place

---

10. The Non-Intervention Committee was created at the urging of the French and British administrations and was endorsed by practically all the European governments, including the Germans, the Italians, and the Soviets, with the aim of preventing the participation of foreign powers in the war. When Hitler and Mussolini signed the Non-Intervention Pact in August 1936, both had thousands of fully equipped troops participating actively and decisively in the conflict.

fundamentally on the international level. This was due to the fact that following the Falangist victory in the 1936 war, the Spanish Republic fell into a severe internal crisis from which it would never recover. In the event, from 1942 onward the Spanish Republic provided no subsidies to the Basque government, converting it into an autonomous institution and one that was necessarily self-sufficient in economic terms. At the same time, from a political or strategic perspective, following the occupation of Western Europe by German troops starting in June 1940, the Euzkadi National Council (Consejo Nacional de Euzkadi)[11] was created in London, and it was this body that managed the process of negotiations with the British government and with the French Imperial Defense Council.[12] The Euzkadi government's policy necessarily became internationalized as a consequence of the victory of the insurgent forces in Spain and the subsequent outbreak of World War II.

Conversely, international pressure also had a decided influence on the adoption and reaffirmation of the policy of national unity. Both the French authorities in Paris before the occupation and those of the French Imperial Defense Council in British exile, as well as the British government itself and the Argentine, Uruguayan, Cuban, American, and Venezuelan governments, among others, singled out the Basque refugee populations in their respective immigration decrees, reports, or policies, at the same time that they identified the Basque government (or the Euzkadi National Council in its place between June 1940 and October 1941) as a valid political interlocutor, consequently negotiating and ratifying bilateral accords.

In sum, one of the basic aspects relevant to the active policy of Agirre's program of government, drafted in the spring of 1940 and so before the occupation, was the defense, maintenance, and implementation of an "international policy of close relations with

---

11. Following the occupation of Western Europe by German troops in the spring of 1940, *Lehendakari* Agirre had to adopt a false identity and go into hiding until he was able to escape from Europe in October 1941. The Basque government had adopted in Paris an emergency protocol in virtue of which, if the prime minister disappeared, a National Council would be created that would represent the Basque government until normality was restored. The council was created in London in June 1940 and carried out the tasks of government under the leadership of Manuel Irujo until Agirre reappeared in Uruguay in October 1941.

12. Conséil de Défense de l'Empire Français.

the democratic powers, contributing efficaciously to the creation of the new international order."[13] Internationalization thus meant, first of all, active and direct military intervention alongside the Allied forces and in opposition to the Axis powers during the global conflict, and subsequently, once the war was over, active political participation in shaping a federal and democratic Europe. Internationalization meant interventionism both in times of war and in times of peace.

Among the basic strategic assumptions of this interventionist policy, along with its practical consequences, we may highlight the fact that active intervention in the conflict through the secret services dedicated to counterintelligence in Europe and the Americas (and in Europe also to evacuating refugees and caring for prisoners in Spanish prisons) demanded a strong internal organization and, likewise, the creation of a network of delegations abroad (fundamentally in the Americas) that could act as embassies under the Euzkadi government's coordination in defense of the Basque population's interests. Accordingly, the fundamental mission of these delegations was to aid the Basque refugees and secondarily to build diplomatic networks on the political level. These delegations, the majority of which were created in the capitals of Western Hemisphere countries, operated as centers of coordination for all governmental tasks in those countries.

The translation of these fundamental ideological and political principles into concrete strategy entailed the will to open diplomatic negotiations with the Allied governments starting from the very day war was declared. Following the Allied victory in 1945, the survival of the Spanish totalitarian regime forced the Euzkadi government to maintain in exile its struggle for the restoration of democracy in the Basque Country, an idea that Agirre had already advanced as early as September 1944:

> I am satisfied with the Basques' contribution to the struggle against the Axis. This struggle has been conducted in many places, we have done our duty, and it has earned us esteem and affection. This struggle should not cease even when the war does, since dangerous covert nuclei clothed in garments of deceit will still remain and could serve as the basis for preparing a new hecatomb. Second, our people want national freedom, and in

---

13. Draft program for the government of Euzkadi, Paris, April 12, 1940. Text included in Manuel Irujo's letter to Juan Ajuriaguerra, London, April 12, 1940.

accordance with this, the Basque government has followed a practical program, as I have said to all of you many times, preparing the most perfect possible instrument of struggle with which to drive Franco's regime out of Basque territory and put an end to his tyranny. Day by day, the spirit and the organization of our people is growing stronger, and today they have the organization and instructions to implement the plans when the occasion offers itself or when they receive the order. Some of them you know; others you will get to know little by little.[14]

Human Rights and Democratic Principles

The cause of freedom, human rights, and democracy was consubstantial with the political program of the Basque Nationalist Party (Partido Nacionalista Vasco, the political party that led the Basque government-in-exile between 1936 and 1975) and with that of the Basque government in general, with the consequence that in the opinion of the nationalist leaders, it occupied a higher plane than Basque national interests:

> We could under no circumstances put forward an exclusively specific motive having to do with our Basque concerns in order to refuse to join in a labor of collaboration in favor of the cause of democracy. This was what we thought when we went to fight in the Peninsula. In the same way, we have taken part and collaborated as far as has been possible for us in the war against Germany and its powers. On the day when that question is posed to us, we will not have the option of turning a deaf ear or answering evasively. It is necessary to cast aside as foolish the supposition that it is going to be possible for us to set the terms of the problem. We are going to take part in a dialogue in which we will have to adapt our problem to the terms set from outside, taking into consideration, more than our specific national interest, the generic democratic and human cause.[15]

Basque nationalist thinking has historically considered one of the fundamental elements of the political character of the Basque states prior to the French Revolution and the liberal revolution in Spain to have been precisely the democratic character of their

---

14. Letter from Jose A. Agirre to Jose I. Lizaso, New York, September 8, 1944.
15. Manuel Irujo, manuscript note, London, June 24, 1940.

institutions,[16] and both Agirre and Irujo and the rest of the nationalist leaders of the Euzkadi government-in-exile considered the
defense of human rights and of their political expression, democracy, above and beyond a mere political or strategic option, a testament to age-old Basque political tradition and together with this,
an imperative of the faith they professed as Christians: "Freedom
that is our due as a people, and freedom that, as men, we claim in
the name of our tradition of Christian toleration and greatness.
Our compatriots cannot express their will; they do not enjoy the
most essential human rights. Personal freedom exists in a state of
constant precariousness. Thousands and thousands are in prison.
Just as many are outside their fatherland. Misery is the inheritance
of many, many homes."[17]

In accordance with this, the Euzkadi government's strategy
had to consist precisely in bringing about a convergence between
the Basque political cause and the global conflict, for the purpose
of offering whatever collaboration was needed to Basque democracy and, at the same time, the rest of the European democracies,
including that of Spain. Irujo expressed it in this way:

> Moreover, even considering the subject from the exclusively
> Basque national perspective, on the supposition that we had no
> ties and emotions that joined us to the universal cause of democ-
> racy, it would be necessary to ask, "Is it the case that we have
> another patriotic solution that we can oppose to this one? The
> triumph of democracy is our victory. Is it perhaps permissible
> for us to renounce it, on the basis of the fact that we may not be
> entirely satisfied by the formula under which it is initially pro-
> posed?" Simply stating this makes clear how unacceptable such
> a supposition is and leads us to the same conclusion reached
> earlier. It is necessary, then, to study the manner in which the
> subject can be put forward most advantageously for our views.[18]

In effect, in 1939, in the context of armed conflict on a global
scale, the struggle against totalitarianism in Europe implicitly
entailed the struggle for democracy around the world and the protection of human rights in their full scope, both in Euskal Herria
and in France and Spain, but also in Portugal and the other nations

---

16. Letter from Jose I. Lizaso to Jose A. Agirre, London, October 24, 1941.
17. Message from Jose A. Agirre to Francisco Franco, Paris, October 13, 1939.
18. Manuel Irujo, manuscript note, London, June 24, 1940.

oppressed by the occupation.[19] In Irujo's opinion, this collaboration was natural, given that "it is easy for us, and in this way, we will collaborate effectively in the labors of these countries, which in fighting for their own interests are also fighting for our rights."[20] This idea did not change following Agirre's disappearance at the time of the battle of Dunkirk in the spring of 1940. In Irujo's words, "At this moment, in addition, our country is enrolled in the cause of the most universal and human interest, as is the cause upheld by democracy in its fight for human dignity."[21] Accordingly, above and beyond its ideological doctrine or orientation prior to the global conflict or the war of 1936, the Basque government's active involvement in the world political scene and the subsequent diplomatic dispute that would take place at the United Nations until 1955 would involve Basque political nationalism in general and the Basque government in particular in the fight for human rights both in Europe and in the Americas.[22]

The actions of the occupying forces on the continent and of the collaborationist governments, like the Vichy regime in France and General Franco's regime in Spain, themselves gave rise to the persecution, arrest, or internment, and in many cases execution of the Basque civilian refugees on the continent, all of which logically motivated the Euzkadi government to redouble its efforts and its collaboration with international organizations like the Red Cross and the different London councils of the occupied states for the purpose of stopping the notorious violations of human rights in the occupied zones and under totalitarian regimes:

> It is appropriate that the English and French consuls stationed in Basque territory and both embassies accredited in Madrid receive reports of our dead, of our prisoners, details of persecutions, references to the effect produced by the Spanish-language broadcasts of English and French radio. Remember that it is from those reports that the most formidable attack on the Nazi regime has been composed, published recently by England and containing the persecutions to which Hitler and his supporters have subjected the German people.[23]

---

19. Letter from Jose I. Lizaso to Jose A. Agirre, London, October 24, 1941.
20. Letter from Manuel Irujo to Jose A. Agirre, London, January 4, 1940.
21. Letter from Manuel Irujo to Juan Olazábal, London, June 6, 1940.
22. Letter from Jose A. Agirre to Manuel Irujo, Paris, December 29, 1939.
23. Letter from Manuel Irujo to Jose A. Agirre, London, January 4, 1940.

The affirmation of democratic principles and values demanded, in these circumstances, their active defense. In accordance with this, the defense of individual rights would become the leading expression of resistance in exile, which would, in turn, decidedly promote collaboration among the Galician, Catalan, and Basque national councils in exile. This is true of Galeuzca, an institution created to coordinate the efforts of Galician, Basque, and Catalan politicians and institutions in exile with the objective of defending human rights and restoring a democratic government in Spain that would respect the realities and the historical, political, and cultural rights of these three nations.[24] One of Galeuzca's first manifestations in exile was the agreement reached and signed on May 9, 1941, to reconstitute the organization in Buenos Aires. Galeuzca would be committed first of all to the fight for human rights both within Spain and abroad, both in Europe and in the Americas, both during the course of World War II and at the future United Nations. This meant as the first priority combatting the totalitarian regime that held sway in Spain and any other regime not based on the strict recognition of individual rights and democratic principles of government.[25] Where foreign policy was concerned, Galeuzca's members proclaimed their attachment to the Allied cause and their opposition to any expression of despotism:

> The representatives in South America of the local organizations of Basque, Catalan, and Galician nationals, gathered together to consider the situation created in their respective regions by the Spanish war and the subsequent current European war and to study how to coordinate their activity in order to obtain their national claims, the common establishment of the civil rights of their fellow citizens, the safeguarding of their cultural and economic heritages, and the implementation of social justice in accordance with democratic standards of law and the legal traditions of their peoples adapted to the modern concepts of the social value of property, work, and wealth, have fully agreed, following lengthy and objective analyses of the forces currently in conflict, in judging that the group of democratic nations led by the Anglo-Saxon peoples represents the best guarantee for the development of the other peoples in a context of peaceful evolution and the gradual and progressive incorporation

---

24. Galeuzca convention of agreement, Montevideo, May 9, 1941.
25. Goiogana, Legarreta, and Irujo, *Un nuevo 31*, 15–55.

of the various human groups—independent of their size and strength—into the enjoyment of freedom and of the benefits of civilization and the affirmation of their personality on both the individual and the collective level.[26]

The Republic of Republics as Political Project: A Federation of European Nations

As can be inferred from the political and doctrinal principles of the Basque Nationalist Party's political program, the only valid or democratic state model was a republic. From the Basque nationalist perspective, monarchy was a crime, a form of denial of democracy: "The Basque and Catalan democrats are not Monarchist. They will not support any restoration of the Monarchy. From the Basque and Catalan point of view, the Spanish Monarchy is the negation of democracy. We still remember several centuries of very bitter experience under that regime, and if anything was wanting to stiffen our resolution today, it is to be found in the text of the Abdication of Alfonso XIII a few days before his death, foreshadowing a totalitarian absolute Monarchy for his son, Don Juan."[27] Consequently, having ruled out the monarchical formula as a promising model for the restoration of democracy in Spain, the forces and institutions that made up Galeuzca made the republican creed their own:

> b) A republican form of government and a regime of representative democracy with universal and direct suffrage, freedom of conscience and of worship, freedom of thought and of the press, justice on a popular foundation, guarantees for civil rights, labor, and legitimately acquired property, freedom of occupation, of residence, of contract, and disposition of property in accordance with the particular laws of each state, laws which will under no circumstances be able to undermine, decrease, or adulterate the common minimum standards established in the pacts of federation or confederation.[28]

---

26. Galeuzca convention of agreement, Montevideo, May 9, 1941.

27. Appendix 1 to the "Declaration of the London Delegation of the Government of Euzkadi," in a letter from Jose I. Lizaso to J. MacDonald, London, March 7, 1941.

28. Galeuzca convention of agreement, Montevideo, May 9, 1941.

Nevertheless, it was also the case that not just any republican model would satisfy the Basque political forces, but only one that was respectful of the political rights of the nations that made up the Spanish state. The only democratic political formula for the Basque case was consequently a federal republic. Irujo expressed it this way in late 1941:

> The concurrence through a voluntary pact of the different peoples of the Peninsula is the definition of full democracy, which will cease to be such if they are obliged to be part of the confederation by force. The spiritual declaration of independence of the Spanish-speaking countries of the Americas is well put and carries within itself a great deal of political meaning. On these suppositions, you conceive the political organization of the Peninsula in the style of a republican and democratic community made up of diverse peoples, formed under the influence of distinct races with their singular characteristics, bound to one another by a voluntary federal pact, with cultural, historical, and family ties in the Spanish-speaking republics of the Americas. I must tell you with satisfaction that your political conception, summarized in the preceding lines, forms a common front with those closest to ours with which I am familiar among Spanish thinkers and politicians.[29]

Along the same lines, in the international context, the proclamation of the Basque people's right of self-determination entailed the defense of the same right for all the peoples of Europe, at the same time that maintaining an active ideological and strategic confrontation with the Spanish, German, and Italian totalitarian governments meant taking a position in opposition to the dictatorships of Antonio de Oliveira Salazar in Portugal (1933–68), Rafael Trujillo in the Dominican Republic (1930–61), Juan Domingo Perón in Argentina (1946–55), and Marcos Pérez Jiménez in Venezuela (1952–58), and in opposition to totalitarianism as a political, social, economic, and cultural stain on the global level in the forum of the United Nations.[30] With regard to Oliveira Salazar, Irujo wrote to Agirre:

> Your tactical position as a realist leads you to think about the Portuguese dictator. Our information, from Portuguese

---

29. Letter from Manuel Irujo to Arturo Barea, London, November 10, 1941.
30. Goiogana, Legarreta, and Irujo, *Un nuevo 31*, 15–55.

democratic sources, is that he is just another tyrant, intelligent, skillful, patriotic, no less worthy to be opposed than any Franco of the moment. He has not committed mass murder because he has not found himself caught up in a civil war, nor has he needed to fall back on that disagreeable resource. He makes use of the patriarch of Lisbon as Franco makes use of the Spanish episcopate. He is as worthy to be extirpated as any other totalitarian power might be.[31]

Moreover, the *lehendakari* adopted this perspective: "The Franco-Salazar Iberian pact, based on suspicious and fearful totalitarian regimes, is an anticipation of the democratic pact of the Peninsular nations, based on freedom and on trust. I believe that, if we are firm in upholding our national banner and march in good unity with the Catalans and the Galicians, the result will without any doubt be obtained."[32] The defense of this doctrine likewise meant the end of the collaboration agreements with the American administration in 1949, in the context of the Cold War and only months before the outbreak of the Korean War, given that starting in 1949, the political and strategic objectives of U.S. President Dwight D. Eisenhower's new Republican administration did not match the objectives of defense of human rights and democratic principles characteristic of the Basque government.

Anticipating by several decades the political project of the Europe of the Peoples on the international level, as well as that of the federation of Iberian nations in the Peninsular context, the signers of the Galeuzca Pact were to promote "a policy of collaboration and good will, fostering international relationships of all kinds and promoting the creation of supra-state organizations that, considering peace to be indissoluble, will have at their disposal the authority and the necessary means to preserve it, to sanction violators, and to ensure the free life of institutions and peoples."[33] This meant unconditional support for the work of the nascent United Nations following the Allied victory and, at the same time, opting for a federation of Iberian nations on the basis of a pact and as a guarantor in any event of the right of self-determination of the parties or nations that might form part of it, "to which faculties of a supra-national order may be delegated, such as the coordination

---

31. Letter from Manuel Irujo to Jose A. Agirre, London, January 28, 1942.
32. Letter from Jose A. Agirre to Jose I. Lizaso, New York, September 8, 1944.
33. Galeuzca convention of agreement, Montevideo, May 9, 1941.

of services and forces, shared legislation, especially in the social area, collective security, the development and application of international law, and the diffusion and generalization of democratic principles of law and justice."[34] Agirre put these principles into concrete form in a letter to Alfonso Castelao signed in New York on March 2, 1944:

> When I arrived from Europe in late 1941, that was one of my concerns. I immediately contacted Pi y Suñer in order to reach a strong Basque-Catalan understanding without loss of time and with an explicit invitation to the Galician organizations. At that time, Pi was the only exponent of Catalan will abroad. I composed a joint manifesto, the central ideas of which were: a) the reality of our nationalities with their right of self-determination; b) the creation of a policy of the peripheries favorable to the voluntary integration of a Peninsular political form in which Portugal might take its place when the time came; c) an invitation to reflection and to a pact addressed to Spanish democracy; d) our total and enthusiastic adherence to the Allied cause.[35]

In a document titled "Principios para una declaración conjunta de la democracia peninsular" (Principles for a joint declaration of Peninsular democracy), Irujo included in a declaration of the democratic principles that should guide a democratic restoration in the Iberian Peninsula, as well as, in general terms, in the continent as a whole, the establishment of a federal order in Europe in the political and economic spheres, based on the transfer of powers from the member states to the confederation. Basically, the proposal meant a transfer of the Basque, Catalan, and Galician political problem to the European level, since from the perspective of the political demands of the continent's peoples, the Basque people's demand for the right of self-determination was and remains the same as the demands of peoples such as the Scots, the Irish, the Tyroleans, the Frisians, the Ostrobothnians, and the Flemish.

> Democratic affirmation, along lines of universality and solidarity, for men and peoples.
> Support for England, Russia, China, and their allies in the current war.
> Acceptance of the Atlantic Charter.

---

34. Galeuzca convention of agreement, Montevideo, May 9, 1941.
35. Letter from Jose A. Agirre to Alfonso R. Castelao, New York, March 2, 1944.

Agreement to establish a federal order in Europe on the basis of coexistence and a hierarchy of sovereignty, with formulas of economic rapprochement, military defense, and the aim of a just and lasting peace.

Study of a Confederation of the West as a viable formula for the European Federation and in order to signify our "WESTERN" character.

Franco does not represent the country. Claim for the body of citizens the faculty to grant this representation.

Denounce the system of oppression to which the body of citizens is subjected. In Spain there are more prisoners than in any other country in Europe outside of Russia and Germany.

Protest against the execution of hostages by Germany.

Highlight the actions of Franco's regime designed to definitively hand over the Peninsular territory and the colonies to Germany as a military base.

Reveal the maneuver against Portugal. We democrats will not take advantage of the force wrapped up in them. We aspire to a community of nations in which Portugal may participate, in the freest possible manner, occupying the place that corresponds to her.

Also denounce the grand maneuver that, working through the Committee of Hispanic Identity [Junta de la Hispanidad], wraps up Nazi propaganda in the Americas in imperial aspirations, which we do not feel and the enticements of which we need not make use of in any way.

The declaration should remain open for the adherence of all who are in agreement with its content: no exclusives or monopolies.

The right of self-determination of the Peninsular peoples, concretely of Catalonia and Euzkadi.

Put on record as a fundamental emotion that the democratic basis that we share will give us a way to channel our differences, reaching an agreement that can establish a regime of juridical community founded on Saint Louis's motto: "All human freedoms are in solidarity with one another."[36]

The idea of a European political and economic confederation constituted, from this perspective, an optimal solution:

[a] community of free nations, federated with one another for the development of a joint economy, the security of a lasting

---

36. Declaration of principles elaborated by Manuel Irujo for Peninsular democracy, London, November 24, 1941.

peace, and the implantation of an effective social justice. If that solution is the best, we do not aim to oppose it to another that we might characterize as good. In the event that historical prejudices, national ambitions, or economic cravings pose difficulties for it, or on the—probable—supposition that it will not possible to attempt it while there is no choice but to subjugate Germany and Italy as conquered nations, we will be enchanted to join the Confederation of the Continental West, situated between the Rhine and Gibraltar, made up of the current states of Holland, Luxembourg, Belgium, France, Spain, and Portugal, and perhaps the German Rhineland. This confederation totals 100 million inhabitants. Its colonial empires come to 150. They would be 250 million human beings ordered by one great confederal law.[37]

Also, Irujo added, by "one fundamental economic law. One basic monetary law. One colonial statute. One system of common defense. The border at the Rhine. The customs service is a country's first line of trenches, at the Rhine, which is where the age-old enemy of European peace is encountered."[38]

"The huge superstate would reach from the Rhine, Europe's central Atlantic river, to the Congo, Africa's central Atlantic river. The conception is difficult, marvelous, splendid."[39] As Lizaso pointed out to Agirre by letter, the obvious difficulties in implementing this project and political realism were not to get in the way of delineating the basic motivating principles of Basque national policy, and as political practice would demonstrate later, the postwar European scene designed by the victorious powers would favor a model of European community, distant still from any type of political confederation of states and very far from the future European Union, but in line with those ideas.

> When you have read these documents and your first impulse is to characterize the idea as an unrealizable dream and a fantasy, meditate . . . and read them again. I say this to you because the same thing happened to me, and the second time it no longer seemed like such a dream to me. The conception of a Western Confederation is Manuel's (Irujo). Manuel dreams a lot, but

---

37. Letter from Manuel Irujo to Francisco Belausteguigoitia, London, September 16, 1941.
38. Ibid.
39. Ibid.

even if this is nothing more than that, it is a practical dream. As
someone who has shared his disquiet in this regard, I judge that
it is truly the right idea to frame our problem in this way, as a
matter of doctrine and as a matter of tactics.[40]

In effect, political projects for small federations as proposed
solutions to the problems raised in Europe's especially problematic areas, "like the Baltic, Danube, and Balkan federations, with
110 to 140 million inhabitants, which cover the territories between
the Baltic and the Mediterranean, with all the countries pinned
between Russia and Germany,"[41] were already in fact firm diplomatic proposals, even if Eastern Europe's historical process would
be subsequently marked by its position as the anteroom of the
Cold War, and its politics would be marked by Stalin.

The realization of this political project would respond to
many of the political problems that remained unresolved on the
continent,

the Galaico-Portuguese problem, the Basque problem on both
sides of the Pyrenees, the Walloon problem, the unity of Morocco,
the affective, spiritual incorporation of all the Ibero-American
republics into a state organization from which they draw their
origins, without the need to fear it like Spanish imperialism. The
colonial problems of Portugal and Holland, so often held up to
ridicule, would be automatically resolved. Catalonia and Andalusia would be the privileged countries of the Confederation
with regard to their further possibilities in Africa, due to their
geographical nearness, historical background, and racial kin-
ship. The Iberian Peninsula would fulfill its geopolitical objective
of being a bridge between two continents and a barrier between
two seas, on which it has always turned its back.[42]

As Dr. Leyre Arrieta discusses in depth in her article, the
Basque government would participate very actively in constructing the political basis for the future European Union, which would
turn out to be a Europe of states and not the Europe of peoples they
had dreamed of.

---

40. Letter from Jose I. Lizaso to Jose A. Agirre, London, October 24, 1941.
41. Letter from Manuel Irujo to Francisco Belausteguigoitia, London, September 16, 1941.
42. ibid.

Conclusion

The war and the atrocities committed by the Spanish, German, Italian, and Vichy regimes on Basque soil between 1936 and 1945 internationalized the political activity of the Euzkadi government led by *Lehendakari* Jose A. Agirre. This government likewise made a great effort to internationalize the Basque case by launching a militantly interventionist policy in the context of World War II. With regard to the fundamental principles of the comprehensive defense of human rights and the rights of peoples on the international level and the defense of the rights of the Basque citizens oppressed under General Franco's iron dictatorship, the Basque government opted to participate actively in World War II, in both the military and political spheres, by creating a dense counterintelligence network at the service of the Allies, one which came to include hundreds of agents on three continents, and by creating a battalion that fought in the last battles to liberate the European continent from German occupation in 1945. Starting in 1945, the Basque government participated actively in the international arena, defending the creation of a European political space that was respectful of human rights, a political project that would subsequently crystallize in the creation of the European Community and, much later, the European Union.

4

Agirre: A President Hunted by the Dictatorships

Nicholas Rankin

This chapter about the escape of *Lehendakari* Agirre from Nazi-occupied Europe to the freedom of the New World is more an informal article than a scholarly essay because I am a journalist rather than an academic, and also because I just finished my fifth book two days ago—a 600-page book about Gibraltar at war between 1935 and 1945—and so this presentation is a rather rapid change of gear. I delivered *Defending the Rock* to Faber yesterday and now can start to begin work on the second half of my two-book contract, a work provisionally entitled *The Most Secret Formula*. I see that as-yet-unwritten book about the Basques and the Allies fighting for freedom in World War II as being in some way the continuation of my second book, the biography of George Lowther Steer, *Telegram from Guernica* (or *Crónica desde Guernica* as it was called in Spanish translation), published nearly fifteen years ago. I want to take the story on further from the summer of 1937. While not being a full biography, I do want to write about José Antonio de Agirre in World War II, how his experiences shaped him and his worldview, and made him an international figure.

Agirre was a cheerful man with an almost child-like optimism. But he had to endure some severe hammer-blows in his life. Was ever fate like his? Never to see home again. Never to see the freedom in which he believed and which he fought for all his life, without hatred, but with Christian faith and fortitude. His life is a mountain pilgrimage with great highs and many lows. To be disappointed and let down by people he thought were friends and allies. To see the young people, the future, drifting away from decency and turning, in desperation, to violence and murder. To drink deep from the bitter cup of failure. But not to despair… It is a kind of Christian story: humiliation and crucifixion, with a triumph after death.

You all know how this Agirre story started, the vigorous young man from Bilbao, the soccer player, the energetic mayor of Getxo who announced the coming of the Spanish Republic, the charismatic young leader who turned the PNV/EAJ (Basque Nationalist Party) from a reactionary Carlist party into something more modern and progressive and democratic. You know how the Statute of Autonomy was only gained in wartime in October 1936, after the military uprising against the Spanish Republic three months earlier, and how the little Republic of Euzkadi was under attack and blockade from the very beginning. And you all know how Agirre ran a brilliant anti-fascist coalition government in wartime (like a Basque Churchill, he was both Prime Minister and Minister of Defense) and how Euzkadi fought gallantly for nine months before being overwhelmed in the summer of 1937 by Franco's forces, heavily supported by the planes and tanks and technology provided by Adolf Hitler and Benito Mussolini. Agirre was proscribed, had his property confiscated, was fined 20 million pesetas *in absentia*. His family took refuge in France, his second child Joseba Andoni was born in Paris in 1938, and the seat of the Basque government-in-exile was in Barcelona in autonomous Catalunya until that too was defeated by the combined forces of Fascism. Once again, exile beckoned: Agirre and Lluis Companys had to cross the Pyrenees in winter, on February 4, 1939, to reach sanctuary in France. When the civil war ended with Republican defeat in April, the little Basque republic was now scattered, its people in diaspora as evacuees, refugees, some as inmates of camps and prison, others shot by Francoist firing squad.

Robert Louis Stevenson once described the Polynesians in the modern world as "a shopful of crockery launched upon the stream of time, making their desperate voyage among pots of adamant and brass" and that too was the situation of the defeated Basques, with their problems being dealt with and handled as best they could by the Basque government-in-exile, now based at 11 Avenue Marceau in the 15th *arrondissement* of Paris.

World War II broke out in September 1939, and to begin with the fighting was far away, at first in Poland, and then in Norway and Denmark. However, Agirre knew whose side the Basques must be on, declaring "There can be no neutrality in a fight between freedom and oppression." He committed the Basques to the French and British Allies: "Our duty as a people is to put ourselves on the sides of the democracies . . . The defeat of the totalitarians will be the first base of our road to independence."

On May 8, 1940, the Agirre family went on vacation to Belgium. There were a lot of Basque exiles in Belgium (including 5,000 Basque children evacuees and fifty priests with them) and Agirre's mother and his wife's mother were living there too, in the city of Leuven (Louvain). The families arranged to meet in some rented houses at the holiday resort of La Panne, which is on that broad stretch of sandy beaches that runs up the North Sea coast where France and Belgium meet. They left by train from Paris. Agirre was thirty-seven years old and was with his wife Mari Zabala and their two children, Aintzane and Joseba Andoni, who were, respectively, just five and nearly two. It being wartime, Agirre had special papers to get him and his family out of France and back in again afterward. The families and friends were all going to get together for a week in the sunshine on the beach—many would see little Joseba for the first time—and then they would return to Paris.

Massive and disastrous events overtook them. As we know, on May 10, 1940 Adolf Hitler launched *Fall Gelb*, Operation Yellow, the German *blitzkrieg* attack on Western Europe. There were two prongs: the attack on Belgium was really a feint, to draw the British army into the matador's cloak, and the real attack was on the German left, through the Ardennes and straight for the sea, the *sickelschnitt* or scythe-cut (*bon cop de fals* as the Catalans would say) to cut off the British and French armies, to trap them against the sea and then eliminate them.

Early on the morning of May 10 the Agirres were woken by the sound of aerial bombing. They saw huge clouds of smoke as the oil refineries of Dunkirk were set on fire. Then they saw the French troops marching into Belgium to go and fight the Germans. Forward to victory! Among the most optimistic spectators was Agirre's sister Encarnación. "Don't worry, the Allies will win!" she said. The other optimist was Cesareo Asporosa of the Basque Commercial delegation, who had been made the group's treasurer, keeping the money for a growing group: nine children, some very old people, students, priests, women, forty-six Basques in all. Then there was movement the other way, as hordes of Belgian refugees, fleeing the German armies, started pouring past the house going south toward France. Some of them remembered the killings of 1914 when the Germans last invaded, and imagined even worse again. The war-zone was no place for a holiday.

On May 17 the Basque group set off walking toward the French frontier. They saw the bombing of La Panne and the strafing of civilians by fighter planes of the German Air Force. "We had seen all of it before," Agirre wrote later, remembering what the Condor Legion had done in the Basque Country at Durango and Gernika and Otxandio and Eibar and all the other places. But the women were terrified and some of the children vomited at the blood and injuries that they had certainly never witnessed before. When one German plane was shot down and the pilot parachuted to safety, every available French and Belgian gun riddled him with bullets. The Basques hid under the trees until the German planes went away at 5 o'clock.

They slowly made their way to the border between Belgium and France, reaching it at 8pm. It was closed until early the next morning. Hundreds of refugees started camping by the side of the road and in the fields. Some of the Basques took their bicycles to go back to the house in La Panne to get food. The night was cold. Airplanes dropped flares. When people tried to cross the fence the guards beat them back. One man with a club was brutal, shouting and swearing, belaboring people. At five in the morning they shuffled forward. Agirre had his special French papers but all the other Basques had Spanish Republican passports, expedited by the Basque autonomous government. *Non, invalid.* France had recognized Franco and his Nationalist regime, so these were the wrong kind of passports. Only Belgians, Dutch, French, and English could pass the frontier. Agirre gave an elegant argument to the border guard—these people attacking you are exactly the same people who attacked us first and you cannot leave an innocent bunch of exiles to their mercy—but it cut no ice. Soon the Belgian police started building a wire cage for all the refugees, and the Basques were herded in with thousands of others, many of them terrified Jews. There was neither food, nor water, nor a roof to shelter them. People fainted with exhaustion, hunger, and thirst. Some died. Agirre looked at the panic-stricken Jews. "I saw their women and children as I saw my own. I was their companion in sorrow." They were three days in the cage. Not everybody behaved well. Finally they got through to French territory, and then found another fence on the outskirts of Bray Dunes. Agirre sent a telegram to the

Basque government in Paris, but in the chaos of the capital they did not manage to send a bus or any cars to rescue them.

They walked all day, then sheltered in a barn packed with other refugees. Agirre could not sleep. (One of the Basque priests was snoring loudly. This man had been arrested and nearly shot by the Belgians because there was a rumor that German parachutists had dropped from the sky disguised as priests and he happened to be carrying some advertisements for agricultural books in German. The Prior had only just managed to rescue him from the *paredón.*) Agirre was outside the barn having a smoke when German airplanes dropped scores of thermite incendiary bombs in the darkness. This too was something he was used to. These were the very same make of incendiary bombs that had burned Gernika three years earlier. Aluminum, as long as your forearm, sputtering fire. With handfuls of earth, he smothered the bombs near the barn so they were no danger to the hundreds of refugees sleeping inside. It was the night of May 21, 1940.

The next day, Agirre and a Jesuit priest he calls "Alberto"[1] in his book but whose real name was Luis Chalbaud, walked the five miles into Dunkirk. The city seemed dead, its streets wrecked by bombs. There was a pall of smoke. No one would give them any food or water. They found a priest in the cathedral who gave them the big picture, that they were all cut off, encircled by the Germans who had reached the sea and were now besieging Calais. The two Basques walked back to the barn, starving. They decided they could not tell the women and children they were trapped.

Order was breaking down in the villages. The great nation of France was beginning to collapse. Ten million people were on the roads, fleeing in terror and panic before the advancing Germans. In Britain, the Royal Navy was planning the mass evacuation of troops from the beaches of Dunkirk, Operation DYNAMO, which would start on May 27 and last until June 4, an epic tale in British history.

The Basques sheltered at Bergues and then decided to go back to La Panne and Bray Dunes. The roads were crammed with refugees. Allied soldiers who had lost all discipline were looting and getting drunk. Others were destroying their vehicles and

---

1. On page 45 of the 1991 University of Nevada reedition of the 1945 American translation of Agirre's book, *Escape via Berlin*, the editor, Robert P. Clark, erroneously states that "Father Alberto" was Canon Alberto Onaíndia. He was not there, but in Paris.

equipment, setting them on fire. Agirre went down to the beach where more orderly French and British soldiers were holding themselves together. He explained his situation to a British colonel at 6:30 am on May 29. "I can't promise you anything . . . I'll try to help you," said the officer. Agirre went back to the families and then the French police burst in with guns drawn, accusing the Basques of being spies. Agirre skillfully managed to talk his way out of that.

The *lehendakari* went back and forth to the beach, seeing the little ships taking soldiers off, watching Ju-87 *Stukas* dive-bombing and strafing the troops in the sand dunes. He met hysterical French officers, their faces twitching uncontrollably from having seen a shipload of men hit by a bomb: "a bursting fountain of arms and legs and blood." They went to La Panne, which the Nazis started shelling with their field-guns. Is there anything more terrifying than the helplessness of being shelled and bombed? The Basques took casualties. Asporosa was killed, Agirre's sister Encarna wounded by a splinter in the shoulder. His family was bleeding, and he had his wife and frightened children to comfort and protect, somehow, in all this chaos, milling about among what Churchill called "the shattered states and bludgeoned races."

Agirre watched a battalion of Guardsmen from the British Expeditionary Force marching toward the beaches, disciplined, in step, singing, while bombs went off and enemy fighters zoomed down. At that moment Agirre says he knew the democracies would win the war. "People who can sing in the middle of such gunfire cannot be vanquished." It was as Churchill said in his speech after Dunkirk: "We shall never surrender."

When more German shells hit the house in which the Basques were sheltering, Encarna Agirre was wounded again, this time in the stomach. She died two days later. Her brother, Juan Agirre, went with Sabin the Basque policeman to look for Cesareo Asporosa in the morgue, because the dead man's coat contained all their money. They found his body among the eight hundred corpses and their dollar bills were still there in the lining of his overcoat that was too shabby for anybody to bother looting.

So the British and French retreated, the Germans advanced, and the little group of Basques were going nowhere. In total, 338,226 Allied fighting men were evacuated from Dunkirk but none of the Basques. It was not for want of trying. In the United States, Manuel Ynchausti was badgering the State Department, and in London, José Ignacio Lizaso and the Basque delegation were also frantically trying to find Agirre. They had been in touch with the British Admiralty and orders had been given to the Royal Navy to pick them up, but the beaches were utterly chaotic.

I think George Steer was looking for them too. Steer, the author of *The Tree of Gernika: a field study of modern war*, had just become a father for the first time. His son George Barton Steer was born on May 14 and Steer senior wanted to invite Agirre to the christening in St Paul's Cathedral on June 8, to be the boy's other godfather with Emperor Haile Selassie of Ethiopia. There was already a connection between the two men, engineered by Steer. You may recall that Agirre had the use of a small Curtiss biplane with a French pilot, M. Lebaud, bought by the Basque government for £5,000 from Haile Selassie after his defeat in Abyssinia, a plane called the *Negus*, which means "Emperor" in Amharic. This was the aircraft that plucked Agirre out of Santander on August 24, 1937 and flew him to safety in Biarritz.

But Agirre and his family could not be rescued from the beaches of Dunkirk in 1940 because the task was like trying to find a needle in a haystack that was already on fire and, besides, the priority was soldiers before civilians in this colossal military disaster. The British Army was going backward in 1940, in fighting retreats or withdrawals. My own family's soldiers were caught up in it: my maternal grandfather and my paternal uncle were both evacuated from Dunkirk, at the same time as my father was being evacuated from Norway.

Last year was the seventy-fifth anniversary of the Dunkirk evacuation and I went over to Belgium with Ane Roteta of Basque TV to film a little report about the trapped Basques. We looked for some of the places where they had been, using my grandfather's contemporaneous map, marked with the route he and his men had followed to retreat to the beaches. And at the seventy-fifth anniversary I came back by sea too, as part of the reenactment that the Dunkirk Little Ships Association carries out every five years. I came back on a gray Motor Torpedo Boat that had been at Dunkirk, MTB 102. And we crossed the English Channel from Dunkirk in France to my home town, to Ramsgate in Kent, which is where the little ships and the destroyers brought so many of those men in 1940. As we skirted the Goodwin Sands and approached Ramsgate Royal Harbour, we could see hundreds of people waiting on the harbor wall to cheer and clap the little ships back in. It was extremely moving.

Back to Agirre. This is the moment of truth on June 1, exactly seventy-six years ago today. The Basques are trapped on land because they cannot escape by sea. If he is caught, Lehendakari Agirre may well be shot. They have a family conference, and decide it will be safer for his whole family if he gets away, on his own. There is a Catalan man there, with his wife and a motor car, who is desperate to take the Jesuit Luis Chalbaud with him to Brussels (he is a freemason and he thinks the priest will be good camouflage) but the Basque priest says he will only travel with him if they take his president as well. Agirre borrows his brother's Belgian student identity card. The first step. The private car gets to Brussels through roadblocks and they go to the Jesuit college of St Francis Xavier, where Agirre starts to grow a moustache. The second step. He is beginning to change, to grow a new personality. Step three: he starts rereading Ignatius Loyola's *Spiritual Exercises.*

José Antonio de Agirre now enters one of the most interesting and perilous parts of his life. He was in grave danger and must either adapt or die. He must improvise and live on his wits in order to avoid the fate of the Republican politicians Julián Zuzagagoitia and Lluis Companys, who were both handed back to Franco and executed in the autumn of 1940. Agirre had many enemies. General Franco and the German Gestapo, of course, but also the right-wing Vichy French government headed by Maréchal Pétain, the former French ambassador in Madrid. The French, eager to keep in with Franco's government, began turning on the Basques, interning thousands, closing down their offices in Paris. Informers and police agents were also sniffing out subversives and troublemakers.

Agirre needed to disappear and he was helped enormously by the Panamanian consul in Brussels, a man called Germán Gil Guardia Jaén, who gave the *lehendakari* a provisional Panamanian passport in the name of Dr. José Andrés Alvarez Lastra (whose initials are of course the same as Jose Antonio de Agirre y Lecube.) Agirre now became Dr. Alvarez, hidden behind a moustache and thick-rimmed spectacles, a neutral Panamanian seeking to get back to his homeland at the junction of the two American hemispheres. Anyone wishing to get there would normally take a plane or ship from Lisbon, but to reach Portugal he would have to travel first through Spain, which was impossible for a proscribed and hunted person like Agirre. So, if he could not go West over the Atlantic, he would go East, and try to get to the Americas via the Pacific. At that time, Hitler's Nazi Germany and Stalin's USSR were allies, following the

Ribbentrop/Molotov Pact of August 1939, so it was not impossible, perhaps, for a neutral to take the Trans-Siberian Railroad and try to cross over from Vladivostok. That was the vague idea, anyway, which impelled Jose Antonio Agirre into the belly of the beast, traveling to Berlin in January 1941.

At this extraordinary moment, Agirre is both actor and observer. He is an actor in that he is playing a role as a doctor from Panama as well as actively pursuing his own escape from the continent, and he is also an observer because for the first time in his life he starts keeping a daily diary, from January 7, 1941 to May 28, 1942. (The Sabino Arana Foundation published a brilliant facsimile and transcription of the diary in 2010, ably edited and introduced by Iñaki Goiogana.) The diary, which would be expanded in the book that Agirre went on to publish in 1944, begins with Agirre taking two trains to get to Hamburg, before arriving in Berlin on Sunday, January 12, 1941. He would remain in the capital of Nazi Germany for the next four and half months.

The whole experience is fascinating and unique and I cannot do justice to it fully in this brief chapter, but I wish to pick out just a couple of moments from the month of March 1941. For example, in the middle of the night of March 12–13, after a day of eating alone and reading theology and history, Agirre had to go down to the air-raid shelter in the cellar when the anti-aircraft guns started firing. (Field-Marshal Göring once famously said that if the British Royal Air Force or RAF ever bombed Berlin his name would be Mayer. Well, the RAF *was* bombing Berlin, Herr Mayer.) The people were also on short commons in the Third Reich during the war. Agirre records being in a restaurant in which the cigarettes and the cocktails were all *ersatz,* because the real things were no longer obtainable, and a bullying Nazi party woman member was collecting for the Winter Relief Fund. This does not feel like sumptuous victory.

On March 14, Agirre went out of curiosity to St Hedwig's Cathedral in the Opera Square (where the Nazis had burned books in 1933) in order to be a silent presence at a funeral mass, attended by most of the diplomatic corps, for the late King Alfonso XIII of Spain, who had died in Rome the month before. Agirre the good Catholic and Republican prayed for the soul of the man whose ancestors had taken away his country's liberty. He watched a dozen Falangists, men and women, standing by the ceremonial tomb, wearing the red beret of the Carlist Requetés. When he went to sleep that night the thing that he remembered most clearly and bitterly was the thought that these right-wingers *dishonored* the *txapela*, the Basque beret. "The beret has always stood for freedom and democracy, and never oppression," he wrote in his book. "With berets like these on their heads, thousands of young men have died defending liberty."

On March 27, Agirre joined a crowd in the Wilhelmstrasse in front of Hitler's Chancellery, where the Führer was about to appear on the balcony with the Japanese Foreign Minister Yosuke Matsuoka. A man from Himmler's SS handed the *lehendakari* two flags, one with a Nazi swastika and the other with a Japanese Rising Sun. Agirre looked around to see what the other Nazis in the crowd were doing and then copied them, waving the little flags and shouting. With dry irony the democrat noted: "It was thrilling to be there, as I happen to have a very strong voice." Quietly to himself he thought the two men on the balcony looked like a gypsy organ-grinder and his monkey.

On May 14, 1941, Agirre was joined in Berlin by his wife and children who were traveling on Venezuelan passports also with false identities. Nine days later they got to Gothenburg in Sweden, still hoping to travel via Russia and perhaps Japan to the United States. On June 21 those plans were completely wrecked when Hitler launched Operation BARBAROSSA, the invasion of the Soviet Union.

The Basque Maecenas, Manuel Ynchausti, came to the rescue again, finally managing to arrange passage from Sweden to Brazil for the disguised Agirre family on the Swedish American Line cargo ship S.S. *Vasaholm*, which sailed on July 31, the feast-day of the Basque who founded the Jesuits, St. Ignatius Loyola. There were only eight passengers, the four Basques and four Polish Jews. On August 14, 1941, in mid-Atlantic, the Poles summoned Agirre to listen to something remarkable on the wireless. The US President, Franklin D. Roosevelt, had met with the British Prime Minister, Winston Churchill, at Placentia Bay in Newfoundland and they had issued a statement of their shared ideals (the United States had not yet joined the war, but was supporting the UK with Lend-Lease supplies). Agirre listened with pleasure to this "Atlantic Charter." The British and Americans did not seek territorial aggrandizement or any territorial changes not approved by the people, and said that "they respect the rights of all countries to choose freely their form of government, and wish to see restored the sovereignties and self-government taken away by force." This was music to the ears of the first *lehendakari* of autonomous Euzkadi, suppressed by Franco with the help of Hitler and Mussolini.

On August 27, 1941 the *Vasaholm* reached Rio de Janeiro. Agirre was still Dr. Alvarez, traveling on a fraudulent passport, so all those identity and status problems had to be sorted out before he could travel legally and openly to the United States. On October 9, 1941, Agirre quietly crossed from southern Brazil into Uruguay. It was five years and two days since he had taken the oath of office as *lehendakari* under the oak tree at Gernika. Now he could take off his false glasses and shave off his moustache and emerge once again as the *lehendakari* of the Basques, the man who had escaped from the grip of the Nazis and Falangists, a real-life Victor Laszlo figure as portrayed in the 1942 film *Casablanca*, an inspiring and charismatic leader whose war-work would be to persuade not just the Basques but many Spanish-speakers in the South American Republics that they should wholeheartedly support the democratic Allies rather than the totalitarian Axis.

Jose Antonio Agirre told his story in a book that exists in three editions. The Spanish, first published by Ekin in Buenos Aires in 1944, is called *De Guernica a Nueva York pasando por Berlin*. The American English edition, published by Macmillan in 1945, is entitled *Escape via Berlin*, and the British English edition, brought out by Victor Gollancz in the same year, is called *Freedom was Flesh and Blood*.

I think it is important to know where this latter rather unusual title comes from. It is taken from a poem by Cecil Day Lewis (father of the actor Daniel Day Lewis), which appeared in his collection *Overtures to Death*, published by Jonathan Cape in 1938. The poem is called "The *Nabara*" and a footnote says "The episode upon which this poem is based is related in G.L. Steer's *The Tree of Gernika*."

The *Nabara* was a ship, one of nine big deep sea fishing trawlers that the Basques had converted into warships for their tiny auxiliary navy run by Joaquin Eguia. The *Nabara* was escorting the passenger ship *Galdames* on March 5, 1937 when it was attacked by the rebel or Francoist cruiser *Canarias* off Cape Matxitxako. Outgunned and outranged, the *Nabara* heroically fought on to the end against the 10,000-ton cruiser though nearly two-thirds of Basque sailors in her crew were killed and the rest wounded. The *Nabara*'s captain, thirty-year-old Enrique Moreno, chose to go down with his ship rather than surrender to the Spanish Nationalists. C. Day Lewis wrote (and José Antonio de Agirre quoted in his book) these lines about their gallant fight:

> They bore not a charmed life. They went into battle foreseeing
> Probable loss, and they lost. The tides of Biscay flow
> Over the obstinate bones of many, the winds are sighing
> Round prison walls where the rest are doomed like their ship to
>   rust –
> Men of the Basque country, the Mar Cantabrico.
>
> Simple men who asked of their life no mythical splendour,
> They loved its familiar ways so well that they preferred
> In the rudeness of their heart to die rather than to surrender...
> Mortal these words and the deed they remember, but cast a seed
> Shall flower for an age when freedom is man's creative word.
>
> Freedom was more than a word, more than the base coinage
> Of politicians who hiding behind the skirts of peace
> They had defiled, gave up that country to rack and carnage:
> For whom, indelibly stamped with history's contempt,
> Remains but to haunt the blackened shell of their policies.
> For these I have told of, freedom was flesh and blood—a mortal
> Body, the gun-breech hot to its touch: yet the battle's height
> Raised it to love's meridian and held it awhile immortal;
> And its light through time still flashes like a star's that has turned
>   to ashes,
> Long after *Nabara's* passion was quenched in the sea's heart.

Bibliography

Aguirre y Lecube, José Antonio de. *Obras Completas*. 2 vols. Donostia: Sendoa Argitaldaria, 1981.

———. *De Guernica a Nueva York pasando por Berlin*. Madrid: Foca, 2004.

———. *Escape via Berlin: Eluding Franco in Hitler's Europe*. Reno: University of Nevada Press, 1991.

———. *Freedom was Flesh and Blood*. London: Gollancz, 1944.

———. *José Antonio Aguirre Lekube. Diario 1941–1942*. Edited by Iñaki Goiogana. Bilbao: Fundación Sabino Arana/Sabino Arana Kultur Elkargoa, 2010.

Ajuria, Peru, and Iñigo Camino. *José Antonio de Aguirre, retrato de un Lehendakari, fotografías inéditas del primer presidente de los vascos*. Prologue by Lehendakari Juan José Ibarretxe. Bilbao: Fundación Sabino Arana/Sabino Arana Kultur Elkargoa, 2004.

Day Lewis, C. *Overtures to Death and Other Poems*. London: Jonathan Cape, 1938.

Bidasoa, Instituto de Historia Contemporanea. *El combate de Cabo Matxitxako*. Bidasoa: 1977.

Mees, Ludger, José Luis de la Granja, Santiago de Pablo, and José Antonio Rodríguez Ranz. *La política como pasión: el lehendakari José Antonio Aguirre (1904–1960)*. Madrid: Tecnos, 2014.

Stevenson, Robert Louis. *A Footnote to History: Eight Years of Trouble in Samoa*. London: Cassell, 1892.

5

Agirre in Berlin and How He Was Able to Escape the Gestapo

Ingo Niebel

On May 23, 1941 the Panamanian lawyer José Andrés Álvarez Lastra, the Venezuelan widow Mari Arrigorriaga de Guerra, and her two youngest children, Gloria and José, embarked on a ship in the German port of Sassnitz that would bring the passengers to Sweden. The officers of the German border police, the Grenzpolizei, who controlled passports and visas, did not know that in fact the four Latin American travelers belonged to one and the same family whose head was wanted by the Spanish police. Since the Spanish Civil War (1936–1939) the Geheime Staatspolizei (Gestapo, Secret State Police) had been in close contact with the security authorities of the Spanish Generalissimo Francisco Franco. Although the Grenzpolizei belonged to the Gestapo, the Basque president, José Antonio Agirre Lekube, his wife Mari Zabala, together with their daughter Aintzane and son Joseba Andoni managed to escape. When the *lendakari* set foot on the ship that brought him to the Swedish port of Trelleborg that May 23, he put an end to nearly twelve months living with a false identity, hiding from Spanish and German agents who were on his trail.

On June 1, 2016 "The International Legacy of Lehendakari Jose Antonio Agirre's Government" congress took place in Berlin. The organizers asked me for a contribution to their publication with an overview of the actual status of my investigations on the time the Basque president spent hidden in German-controlled territory between 1940 and 1941.[1] Only some days before

---

1. I owe my thanks–*mil esker*–for this opportunity to Professors Xabier Irujo

the event started, the Basque magazine *Zazpika* published my Spanish-written reportage "Agirre in the archive of the Gestapo."[2] The Euskal Etxea (Basque Club) of Berlin and the German-Basque cultural association Gernika, Deutsch-Baskischer Kulturverein, contributed to the congress with several of their own activities, remembering the seventieth anniversary of Agirre's successful escape through the German heartland with the webpage "AgirreInBerlin.eus." For this purpose, the Euskal Etxea of Berlin gave me the task of translating those parts of Agirre's original diary that dealt with his stay in Hamburg and Berlin (January 7, 1941 – May 23, 1941) into German.[3] On the other hand, I was asked to collect the essential information for two historical maps that show the most important places Agirre frequented when he was in Berlin. The first map reproduces the addresses and houses in the district of Charlottenburg, where he lived under a false identity in a small hotel. The other map contains such places he visited in the then political center of Berlin and that he mentioned in his diary.[4]

In this chapter I resume my publications on Agirre in Nazi Germany in a more academic style, namely including sources. So far, we only see the tip of the iceberg while my investigations into this topic continue as part of a wider publishing project on the lehendakari in German-controlled Europe. Its main questions remain why and how the well-known politician was able to escape from the Gestapo, which was supposed to be "omnipotent" according to its own propaganda and to those historians and journalists who do not question that description.

Although the German abbreviation of Geheime Staatspolizei, Gestapo, is very useful for drawing the attention of the public, it is

and Mari Jose Olaziregi, to Unai Lauzirika for bringing us together, and to Dr. Uschi Grandel for the revision of my manuscript.

2. Ingo Niebel, "Agirre en el archivo de la Gestapo," *Zazpika*, May 22, 2016. The maps and further information in Basque, German, and Spanish can be downloaded from www.agirreinberlin.eus/karten/, last consulted October 18, 2016.

3. See http://www.agirreinberlin.eus/kritische-edition-der-tagebuecher/, last consulted October 18, 2016. My translation is based on the excellent transcription and edition of Agirre's diary done by Iñaki Goiogana. See Sabino Arana Fundazioa (Ed.), *José Antonio Agirre Lekube. Diario 1941-1942* (Bilbo: Sabino Arana Fundazioa, 2010).

4. Agirre's complete works and the electronic edition of his diary can be found here: www.lehendakariagirre.eu, last consulted October 18, 2016.

more accurate to use the term Sicherheitspolizei/Sicherheitsdienst (Security Police/Security Service), known as Sipo/SD, if we take into account current scholarly research on the Nazi repression apparatus. The reason for this decision will be explained later in a special section on the Nazi Intelligence Community in 1940–1941. For the first time I will publish information in English about the ID cards that the Sipo/SD filed on Agirre, and his deputy Jesús María de Leizaola.

As you have noticed, I use the older orthography *"lendakari"* referring to Agirre instead of the modern *"lehendakari."* This is a conscious decision and not in line with actual Basque newspapers because I believe that his competences as a president differ widely from those of his successors from 1980 on, when the second Autonomy Statute became effective. The most important difference was that Agirre became commander-in-chief of all military units and militias fighting on the soil of the Basque Country against the Francoist rebels and their allies from Nazi Germany and Fascist Italy. For the same reason I use also the orthography of Euzkadi instead of Euskadi.

It is also necessary to take a short look at Agirre's own biography and his contacts as Basque president with the Germans during the Spanish Civil War. This is a new aspect of that part of Basque history as well. I found the cited documents during my research on different topics related to Basque history in German and Austrian archives. These are the German Federal Archive, the Bundesarchiv (BArch, Berlin), and its Military Archive (BAMA, Freiburg i.Br.), the Political Archive of the German Foreign Ministry (PAAA), and the Austrian State Archive (ÖStA). Generally, there are no entries on the "Basken" and "Aguirre" in the registers of these archives. Therefore, the research is very time-consuming because the interesting documents on Basque history are "hidden" among the papers dealing with German relations with Spain and France.[5]

Because of space and time, I will not go into further details on Agirre's stay in Berlin. I will only mention some specific aspects that are helpful to understand how he got reunited there with his wife Mari Zabala, daughter Aintzane, and son Joseba Andoni, just ten days before they left the Reich by ship heading toward Sweden.

---

5. In the published version of my PhD thesis I refer to the situation of the archives. See Ingo Niebel, *"Gebildet … freier baskischer Staat." Das Baskenland während des Spanischen Bürgerkriegs 1936/37* (Bonn: Pahl-Rugenstein, 2014).

A President-in-Exile Went into Hiding

On May 8, 1940 Agirre traveled with his wife Mari and the two children from the French capital of Paris, where they used to live, to the Belgian coastal town of Le Panne, where they met with his mother, brothers, and sisters, who also lived in exile, but in Belgium. Initially, the lost war in the Basque Country against the overwhelming military superiority of the German Condor Legion, the Italian Corpo Truppe Volontarie, and the Francoist rebels had forced him to seek exile in Santander and Catalonia. Ultimately, the triumph of Franco, achieved in 1939 thanks to the support granted by the Nazi Führer and German Reichschancellor Adolf Hitler and the fascist Duce Benito Mussolini of Italy, drove Agirre into his second exile in France. Despite the defeat, the president looked for new opportunities to convince western democracies to fight against the European Fascisms.

Two days after Agirre's arrival at Le Panne, Hitler ordered his Armed Forces, the Wehrmacht, to attack the western neighbors of Germany. The offensive caught the Agirre-Zabalas and their relatives by surprise. With the German bombs, death and chaos descended. Finally, the Basque president managed to unite several dozen family members and compatriots in the Belgian village but they could not cross the Belgian-French border because it had been closed already by the French authorities. Twelve days after the beginning of Operation Yellow, the German Panzers reached the French coast near Calais. Agirre realized that not only the British Expeditionary Force was caught in the area of Dunquerque but also he and his companions were also trapped because there were no means to leave the pocket. So the thirty-six-year-old politician decided to follow the advice of his family, who insisted that he had to leave without them. Together with a befriended priest he went back to Brussels in the car of a wealthy couple. Agirre destroyed his identity documents and operated as a Belgian student.

In the Belgian capital he hid first with the Jesuits, whose school and university he had attended in the Basque Country, but when the Sipo/SD started raiding the institutions of that Catholic order, considered by Nazi ideology as an enemy, the Basque moved to Antwerp, where his government had installed a commercial delegation during the Spanish Civil War. He had changed his appearance, wearing a pair of false glasses and a real moustache. Thanks to the consul of Panama, German Gil Guardia Jaén, he had got a real passport of that American Republic that documented his false identity of the landowner and lawyer, José Andrés Álvarez Lastra. His new name corresponded with the initials of his real name, so he could use his clothes marked with these letters. In Antwerp the Basque lived in the house of a Belgian family who did not know his real identity. He forged some letters from Panama in which his nonexistent relatives asked him to abandon the European continent and to come back.

At the end of the fall, Agirre/Álvarez had to look seriously for an escape route because the Germans had put in place their repression machinery in Belgium and were searching for hidden enemy aliens and other opponents of the German Reich.

Sipo/SD with Its Very Own Problems

When, on January 30, 1933, the elderly president, Paul von Hindenburg, appointed the leader of the German National Socialist Workers Party (NSDAP), Adolf Hitler, chancellor of a right-wing coalition government, the Nazi Heinrich Himmler, chief of Schutzstaffel (SS, Security Units) tried to get control over the entire police and all intelligence organizations. At the beginning of World War II, Himmler and his fugleman, Reinhard Heydrich, had almost achieved that goal. The SS controlled a vast economic and industrial imperium based widely on the exploitation of the inmates of concentration camps. Another pillar of the SS empire was the uniformed police forces. In a third one and under the denomination of the Reich Main Security Office (RSHA, Reichssicherheitshauptamt), Himmler and Heydrich had concentrated all the other police organizations and intelligence agencies, except the military ones. In the NSDAP there existed officially only the secret service of the SS, the Sicherheitsdienst (SD, Security Service), which had absorbed all other former intelligence structures of the party. Himmler and Heydrich consolidated the Gestapo and Kriminalpolizei (Kripo, Criminal Police) into the Sicherheitspolizei (Sipo, Security Police). Though both belonged to different offices (Amt) inside the RSHA, they shared police work. The Gestapo, known as Amt IV, used to investigate and fight against all potential enemies of the Nazi state, while the Kripo (Amt V) specialized in typical criminal investigation labor, such as searching for someone, for instance. The SD was split into Amt III, which as the SD-Inland monitored the political, social, cultural, and economic situation inside the Reich, while the SD-Ausland (Amt VI) acted as an intelligence service abroad. In its Amt VII the SD monitored and investigated its enemies from an ideological point of view. But this administrative separation between the aforementioned offices should not be overestimated because in fact they collaborated if necessary, despite all existing internal and personal rivalry.

In the hypothetical case that some institution would have wanted Agirre to be arrested, the Gestapo would have issued the warrant and perhaps set up a taskforce of its own officers and those of the Kripo. Had it been necessary, further experts from the SD could have been called in. "Sipo and SD formed an amalgam," concludes the US historian George C. Browder, a specialist on the Nazi police system.[6]

But when Operation Yellow started, Himmler and Heydrich had a serious problem: The High Command of the Army (OKH) excluded the Sipo/SD from acting as a special police force behind the advancing Army Groups. The reason for that decision came from the experiences during the invasion of Poland in 1939. The Sipo/SD execution squads had liquidated the Polish intelligentsia and Jewish citizens by means of mass murder. This had caused a certain amount of upset among lower ranking army commanders although others had supported the killing operations of Himmler's men.

This kind of warfare against the civilian population did not fit into the plans the OKH had regarding the occupation of the western democracies. It had planned to maintain their civil administrations, which would then act on behalf of the German Military Commanders. The strategists in Berlin thought that they could install and protect the new German order with their own military police forces and secret service without the Sipo/SD. At their disposal they had the Feldgendarmerie, which acted as the traditional military police, controlling the soldiers and their discipline, military traffic, and last but not least the transporting of prisoners of war. The military intelligence branch, the Abwehr, had its own police, the so-called Geheime Feldpolizei (GFP, Secret Field Police). Due to the compromises the Wehrmacht had to find with

---

6. George C. Browder, *Foundations of the Nazi Police State: The Formation of Sipo and SD* (Lexington, KY: University of Kentucky, 2004), 7; Michael Wildt, *Generation des Unbedingten.Das Führungskorps des Reichssicherheitshauptamtes* (Hamburg: Hamburger Edition HIS, 2013).

the SS, this military unit was also integrated with Sipo-Personal. The conscripted officers of the Gestapo and Kripo had to wear the military uniform of the GFP, got military ranks, and were subject to military discipline. Though Himmler and Heydrich had a foot in the door of the military intelligence structure, they could not enter the western countries with their especially prepared Einsatzgruppen and Einsatzkommandos. The RSHA provided these Sipo/SD units with all kinds of information on the political, ideological, and military enemies that they needed before invading a foreign country and acting against potential enemies located in society and the state.

When the Wehrmacht occupied Paris on June 14, 1940 the Abwehr had other priorities rather than spending too much time on the political enemies of the Reich because the Oberkommando der Wehrmacht (OKW, Supreme Command of the Armed Forces) planned to continue the war with the invasion of England. So the military had other priorities than the Sipo/SD could have had. Despite the exclusion, the chief of the RSHA, Heydrich, managed to send two smaller commandos of his men in GFP uniforms to Paris. In the meantime, Himmler tried to lift the ban imposed by the OKH on the Sipo/SD in France and Belgium.

Although there were serious problems between the SS and the Wehrmacht, the latter did not hesitate to arrest political enemies as happened in the case of Lluis Companys. The president of the Generalitat, the Government of Catalonia, was detained because the Francoist police officer Pedro Urraca, based in the Spanish Embassy in Paris, had monitored the most important figures of the Spanish republican exile before Germany started her war against France. When he asked the German Military Administration for support to detain people like Companys, he got it, including from the officers, probably from the GFP or Feldgendarmerie, who escorted him and the detainees to the Basque border town of Hendaia (Hendaye). The prominent Catalan and homologue of Agirre did not hide himself nor did he escape to the unoccupied zone of France because he did not want to leave his mentally ill son, who was in a French hospital, behind. The Germans arrested and delivered him to the Spaniards, who held him in prison until October 1940. In a farce of a trial without any legal guarantees they condemned Companys to death and executed him on October 15.

Although Agirre arranged to escape the control of both Francoists and Nazis, he was not safe.

Agirre in the Archive of the Gestapo

"We do not even know if the Gestapo tailed him seriously although we can confirm that the Francoist authorities tried to discover his whereabouts," affirms the German historian Ludger Mees in his biography on the lendakari.[7] Other authors prefer to accuse Agirre of being a philo-Nazi, taking some of the entries in his diary out of the context. The Basque summed up his time in Germany in his autobiographical book *De Guernica a Nueva York pasando por Berlín*, published in 1943 in Argentina. "Thank God, I do not know the internal mechanism of the Gestapo," recognizes Agirre, because he believes that the German secret police did fulfill its duties.[8]

But his brother Juan was arrested by the Sipo/SD, as he also remembers in his autobiography.[9] So Himmler's men were on his tail. At least they knew his relatives and where they had to look and whom to interrogate. If they lost him then, it was because the lendakari had run the rumor that he was already in England. The other reason may be that the Sipo/SD did not consider him significant enough for initiating a major search. Due to the fact that Nazi Germany had occupied nearly all of her neighboring countries, the RSHA had serious personal problems when it came to achieving its main goals of liquidating communists, Jews, and foreign agents considered the main threats to the Reich's security.

Perhaps the fact that Agirre was not so important for the Sipo/SD hurts Basque feelings and the importance that this politician has for the history of Euskal Herria (the Basque Country), but it is the conclusion that can be drawn by analyzing three specific Gestapo documents that I discovered in 2016.

It was on August 26, 1937 when an unknown Gestapo officer filled in by hand the first of two ID cards with the family name "Aguirre."[10] The sentence "A. was 'president of the Basque Republic'" confirms the identity of this person whose first name is not given. "After the conquest of Santander, on 24.8.37, he escaped to Paris," continues the information. No source is given but the

---

7. Ludger Mees, *El profeta pragmático. Aguirre, el primer lehendakari (1939–1960)* (Irun: Alberdania, 2006), 64.

8. José Antonio Aguirre, *De Guernica a Nueva York pasando por Berlín* (Bilbao: Ikur, 1992), 186–87.

9. Ibid., 122.

10. BArch, R 58/9673.

information is correct. On that day, the supreme council of his Partido Nacionalista Vasco-Eusko Alderdi Jeltzailea (PNV-EAJ) or Basque Nationalist Party, the Euzkadi Buru Batzar (EBB), ordered him, being the lendakari of the then Euzkadi'ko Jaurlaritza (Government of the Basque Country), to leave the province of Santander. On August 25 and 26, 1937 the Basque militias, organized by the Euzko Gudarostea (close to the Catholic PNV) and Euzko Ekintza (close to leftist Acción Nacionalista Vasca (ANV), Basque Nationalist Action), were ready to surrender to the Italian forces in Santoña. From exile, Agirre and his government unsuccessfully tried to evacuate their comrades from Santander. In France and Catalonia they prepared for the support of the 100,000 Basque refugees in both countries.

The second card that the Gestapo filed on March 16, 1938 refers to this relationship. "Aguirre" is "head of the Basque Government although he has no longer any political importance. He stays in contact with the leader of the Catalans, Companys. Both are in opposition to the communist leadership and monitored." This raises the question who monitored Agirre and Companys, the communists or German agents?

This second card was written by section A3 of the Gestapo, which specialized in "the observation of the Soviet Russians and dealing with alien enemies of the State." In 1937 its head was the SS officer and member of the Kripo, Erich Schröder. In June 1941, he moved to Lisbon (Portugal), where he became the head of SD at the German Embassy. His immediate superior was the notorious Paul Winzer, who was based at the German diplomatic representation in Madrid and headed the Spanish department of Sipo/SD.

The Gestapo officer wrote that second ID card during a very deep internal crisis of the Republican Government. After several military defeats, the president of the Spanish Republic, Manuel Azaña, proposed that a solution should be negotiated with General Francisco Franco's rebels because the war had been lost. He was supported by Basque and Catalan nationalists, such as Agirre and Companys, but also by a part of the Partido Socialista Obrero Español (PSOE, Spanish Socialist Workers Party. Against him stood the rest of the PSOE, the Partido Comunista de España (PCE, Communist Party of Spain), and Prime Minister Juan Negrín. They thought a continuing war would become a major European conflict that would force London and Paris to take part in it on the side of the Spanish Republic against international Fascism.

From these two cards we can conclude that in 1938 the Gestapo considered Agirre of such minor importance that his first name is not even mentioned. That also means that it did not regard "the Basques" in their totality as "enemies," like the Sipo/SD did with "communists" and "Jews."

This interpretation is stressed by the Gestapo card of another known *jelkide* (member of the PNV), Jesús María de Leizaola.[11] The Secret Police payed him more attention than Agirre. The type-written card calls the deputy of the Basque president by his complete name and refers to his "Spanish" nationality. His places of residence are located in Santander and in "France, St. Jean de Luz." The first inscription dates, as in the case of Agirre, from August 26, 1937, and explains that, "after the fall of Santander he fled to France." The second entry is from February 20, 1939, stating that he is a "Basque member of parliament and Minister of Justice." In fact, Leizaola was the Minister of Justice and Culture in Agirre's first Basque government in 1936. The inscription continues that, "in n°5 of 3.2.39 'Die Zukunft' [The Future, IN] is L's article to readers on democratic solidarity." The magazine was published by German exiles in Paris. It aimed to resume the different political sensibilities of Germans and French for creating a united movement inside the widespread anti-Hitler opposition and outside the Kommunistische Partei Deutschlands (KPD, Communist Party of Germany). The Gestapo considered that project so dangerous that it filed a special report on Leizaola. A remark on it is included in the ID card. That document is not in the Bundesarchiv, the German Federal Archive. It has probably disappeared or it was destroyed.

According to the Bundesarchiv, it received the Gestapo cards on Agirre and Leizaola when in 1990 it began to dismantle the so called "National Socialist Archive" (NS-Archiv) of the Ministry for State Security (MfS) of the German Democratic Republic (GDR). This intelligence agency, better known by its popular name "Stasi," collected all kinds of information on the Nazi era, hoping to use it for its intelligence operations against the Federal Republic of Germany (FRG). This activity was done without experts and archivists, who would have been able to process and store such an amount of documents. This explains why the Bundesarchiv does not know where and when the MfS found the cards. The MfS officers gathered them in a new collection titled "persecuted by the Gestapo."

---

11. BArch, R 58/9687.

The institution handling the Stasi files, the BStU, informed me on my request that there are no further documents on Agirre or Leizaola in the remaining archive of the disbanded East German intelligence agency.[12] That means that the MfS did not have any interest in these politicians or their party, the PNV/EAJ.

Agirre in Other German Documents

Although the Nazi regime created several secret agencies and police organizations, there was no institution that coordinated intelligence activities. Perhaps because of that fact, the Sipo/SD, and especially the Gestapo, did not know that the Foreign Ministry had had a picture of Agirre since 1936. Actually, this is the only known image of one of the members of the first Autonomous Basque Government in 1936 recorded by a Nazi institution.

It was part of a large report that the chargé d'affaires at the German Embassy in Alicante, Hans Hermann Völckers, wrote on October 9, 1936,[13] a week before the Spanish parliament approved the Statute of Autonomy for the Basque Country. It was the political price that the Republican forces had to pay for converting the passivity of the PNV-EAJ into an active defense of the constitution against the rebels. These were led by several generals, Francisco Franco and Emilio Mola being the most important at that moment. On July 17 and 18, 1936, together with other officers, they started their coup d'état against the Republic and its democratically elected leftist government. But the rightist putsch failed and transformed into a civil war. Although even the Basque Country was split into two parts, as was the case with the "dos Españas," the two Spains, the PNV-EAJ tried to remain neutral in that conflict, considering it a war among Spaniards. Its leadership expected that one of the Spanish sides would win rapidly, so that it its executive committee, the EBB, would not have to take any decision whom it should support. In September, the time of staying away from the front was over. The rebels began to execute even PNV-EAJ members, despite their being Catholics and mainly bourgeois. They considered the demand of Basque nationalism for self-government as a menace for the unity of their España. The Republican forces also distrusted the Basque

---

12. Information given by phone, October 12, 2016.
13. Politisches Archiv des Auswärtigen Amtes (PAAA), R103004: Pol III 3806 Deutsche Botschaft Alicante an AA, October 9, 1936.

nationalists because of their ideology, their aim to create their own Basque state on Spanish soil, and their offer to the Basque provinces in the French Republic to join it. Finally it were the "dos Españas" which militarized the political conflict of the Spanish state with the Basque Country because until October 1936 no Basque national organization had fought by other than political means for the creation of its own *res publica*, termed "Euzkadi," in the twentieth century. The price Basques had to pay for receiving autonomy was that they had to defend it by arms and side with the leftist parties.

The political idea of Euzkadi became real when, on October 7, 1936, Agirre was sworn in as the president of the Euzkadi'ko Jaurlaritza, the Government of the Basque Country. The ceremony took place in the city of Gernika (Guernica) under the old oak tree where in former times the Spanish kings had to swear to respect Basque self-government. In the nineteenth century three civil wars were necessary to abolish Basque liberties, imposing Spanish rule on the region, and starting to eliminate Basque identity. Now, in 1936, it was Agirre who brought back to his fellow Basques the right to govern themselves by their own institutions.

For that reason Völckers included in his report the picture of Agirre, which was on the top page of the then republican newspaper ABC, and the entire text of the Statute. But he declined to translate and analyze it, arguing that "in the case of a victory of the Government of Burgos it will disappear again from the political reality in Spain;" despite the fact that the German diplomat also recognized that the Statute was a victory for the Government of Madrid because it kept the Basques on its side and it could "make it more difficult or postpone the victory of the Government of Burgos."[14]

From Bilbao, the new *lendakaritza* did not waste any time in communicating the existence of a new Basque entity to the international community. The words "constituted seven October government free Basque state" can be read in a Spanish-language telegram that the Basque Executive sent on November 6, 1936 to the Austrian diplomatic mission at Paris that had dared to address a message to the civil governor of the province of Bizkaia.[15] That position had expired when Agirre became lendakari.

---

14. PAAA, R103004: Pol III 3806 Deutsche Botschaft Alicante an AA, October 9, 1936.

15. OStA, Gesandtschaftsarchiv Paris, Bilbao Akten W. Wakonigg: 8816, telegram sent on November 6, 1936.

One month later, the commander of the German cruiser *Königsberg* sent a cable to the "presidente de Vizcaya" and got back by telegraph an answer that he had to refer to "presidente de Euzkadi."[16] Agirre and his government achieved their goal by implementing the idea that Euzkadi was no longer only a political project but had become a new Basque institution. Though his executive never declared a "Basque Republic," this term started to circulate outside the Basque Country. Even Francoist dailies like the *Hoja Oficial del Lunes* (Gipuzkoa) protested on October 26, 1936 against the "República vasca," the Basque Republic. After the bombing of Gernika by the German Condor Legion and some Italian planes on April 26, 1937, the falangist *Diario de Burgos* referred to Agirre as "presidente de la república de Euzkadi" (president of the Republic of Euzkadi). The philo-Republican Belgian journalist J.-E. Pouterman chose as a title of his report "Passing through the Basque republic." And the special envoy of Reuters news agency, Christopher Holmes, also used the term "Basque Republic." Finally, even the German Condor Legion and Gestapo adopted "Basken-Republik" and "baskische Republik" as synonyms of "Euzkadi." From the ideological point of view of Nazism and Francoism, the concept of "republic" had a pejorative connotation, above all if it was linked to the adjective "Basque."

But despite that, on November 15, 1936 even Völckers directed a message to "Su Excelencia Señor Presidente de Euskadia [sic]", trying to save the life of the former Austrian consul Wilhelm Wakonigg.[17] The Tribunal Popular de Euzkadi had sentenced him to death for espionage. This is the unique document that proves that German diplomacy had taken notice of Euzkadi as a new institution and political actor in the Spanish Civil War. The highest ranking representative of Nazi Germany, who never met Agirre personally, was the commander of the cruiser *Köln*, Otto Backenköhler, who in 1936 also intervened to save Wakonigg from execution. The naval officer describes the then thirty-two-year-old president as a "young man, intelligent, energetic."[18]

---

16. BAMA, RM92/5067: 73, 76.
17. PAAA, Botschaft Madrid (offen), Sa 5b Gefangene in Rotspanien (Beiakte), t.1: Copy of Völcker's telegram to Agirre from November 15, 1936; For further information on the Wakonigg case s. Ingo Niebel, *Al infierno o a la gloria. La vida y muerte del cónsul y espía Wilhelm Wakonigg en Bilbao 1900–1936* (Irun: Alberdania, 2009): 218-230.
18. BAMA, RM92/5062: 8.

All these details show that the Gestapo could have had sufficient material and eyewitnesses, who had dealt with Agirre, for opening a file on him. If it did not do it, it was because of other priorities the Sipo/SD had in 1940–1941.

Agirre in Berlin

On January 7, 1941 Agirre/Álvarez entered Germany. The Sipo/SD had strengthened its control over Belgian territory and society. For the lendakari there was a real chance to leave German-dominated Europe toward Greece thanks to the help of his protector Guardia Jaén. Coming from Brussels, the president took a second train in Cologne to Hamburg.

In the port town consul Guardia Jaen was already waiting for him and brought him to the guesthouse of Frau Mickoleit. Next day, both registered themselves at the police station. They were forced to do so by law or else they could not get the obligatory ration cards. The documents in the State Archive of Hamburg only prove Guardia Jaen's stay in the above mentioned pension.[19]

After three weeks in Hamburg, Agirre moved to Berlin. In the capital of the Reich he lived in the Victoria Hotel Guesthouse at Kurfürstendamm 203/204. Supposedly, he shared a room with Guardia Jaen, who traveled a lot between Hamburg and Berlin, Brussels, and Antwerp, and other places.

The guesthouse was located in the district of Charlottenburg, some five kilometers (three miles) from the Brandenburg Gate and the political center of the capital. Then, as well as now, Charlottenburg was a typical bourgeois quarter, where several Latin American diplomats also lived close to their delegations. For instance, the chancellery of Venezuela's Embassy was located at Kurfürstendamm 186. That diplomatic representation was important for Agirre because his wife and children had adopted the false identity of Venezuelans thanks to the real passports they got in Belgium.

Hiding behind a false identity, Agirre choose a very open way of life as he had done so before in Belgium. He regularly left the guesthouse and almost every day took a walk with diplomats of Panama and the Dominican Republic he had befriended. When he

---

19. Staatsarchiv Hamburg to the author, July 3, 1996. I published my research on Agirre's stay in Hamburg as a part of a larger report on that German town. See Ingo Niebel, "El primer lehendakari de Euskadi," *Igandegin*, July 7, 1997, 6.

was alone, he spent a lot of time in movie theaters. This was a standard method also used by other people who lived underground and who did not want to raise the suspicion of their neighbors. They had in some way a kind of fake normal work life, spending most of the day out of the house. Agirre did not have to commit any misdemeanors to survive because he got enough money from Manuel Ynchausti, a US millionaire of Basque origin. That enabled him to dine out at modest restaurants nearly every day although he tried to save his money as much as possible because of his character and of his security measures, which made it impossible to contact his fellow Basques in the United States directly.

On two occasions, one of which was his birthday on March 6, 1941, he attended the exclusive restaurant Tusculum with his diplomat friends. This place was frequented by members of the Diplomat Corps and the Nazi regime's elite. For this reason, the Abwehr and Sipo/SD had an eye on everybody who frequented the Tusculum. Rumors also called it the "cantina of the Salon Kitty." That establishment was located around the next corner at the Giesebrechtstrasse and could be reached discretely by those clients who looked for the special services that the well educated women who worked in the Salon Kitty used to offer in a luxury environment. It is said that the Sipo/SD had installed microphones in every room, which were connected to recording machines in the cellar of that building.

For a German observer it seemed obvious that Álvarez was conducting a normal life in Berlin and that he was close to such diplomats whose countries were still not opposed to the Reich. Even if the Gestapo checked Agirre's guesthouse and questioned him, there would be no evidence that he had fought against Condor Legion and Franco during the Spanish Civil War.

Agirre in Front of Hitler's Reich Chancellery

The Basque character is said to contain something of the gambler, a feature corresponding to the slogan "who dares, wins." On several occasions Agirre visited the political center of Berlin accompanying one of his diplomats or alone.

The most risky situation he entered into fully aware of the risks was on March 27, 1941. On that day the lendakari went to the Wilhelmstrasse where the famous balcony of the Reichschancellery was and where Hitler used to appear before his people. On that occasion, the Führer appeared together with the Japanese foreign minister Yosuke Matsuoka. As Agirre himself recounts, he was only fifty meters from the balcony in the crowd waving the flags of the two countries and shouting what hethought he could make out from the people around him. Between the mass and the building the Nazi garde du corps, the SS, protected the empty security area that was monitored by the Reichssicherheitsdienst (RSD, Security Service of the Reich), a special unit of SS bodyguards. Agirre was lucky that even on that occasion there was no security check to enter the area as is usual nowadays. He could therefore see the man with the moustache and swastika who was responsible for killing people like his sister Encarna at Dunkirk, for forcing people like him into exile, and who was going to murder even more and more humans. When I researched Matsuoka's visit to Berlin, I found one picture in the database of Getty Images that shows the crowd in front of the Reich Chancellery.[20] One of them could be Agirre, but it is nearly impossible to locate him. A similar image was included in the map of the Euskal Etxea.

Conclusion

Call it luck or coincidence, destiny or providence, but Agirre managed to unite with his loved ones in Berlin and to leave Nazi Germany with them. His last indirect kick against the not so almighty Nazi repressive apparatus was that leaving Berlin by car, he had to cross Oranienburg, a city north of the capital, in which the Sachsenhausen concentration camp was located. Two years after Agirre's escape the SS incarcerated there, in the area for very important prisoners, his former Spanish political rival, Francisco Largo Caballero. The socialist had been the president of the Republican Government when Agirre became lendakari of Euzkadi. Largo Caballero survived that time in the hand of the Black Death head order.

It would be too hypothetical to wonder what would have happened to Agirre if the Sipo/SD had caught him. I think if that had occurred in 1940, the Nazis would have handed him over to

---

20. See   www.gettyimages.fi/detail/news-photo/germany-free-state-prussia-berlin-a-crowd-on-wilhelmplatz-news-photo/548790245#germany-free-state-prussia-berlin-a-crowd-on-wilhelmplatz-cheers-picture-id548790245, last consulted November 15, 2016.

the Francoists, hoping that with this "gift" General Franco would officially join the war on their side, and permitting an attack on Gibraltar. As we know, the Caudillo did not dare to make that step. At the end of 1940 that changed the expectations the Germans had in Franco. Perhaps they would have treated Agirre as they did Largo Caballero, thinking that in some way he could be useful.

I think there are two main reasons for Agirre's successful escape. On the one hand, he did not act as it was expected. He went under the radar of his Francoist enemies in Paris and later did not use the traditional escape routes but dared to enter Hitler's Grand German Reich. There, on the other hand, he could pose as a Latin American lawyer thanks to the financial and logistical support he received from both diplomats and his Basque friends in the United States. Finally, he left Germany with his family only one month before the Wehrmacht started the invasion of the Soviet Union on June 22, 1941. That new German military campaign would have made his situation in Berlin even more difficult because he was together with his wife and children who, according to their false identities, belonged to another family. And, above all, the Sipo/SD had sufficient other people to look for than wasting its time on the Agirre-Zabalas.

These are academically based explanations. Whoever reads Agirre's diary will discover how strong his Catholic faith was. A secularist may interpret his prayers in Germany as some sort of self-relaxing in a situation full of tension and uncertainty, but perhaps they were really so strong that Saint Ignatius of Loyola, the Basque founder of the Jesuit order, gave a helping hand from up on high so that his student and his relatives could get out of that empire of evil. Who knows?

Bibliography

Aguirre, José Antonio. *De Guernica a Nueva York pasando por Berlín*. Bilbao: Ikur, 1992.

Browder, George C. *Foundations of the Nazi Police State: The Formation of Sipo and SD*. Lexington, KY: University of Kentucky, 2004.

Mees, Ludger. *El profeta pragmático. Aguirre, el primer lehendakari (1939–1960)*. Irun: Alberdania, 2006.

Niebel, Ingo. "El primer lehendakari de Euskadi." *Igandegin*, July 7, 1997.

———. *Al infierno o a la gloria. La vida y muerte del cónsul y espía Wilhelm Wakonigg en Bilbao 1900–1936.* Irun: Alberdania, 2009.

———. *"Gebildet ... freier baskischer Staat." Das Baskenland während des Spanischen Bürgerkriegs 1936/37.* Bonn: Pahl-Rugenstein, 2014.

———. "Agirre en el archivo de la Gestapo." *Zazpika*, May 22, 2016.

Sabino Arana Fundazioa (Ed.). *José Antonio Agirre Lekube. Diario 1941-1942.* (Bilbo: Sabino Arana Fundazioa, 2010).

Wildt, Michael. *Generation des Unbedingten.Das Führungskorps des Reichssicherheitshauptamtes.* Hamburg: Hamburger Edition HIS, 2013.

6

The Vatican and Euskadi during the
Spanish Civil War, 1936–1939

Hilari Raguer i Suñer

A civil war, a war between brothers, is always horrible, and the Spanish Civil War was no exception, but especially not in Euskadi. The insurrectionists proclaimed to the world that they were fighting in defense of religion and of Christian civilization, but they attacked the Basques, who were much more Catholic than they were. The military uprising was not in favor of religion, nor in favor of the monarchy, but against the Popular Front government. Not a single one of the proclamations declaring a state of war issued in every city in which an uprising took place invoked religion. Very quickly, however, the revolt turned into a crusade: for one reason, because everywhere the coup failed, except in Euskadi, a ferocious religious persecution was immediately unleashed, allowing the rebels to present themselves to international opinion as defenders of religion, and of order and property as well.

A member of the Passionist order, Fr. Francisco Gondra, better known as Aita Patxi,[1] constantly mentions three groups in his memoir of the war: "us," "the Spaniards," and "the *requetés*." "We" are the Basques; "the Spaniards" are the insurrectionists who were invading Euskadi; "the *requetés*" are the Navarrese Carlists, Basques who had nevertheless joined the Spaniards to attack their Gipuzkoan brothers. The name "Spaniards," let it be noted, had not the slightest connotation of hatred for Aita Patxi: he twice offered in prison camps to take the place of prisoners who were going to

---

1. See Hilari Raguer, *Aita Patxi: Prisionero con los gudaris* (Barcelona: Claret, 2006).

be shot (like Saint Maximilian Kolbe, but a few years earlier), and in both cases, the beneficiary was a Spaniard. It is interesting to see the way in which this priest, whose charity had no boundaries, conceived the religious dimension of his Basque identity. On one occasion when Franco's artillery and air force were pounding his battalion, the *gudaris* (soldiers in the Basque forces) were fleeing in disorder, and he stopped them, saying, "Don't flee; it's a sin." After he was taken prisoner, he was asked in repeated interrogations, "Caught or crossed over?" Knowing that if he said that he had crossed over, his fortunes would improve, he always answered categorically, "Caught. Never crossed over!" and he said repeatedly, "Desertion is a sin." He was scandalized to recount, as if it were the most shameful sin in the world, that another member of his order had crossed over to the Spaniards.

This intermingling of religious faith and patriotism, so deeply rooted in Aita Patxi, was shaken by the civil war in Euskadi. The Basque patriots were told by the religious authorities, including their bishop, that they were sinning by uniting with the Communists.

The case of the Basque Catholics did not fit into the simplistic picture of the civil war as a struggle between God and Lenin: they were fighting against the "crusaders," but they were Catholics. After traveling through wartime Euskadi, a Catalan priest, Josep M. Tarragó (who had founded a Catalan Christian labor union), published a dramatic book in mid-1937, *Le drame d'un peuple incompris: La guerre au pays basque* (The drama of a misunderstood people: The war in the Basque country).[2] In the second, revised and expanded edition (1938), François Mauriac writes in a preface, "Among all the murdered peoples, only the Basque shares with his Master the privilege of being insulted on the cross."

Explaining this contradiction would far exceed the space allotted. For this reason, after a very brief outline of the background of the issue, I will concentrate on the Vatican's attitude, focusing my analysis on a few points that have struck me as most significant for the conclusion I hope to demonstrate: that Pius XI, who felt great admiration and affection for the Basque Catholics, always refused to condemn them, despite strong and repeated pressure to do so, and even protected them in various ways, but in the end, after Eugenio Pacelli had become Pius XII, *realpolitik* took over, and the Vatican surrendered to the general victor.

---

2. Paris: H. G. Peyre, 1937.

Background

Before the civil war, the diocese of Vitoria-Gasteiz included the three Basque provinces: Bizkaia, Gipuzkoa, and Araba. The diocesan seminary was indisputably the best in Spain, both academically and in its solid spiritual formation. Seminary training was very advanced on social issues, based on the Basques' traditional Christian humanism, which promoted cooperatives and had built a Catholic labor union with majority membership, but at the same time, it was very traditional on dogmatic questions. Religious practice was very high throughout the region. The Basque clergy, in which we include the Navarrese, produced numerous candidates for the episcopate. In 1935 the cardinal-archbishop of Seville (Ilundain) and the bishops of Barcelona (Irurita), Tortosa (Félix Bilbao), Orihuela (Irastorza), Segovia (Pérez Platero), Zamora (Arce Ochotorena), Santander (Eguino), Ciudad Real (Estenaga), and Barbastro (Mutiloa), the auxiliary bishop of Valencia (Lauzurica), and the apostolic administrator of Oviedo (Echeguren) were Basques. The bishop of Vitoria-Gasteiz at the time was the Basque Mugica, a Euskara-speaker, but his predecessors (Cadena Eleta, Melo Alcalde, Eijo Garay, and Zacarías Martínez) did not speak Euskara and not only were not Basques, but had made public statements in opposition to Basque nationalism. Hence Bishop Zacarías Martínez of Vitoria-Gasteiz, speaking at the opening of the Urola railroad to an audience that included Alfonso XIII and the dictator Primo de Rivera, said, "The Church also has a blessing for land routes, because they unite men. . . . The Church also gives its blessing to this railway line, so that it may carry the good ideas of peace and work and Spanish identity [*españolismo*], and so that it may never carry the criminal ideas of separatism."[3] The Basque nationalists did not aspire to see the Vatican and the bishops of Vitoria-Gasteiz and Pamplona (Iruñea) at the service of nationalism. Indeed, the Basque Nationalist Party (Partido Nacionalista Vasco, PNV), faithful to Sabino Arana's ideas, had distanced itself from the monarchical integrism of Carlism. However, they rejected the idea that the Catholic faith required them to renounce their nationalism.

Where Euskadi, like Catalonia, is concerned, the Spanish state, in whatever form (monarchy, dictatorship, Franco's regime), has

---

3. Quoted in Ildefonso Moriones, *Euzkadi y el Vaticano 1935–1936* (Rome: Tipogr. Orientale S. Nilo, 1917), 47–48.

practiced a *do ut des* with the Vatican, granting great honors and favors to the institutional Church in exchange for the Holy See's collaboration in repressing nationalism, and the most powerful instrument of this policy has been the appointment of outsider bishops. "For centuries, the Basque people have faced a problem precisely where—at least in theory—they could least expect it: their ecclesiastical hierarchy, whether in Rome or at the diocesan level."[4]

The Second Republic

Before the civil war, the right was synonymous with religion and monarchy, and the left with anticlericalism and republicanism. The Basque nationalists were not monarchists, because the monarchs were antinationalist, but neither were they enthusiastic about the Second Republic, because the majority of republicans were anti-clerical. In the industrial areas, however, the Socialist party, which was republican, was strong. In Eibar (Gipuzkoa) the Republic was proclaimed on April 14, 1931, before it was proclaimed in Barcelona and long before it was proclaimed in Madrid.

In the battle over the religious issue in the Spanish parliament, Nuncio Tedeschini and Cardinal Vidal i Barraquer, who led the defense of the Church, were sure that they could count on the Basque nationalists, who were allied for this purpose with the Navarrese traditionalists, forming the "Basque-Navarrese minority." Over the years of the Republic's existence, the PNV gradually distanced itself from the traditionalist right and drew closer to the left, until when the civil war broke out, it remained loyal to the Republic and opposed the insurrectionists.

Catalonia had obtained its Statute of Autonomy because the left held power there and it was "the bulwark of the Republic" (in the words of Manuel Azaña), while Euskadi's statute was held up because the right predominated there, and according to Indalecio Prieto, autonomy would lead to a "Vaticanist Gibraltar."

On the eve of the February 1936 elections, an incident took place that was characteristic of the political and religious context of the moment, dominated by the Vatican obsession with the

---

4. Manu E. Lipuzcoa, *La Iglesia como problema en el País Vasco* (Buenos Aires: Ekin, 1973), 7.

"union of the Catholics" in defense of the Church.[5] Long before the elections were called, the PNV's leadership had arranged a visit to the Vatican, with audiences with the pope and the secretary of state, in order to explain the problem of Euskadi to them, but when they arrived in Rome, Msgr. Pizzardo, secretary of the Secretariat of State, told them that neither Pius XI nor Pacelli would receive them unless they committed in writing to campaign in coalition with the Spanish Confederation of the Autonomous Right (Confederación Española de Derechas Autónomas, CEDA), supported by the Vatican, which was insisting on the "union of all the Catholics." Pizzardo told them over and over that the elections were between Christ and Lenin. They answered in writing: "The Basque nationalists are not joining with rest of the right for the elections, because religion does not require them to do so, and politics forbids it." The fact was that the CEDA did not limit itself to defending the Church, but also had a reactionary ideology on social issues (due to the influence of Castilian landowners) and was opposed to autonomy. They added that there was no religious problem in Euskadi, since the large majority was Catholic, and their triumph was assured.

Civil War: The Uprising

The uprising of 1936 was like "a knife's edge" (Luis Romero), on which it was impossible to balance without taking sides. For the Basques, it was not their war. They could identify neither with the insurrectionists nor with the Republic, but they could not be neutral: they had to choose one side or the other.

The uprising was not motivated by the defense of religion; not a single one of the proclamations declaring a state of war mentioned it, and the generals involved in the conspiracy were not distinguished by their religiosity. An examination of the Seville, Salamanca, and Zaragoza press shows that religion was not discussed in the first few days, but it appeared as a topic soon after. The failed military coup quickly became a war of religion, because a terrible religious persecution was immediately unleashed in reaction in the republican zone. As Josep Benet said, the uncontrolled murderers and arsonists served up the title of "crusade" to Franco on a platter, and he would find it very useful. It soon

---

5. See Moriones, *Euzkadi y el Vaticano (1935–1936)*.

became evident that both sides were dependent on outside help, because neither army had munitions for a long war, and the rebels believed at the time that the banner of religion, united with those of order and property, would be greatly beneficial to them in international opinion. And so it was. Rebel propaganda began to speak about a holy war and a crusade, and the bishops joined in. The first prelate who used this label was in fact a Basque, Marcelino Olaechea Loizaga, a Salesian and a native of Barakaldo. His father had been a steelworker, and for this reason, when he was named bishop of Pamplona in 1935, he put a blast furnace on his coat of arms, instead of the usual rampant lions and eagles of the aristocracy. It was in a circular in favor of a national subscription, published in the *Boletín oficial del estado* (BOE), the government legal gazette, on August 15, 1936, that he said, "It is not a war that is underway; it is a crusade."[6]

Religion urged the Catholic Basque nationalists to unite with the insurrectionists, but nationalism led them to oppose them. They decided to resist the invading "Nationals," declared enemies of separatism, in which they included autonomy of any kind.

Gomá composed a pastoral letter with the *non licet*—it is not licit for you to ally with the Communists—and got the bishop of Vitoria-Gasteiz, Mugica, and the bishop of Pamplona, Olaechea, to sign it, but the Basque nationalists did not feel themselves bound by that letter. They had not allied with the Communists; rather, they were defending themselves against an aggressor, the declared enemy of autonomy of any kind, and in this defense they found themselves on the side of the Republic, which included Communists. It was not their fault that the Communists were also fighting against the military uprising. In addition, they doubted that Bishop Mugica was acting freely when he signed. In Euskadi, the Catholic nationalists protected people and buildings and maintained public worship. In Euskadi's army, there were chaplains, like the famous Aita Patxi. On September 25, the PNV entered the government of the Republic, with Manuel Irujo as minister without portfolio, on two conditions: the statute of autonomy and the reestablishment of religious freedom.

The Spanish bishops were enthusiastic adherents of the military coup, but they generally did not make public statements until Pius XI spoke on September 14, 1936. Those who acted earlier did

---

6. Alfonso Álvarez Bolado, *Para ganar la guerra, para ganar la paz* (Madrid: Universidad Pontificia de Comillas, 1995), 40n42.

so because the special circumstances of their dioceses demanded it: Mugica of Vitoria-Gasteiz and Olaechea of Pamplona, who published a pastoral letter on August 6 condemning the Basque nationalists' collaboration with the Communists, and Miralles of Mallorca, as a consequence of the landing of Captain Bayo's expedition in August.

The Drama of Bishop Mugica

The bishop of Vitoria-Gasteiz, Mateo Mugica,[7] was considered to be a nationalist and close to the PNV, especially because before the February 1936 elections he had declared that Catholics could also vote for the PNV. When the uprising broke out, he found himself in the eye of the hurricane, and despite his generous contributions and grants to the army, he continued to be held in suspicion. It was not enough that he had signed, along with the bishop of Pamplona, the August 6 pastoral letter composed by Gomá, saying that it was not licit for the Basques to unite with the Communists and combat the defenders of the faith, nor that he had dismissed his vicar-general, with whom he got on very well but who was accused of being a nationalist, and replaced him as he was instructed. Gomá reported to Pacelli on September 4, 1936, that the Defense Committee (Junta de Defensa) wanted Mugica to appear before it in Burgos in order to adopt the necessary measures to subdue the nationalists. Mugica made his excuses, alleging the insecurity of the trip and invoking everything that he had done in favor of the Movement. General Dávila then demanded that Mugica voluntarily retire from his diocese "while the acuteness of the circumstances lasts," with threats if he did not. Gomá, although convinced that Mugica was a supporter of the National Movement, judged that his personal safety was not guaranteed, and he offered to point out the advantages of the secretary of state calling Mugica to Rome. The Basque prelate then suggested the excuse of attending the Missionary Congress that was to be held in Rome, given that he was the national president of the Missionary Union of the Clergy (Unión Misional del Clero).

---

7. See Anastasio Granados, *El cardenal Gomá, primado de España* (Madrid: Espasa-Calpe, 1969), 134–44; María Luisa Rodríguez Aisa, *El cardenal Gomá y la guerra de España: Apectos de la gestión pública del Primado, 1936–1939* (Madrid: CSIC, 1981), 41–53; Alberto de Onaindia, *Hombre de paz en la guerra* (Buenos Aires: Ekin, 1973), 303–36.

I have recently published the correspondence exchanged between Vidal i Barraquer, the bishop of Seo de Urgel, Justino Guitart, and Mugica in relation to Mugica's expulsion and removal.[8] On January 2, 1937, the bishop of Vitoria-Gasteiz lamented the interference of the rebel military men and thanked Vidal i Barraquer for the advice that he had given him (in a letter we have not located) not to resign; at "the Supreme" (the Supreme Sacred Congregation of the Holy Office) they had assured him that the pope would defend his honor and dignity. On April 19, the cardinal of Tarragona expressed his solidarity with the Basque prelate, now in Rome, and congratulated him for not having stepped down: "You did well in rethinking your decision [to resign], even if it may cost you greater sacrifice," obeying the pope (who had promised to defend him). However, the fall of Bilbao on June 15 and with it the fall of the whole of Euskadi led the Holy Father on September 14 to name an apostolic administrator of Vitoria-Gasteiz in the person of Francisco Javier Lauzurica Torralba, auxiliary bishop of Valencia. Mugica found out from *L'osservatore romano*, and he told Bishop Guitart on September 30 that when he heard the news, he resigned everything, and his resignation was accepted. On October 7, Mugica commented to Vidal i Barraquer, in very pained terms, that Pacelli had told him that he could not return to Vitoria-Gasteiz and that they had subsequently named an apostolic administrator. Upon learning as much, Mugica had hurried to submit his resignation. On October 14, the Catalan cardinal told him that perhaps it would have been better to retain the title of bishop of Vitoria-Gasteiz. Meanwhile, the collective letter of the Spanish episcopate dated July 1, which Vidal i Barraquer and Mugica had not signed, had been made public well into August. On June 28, Mugica had replied to Gomá's invitation that he had been away from his diocese for eight months, "with all the painful circumstances," and had no guarantees of freedom and independence.[9] Later on, he would be more explicit: "According to the Spanish episcopate, justice is well administered in Franco's Spain, and this is not true. I have extremely copious lists of fervent Christians

---

8. Hilari Raguer, "Unas cartas de y al obispo Mugica sobre su expulsión y renuncia," *Scriptorium victoriense* 62, nos. 1–4 (2015): 67–75.

9. Isidro Gomá y Tomás, *Archivo Gomá. Documentos de la guerra civil*, vol. 6, *(Junio–Julio 1937)*, ed. José Andrés-Gallego and Antón M. Pazos (Madrid: CSIC, 2004), 254–55.

and exemplary priests murdered with impunity, without trial, and without any legal formalities."[10]

Another Basque prelate failed to sign: Javier de Irastorza Loinaz, bishop of Orihuela-Alicante. In 1935, the Holy See had imposed an apostolic administrator on him *sede plena* and had dispensed him from the duty of residence (apparently due to a delicate issue involving foreign currency). As a good Basque curate, he was familiar with social issues. Gomá did not send him the letter because he was not a bishop with jurisdiction, just as he also did not send it to Segura. However, the latter had resigned his see of Toledo, while Irastorza only had his jurisdiction suspended, and when the apostolic administrator was murdered in 1936, he considered himself to have recovered his full authority. Once the war was over, he appeared in Alicante and, to general astonishment, resumed the governance of the diocese. The Holy See, which was in conflict with Franco over episcopal appointments, recognized him as bishop of Orihuela-Alicante, and he appeared as such in the *Annuario Pontificio* until his death in 1943.[11]

On the occasion of Lent 1937, at the peak of the offensive against Euskadi, the archbishop of Burgos, Manuel García y Castro, published a pastoral letter in which he said that the Basques, who were making common cause with the "godless," were excommunicated. When Mugica, who was no longer in his diocese by then, found out, he was extremely displeased, because the archbishop of Burgos was meddling in the affairs of another diocese. On March 16, he wrote to Pacelli complaining about the archbishop's overreach. However, in 1939 Mugica wrote to Onaindia:

> I have suffered dreadfully for defending my dearly beloved clergy, more than any of you know. . . . I sent what I had written to Cardinal Pacelli; will you believe that in his letter of reply, the cardinal took the archbishop's side, applying to our case the canons that deal with "cooperators" in offenses and crimes, even if the reply does not say that, in effect, the Basques, priests and laity, are explicitly and categorically condemned? I kept quiet,

---

10. Quoted by Juan de Iturralde, *El catolicismo y la Cruzada de Franco*, vol. 3 (Toulouse: Egui-Indarra, 1965), 348–49.

11. See Hilari Raguer, *La pólvora y el incienso. La Iglesia y la Guerra Civil Española (1936–1939)* (Barcelona: Península, 2001), 156–61.

like a dead man; I continued defending my clergy; and now you have all seen what the pope has said about the Basque priests.[12]

These last words were referring to the visit made to the pope toward the end of the war, in December 1938, by the bishop of Dax (Les Landes, France), Clément Mathieu, a French Basque who worked to aid the Basque refugees as head of the Basque Reception Committee (Comité d'Accueil aux Basques). He explained to the pope that the committee was active exclusively in the charitable domain[13] and that the Basque exiles demonstrated a solid Catholicism; the French faithful discovered authentic priests among them. Pius XI interrupted him, saying, "It is useless for you to insist. If there is anything about which I am perfectly informed, it is undoubtedly the Christian vitality of the Basques. However much you could tell me would not be able to add anything to what I already know about that region, for which I feel the greatest admiration." At the end of the audience, Pius XI told Mathieu, "I thank and congratulate all of you for everything you are doing for the Basques," and when he took his leave, he gave the Basque bishop "a donation worthy of kings."[14]

Mugica's expulsion was an error by the "Nationals." While he was in Vitoria-Gasteiz, he had to give way to repeated impositions by the military men; along with Olaechea, he had signed the pastoral letter Gomá composed. In exile, however, he spoke freely and did not sign the collective letter.

The Vatican's Initial Attitude

It is surprising that, despite the terrible religious persecution in the Republican zone, the favors and honors granted to the Church in the other zone, and the confessional tone adopted by the new regime, the Vatican waited two months to take a position, and when it did, it was not one of unconditional recognition. The reason is that at the beginning, it was not evident who would win the war, and if the Republic succeeded in defeating the rebels, a Church that had recognized and morally supported them from

12. Onaindia, *Hombre de paz en la Guerra*, 267.
13. Franco's ambassador, José de Yanguas Mejía, protested to the Vatican because Mathieu had ordered a collection to benefit the Basque refugees.
14. From a note by Bishop Mathieu quoted by Onaindia, *Hombre de paz en la Guerra*, 269.

the beginning would be left in a very bad situation. In addition, from the first moment, the rebels were brazenly aided by Germany and Italy, countries with which the Holy See, despite the respective concordats of 1933 and 1929, had growing problems. Nazi influence exercised through the Falange was especially feared.

The Castelgandolfo Speech

The Vatican took a public position with Pius XI's speech at Castelgandolfo on September 14, 1936, to a group of around five hundred Spaniards who had fled the country. The pope had already had news by then of the shooting of Basque priests, but he was probably not familiar with the scope of the terrible repression unleashed in the so-called National zone, reproduced in every town they occupied. Only in recent years have the numbers been verified, much higher than those of the Republican zone, and much more culpable, because while the repression in the latter took place despite the government's efforts to prevent it, the repression in the former was perfectly controlled and even planned from before the uprising, on General Mola's instructions. I rely for this point on Paul Preston's *The Spanish Holocaust*.[15] For this reason, it has to be understood that when Pius XI alluded to the excesses committed by those who claimed to be defending religion, he was referring above all to the excesses of which the Basque clergy were victims and to the expulsion of Bishop Mugica.

When it became known in Rome that the pope would receive a large group of Spaniards who had fled the country, especially ecclesiastics, and would make a speech to them, expectations were high. The cardinal-archbishop of Tarragona, Vidal i Barraquer, who had taken refuge in the Carthusian monastery of Farneta, near Lucca, wrote to Pacelli on September 2 and took the liberty of explaining to His Holiness his views on the consequences that an unconditional position in favor of the insurrectionists would have for the clergy and faithful in the Republican zone. He said, in addition, that it was necessary to have a great deal of patience with the persecutors; a clamorous act of protest, as well as being ineffective, would constitute "a major obstacle for the ability of priests to return to Spain and work for the conversion of those

---

15. Paul Preston, *The Spanish Holocaust: Inquisition and Extermination in Twentieth-century Spain* (London: Harper Press, 2012).

who, despite their perversion and evil, do not cease to be our brothers."

It should have been Cardinal Vidal i Barraquer who led the group and addressed the pope in the name of them all, but he was a target of such animosity from the Spanish far right for having procured the Church's reconciliation with the Republic that on September 9, Pacelli told him that, "given the special delicacy of the current conditions and also your personal situation, His Holiness does not consider it opportune for Your Excellency to leave your current place of residence for the time being." Vidal i Barraquer was unable to attend the audience at Castelgandolfo, but the pope's speech was made with his arguments very much in mind.

The audience was attended by around five hundred Spaniards, the majority priests and religious figures, headed by the bishops of Cartagena, Tortosa, Vic, and Seo de Urgel. Pius XI was a good orator and usually spoke without notes, but on that occasion he not only read the speech "La vostra presenza" (Your presence)[16] in Italian, but also had it translated into Spanish and distributed to the attendees. He began with some heartfelt words lamenting the victims of the persecution and condemning Communism, but instead of deducing from this condemnation the proclamation that the war was a crusade, as some of those present expected, he expressed his horror at that fratricidal war, "a war between the sons of the same people, of the same mother country." Quoting Manzoni, he said, "It has been well said that the blood of a single man is already too much for all the ages and for all the earth. What is there to say in the presence of the fraternal slaughters that are still being announced?" Papal audiences end with a blessing, but on that occasion, the blessing was preceded by words that would infuriate the fanatical supporters of the uprising:

> Above and beyond all political and worldly considerations, our blessing is especially addressed to all those who have taken up the difficult and dangerous mission of defending and restoring the rights and the honor of God and of religion. . . . A difficult and dangerous mission, we said, also because the effort and difficulty of this defense very easily make it excessive and not entirely justifiable, in addition to the fact that it is no less easy for incorrect interests and egoistical or partisan intentions to be

---

16. Official text in Spanish in *Acta Apostolicae Sedis* 28 (1936): 373–81.

introduced, so as to cloud and alter the entire morality of the action and the entire responsibility for it.

He ended with a Gospel exhortation to love one's enemies and pray for them, in words that seemed to be taken from Vidal i Barraquer's letter of September 2:

> We have, dear children, divine examples and divine precepts for us and also for you . . . we have never been able and are not able to doubt even for an instant what we and you are called on to do: to love these dear sons and brothers of yours, to love them with a particular love made of compassion and of mercy, to love them and, being unable to do anything else, to pray for them, to pray that the serene vision of truth may return to their minds and that their hearts may again open to the desire and the fraternal search for the true common good, to pray that they may return to the Father who awaits them with great desire.

Some fanatics among those present tore up the text they had been provided and threw it away right there. The "National" propaganda services gave the parts of the speech that favored them wide publicity but suppressed the parts that were against them, so that it became an approval and unconditional blessing of the "crusade." When they learned of the Castelgandolfo speech in its mutilated form, the pens of the Spanish bishops, so prudent until then, were unleashed, and pastoral letters in favor of the crusade multiplied.

Magaz's Failure

In August 1936, the Burgos Defense Committee, chaired by Miguel Cabanellas, a Freemason, had sent as its representative to the Vatican the Marquis of Magaz (whom Alfonso XIII and Primo de Rivera had previously sent as their ambassador during the dictatorship in order to obtain the Vatican's help in combatting "Bizcaitarrism" and Catalanism). Magaz demanded the condemnation of the Basque Catholic nationalists. He tried in vain to prevent the episcopal consecration of the Basque Antonio Pildain, characterized as a nationalist, who had been a member of the Spanish parliament and had been named bishop of the Canary Islands in May 1936.

Magaz had been recognized by the Vatican only as an "unofficial chargé d'affaires" (as Gomá was by the Burgos government) and had been received by Pizzardo and even by Pacelli, both of whom he bombarded with a torrent of writings that the papal diplomats did not manage to answer. He energetically protested the pope's failure to receive him. An appearance on *L'osservatore romano*'s list of papal audiences would have been a first step toward recognition of the government he represented. Finally, the Secretariat of State informed him that he would be received by His Holiness on November 23, 1936. However, the audience did not go as he had hoped, because the pope had received information about the Basque priests who had been shot, jailed, and exiled and about Bishop Mugica's expulsion, and he began by snapping at him, "In National Spain priests are shot just as they are in Republican Spain." We do not know the exact words of Magaz's reply, but he was always arrogant, and his words were such that Pius XI, who had a very lively sense of his own authority, suffered an attack of his chronic asthma and nearly suffocated. The attendants brought a glass of water, the audience was suspended, and Franco hurried to change his representative and appoint Magaz ambassador to Berlin. On December 9, Pacelli informed Gomá that the pope had received the Marquis of Magaz and "paternally took up the defense of the innocent priests."[17]

Pius XI had a very high conception of the Basque clergy and of the Basques in general. He believed that they were politically mistaken in allying with the Communists, but despite repeated pressure, he always refused to condemn them publicly. He never made the condemnation of Gomá, Mugica, and Olaechea his own.

Negotiations for the Surrender of Bilbao

Another demonstration, and not the least, of Pius XI's sympathy for the Basque Catholics was his initiative to get Franco to grant favorable conditions for the surrender of Euskadi. On May 6, 1937, Cardinal Gomá received a coded telegram from the Holy See urging him to arrange favorable conditions for the surrender of Bilbao.[18] Simultaneously, the Secretariat of State had commu-

---

17. Granados, *El cardenal Gomá, primado de España*, 146.

18. See Granados, *El cardenal Gomá, primado de España*, 158–65; Fernando de Meer, *El Partido Nacionalista Vasco ante la guerra de España (1936–1937)* (Pamplona: Eunsa, 1992), 415–48; Onaindia, *Hombre de paz en la guerra*, 196–228; José Antonio de Aguirre y Lecube, *De Guernica a Nueva York pasando por Berlín*, 3rd ed. (Buenos Aires: Ekin, 1944), 34–39.

nicated the pope's desire to Magaz, who hurried to transmit it to Franco.

This initiative had significant antecedents. Already on February 13, Pacelli[19] noted that the pope had told him, "On the Basque issue (conditions of Franco's government). If Mussolini agreed, some good counsel of moderation could be given. There are examples: United States, Canada, Switzerland, etc. It could be hinted: begin, for example, with a small parliament, etc., and then see what comes."[20] After Gomá received Pacelli's telegram, he met with General Mola in Vitoria-Gasteiz on May 7, and they agreed on some basic principles for the surrender: the city would be preserved intact, the Basque leaders would be able to leave, the occupying troops would not commit excesses, the soldiers and militiamen who surrendered with their arms would be set free (except for deserters), those guilty of crimes, destruction, or looting would be subject to the courts, and the commanders of Euskadi's army would be considered deserters and would be judged by a court that would act with benevolence. Mola then telephoned Franco, who was in Salamanca, and informed him of what had been agreed. Franco not only gave his approval but softened the final point, changing it to "respect for the lives and property of those who surrender in good faith, including the military commanders," and he even added two clauses of a political nature: Bizkaia would have a decentralized administration analogous to that of other favored regions, and social justice along the lines of the encyclical *Rerum novarum* would be promised, in accordance with the possibilities of the national economy. However, all this would be the case if they surrendered immediately. In order to obtain Basque agreement, Gomá traveled to Saint-Jean-de-Luz (Donibane Lohizune) to meet with Onaindia, but Onaindia had gone to Paris.

The pope's personal involvement appears as clear as day in Pacelli's notes. In the February 13 notes already mentioned, he suggested the intervention of Mussolini (who did in fact intervene through Consul Cavalletti, although it is not clear to me whether this was really on account of the pope's suggestion); but in the

---

19. Among the most important documents in the Archivio Segreto Vaticano recently opened to researchers are the handwritten notes, written in condensed, almost telegraphic style, that the secretary of state, Eugenio Pacelli, took for his own personal use about what Pius XI told him in his almost daily audience with him.

20. Segreteria di Stato, Archivio Storico, Affari Ecclesiastici Straordinari, 1937, posiz. 430, fol. 24.

audience of May 8, the same day as the famous intercepted telegram to Agirre, Pacelli recorded in his habitual synthetic style that His Holiness had told him, "Telegram sent to Aguirre, and another to Msgr. Valeri for him to act in some way (through the French government or with a special envoy) without worrying about the expense. Authorized for all expenses, even with aviation. *Tutto quello che si vuole* [Everything that may be wanted]."[21] In effect, the nuncio in Paris, Valerio Valeri, acted.

Pacelli's telegram to Agirre, sent on May 8, 1937, at 1:40 pm, said:

> His Excellency Aguirre. Bilbao. I have the honor to inform Your Excellency that Generals Franco and Mola, having been explicitly questioned about the matter, have now communicated to the Holy See the conditions for a possible immediate surrender of Bilbao. 1. They are making an effort to conserve Bilbao intact. 2. They will facilitate the departure of all the leaders. 3. Complete guarantee that Franco's army will respect persons and property. 4. Absolute freedom for the militia soldiers who surrender with their arms. Those guilty of common crimes and destruction will be subject to the courts. 6. The lives and property of those who surrender in good faith, even the commanders, will be respected. 7. In the political order, administrative decentralization in the same form enjoyed by other regions. 8. In the social order, progressive social justice, taking into account the national treasury's means, in accordance with the principles of the encyclical *Rerum novarum*. Stop. Trusting in the generous sentiments of Your Excellency and of those dear sons, the Holy Father exhorts Your Excellency to take the said propositions under attentive and solicitous examination, with the desire to see the bloody conflict finally cease. = Cardinal Pacelli =.[22]

This telegram was to have traveled from the Vatican City by way of Paris and Bilbao, but it was sent by way of Paris and Barcelona. There, a telegraph operator with the surname Bermúdez, realizing its importance, stopped it and at 4:35 pm sent it to Francisco Largo Caballero, the prime minister of the government then installed in Valencia, preceding it with another telegram indicating

---

21. Ibid., fol. 45.
22. Transcription respecting the original orthography held in the historical archive of the Fundación Pablo Iglesias de Madrid, Fondo Largo Caballero-LIV-5.

that he would retain the original until he was explicitly authorized to send it on.[23]

The Council of Ministers was to meet that same afternoon, but that morning, Largo Caballero had called a meeting to which neither the Basque minister, Irujo, nor the Catalan minister, Ayguadé, were invited. They decided to keep the document secret, and it was not discussed in the Council of Ministers attended by Irujo and Ayguadé that afternoon. Largo Caballero wanted to be sure that no further telegrams from the Vatican would reach Agirre, and in effect, Pacelli's telegram to Agirre had been repeated from the Vatican. In the Largo Caballero archival collection of the Fundación Pablo Iglesias, Pacelli's telegram to Agirre is followed by another one, dated May 12, from Largo Caballero to the Chief of the Army of the North, Francisco Llano de la Encomienda, ordering that "If by way of London or anywhere else there arrives a dispatch proceeding from Rome, you should intercept it, sending its text by coded dispatch to the General Chief of the Army of North so that he can communicate it to me." At the bottom of the telegram is the following handwritten note: "All this motivated bitter debates in the Council of Ministers, giving rise to the letter that follows." Also on May 12, a telegram from the general director of telecommunications to Largo Caballero reproduced a second transmission of Pacelli's telegram to Agirre, also retained in Barcelona, and informed him that the minister of communications and the merchant marine was sending urgent orders to the head of the Bilbao telegraph office so that, if the famous telegram was sent again by way of Bilbao, it would be not be delivered.

Agirre did not find out about the telegram until two years later, when he was given an article by the Jesuit J. Bivort de la Saudée, "Les martyrs d'Espagne et l'alliance Basco-Communiste" (The martyrs of Spain and the Basque-Communist alliance),[24] in the *Revue des deux mondes*. The author condemned the Basque nationalists' alliance with the Communists, persecutors of the Church, and reproached Agirre for not having answered Pacelli's proposal. The *lehendakari* (Basque president), after gathering information, sent a letter on April 30 to the secretary of state at that time, Cardinal Maglione, assuring him on oath that

---

23. Ibid.
24. *Revue des deux mondes*, February 15, 1940, 703–19.

he had not received that telegram from Pacelli (now Pius XII) nor heard anything about it, since if he had received it, he would not have failed to answer it, because of the political importance of the topic, because of the courtesy owed to the Holy See, to which as a Catholic he was devoted, and because in fact the government of Euskadi throughout the entire war had not stopped trying to enter into direct contact with the Vatican, without success, and would not have failed to take advantage of the opportunity offered. This devout and respectful letter by Agirre received no reply. Given the idyll between Franco and the Church in 1940, Pius XII must have considered it inconvenient to open relations with the lehendakari of the Basque government-in-exile.

At this time Pius XI launched an initiative that is of interest because it reveals that on occasion His Holiness sought to get beyond the received views with which those who surrounded him boxed him in, and also because it touches on the major accusation formulated against the Basque Catholics: their relations with the Communists. In view of the proliferation of fascist movements throughout Europe, the Comintern had changed tactics to promote alliances with all the democratic parties, the Catholics included, in Popular Fronts.[25] The general secretary of the French Communist Party, Maurice Thorez, in his famous speech of April 17, 1936, had said, "*Nous te tendons la main, ouvrier catholique* [We extend our hand to you, Catholic worker]." According to Pacelli's previously mentioned notes, Pius XI told him in his audience of November 16, 1937, that after a sleepless night pondering the issue, he was accepting the Communists' hand, but also extending his own, and with it the Church's social doctrine. The French bishops would have to do something along these lines, he said, and as evidence of the Church's good faith, he was putting a million francs at the French episcopate's disposal for some charitable work. The pope's proposal disconcerted Nuncio Valeri and Cardinal Verdier, since it was the complete opposite of their political strategy at the time. Neither they nor Pacelli could tell the pope that his plan was nonsense, but they endeavored to buy time until the matter was dropped.[26]

---

25. The first Popular Front to win an election was the Spanish one, on February 16, 1936. The French one would win in May.
26. Affari Esteri Straordinari, posiz. 430, fasc. 354, 1937, fol. 64.

Msgr. Antoniutti's Mission

Basque nationalists have very unpleasant memories of Msgr. Antoniutti's mission,[27] and not without reason, but in Pius XI's intention, sending him was another sign of his esteem for the Basque Catholics.

On June 15, 1937, all the attempts at a negotiated surrender having failed, Bilbao fell. On July 21, Pacelli informed Gomá by telegram, "The Holy Father has decided to send Msgr. Antoniutti, Ildebrando, currently apostolic delegate in Albania, to Bilbao with the charge of making a special study, in understanding and agreement with Your Reverend Excellency, of whether and how the return of the Basque children to their families would be possible. Period. I ask Your Reverend Excellency to procure the free entry and movement of the said prelate."[28] On July 25, Pablo de Churruca y Dotres, who had become Franco's chargé d'affaires to the Vatican on June 7, announced by telegram that the archbishop Msgr. Ildebrando Antoniutti would be leaving for Spain on June 26, having been named apostolic delegate with the mission of collaborating on the repatriation of the Basque children who had been evacuated abroad before the final offensive against Bilbao. However, Churruca added, "He undoubtedly also has faculties to examine other aspects of the situation," and he suggested that the authorities at the border and the civil governor of Donostia-San Sebastián be alerted. Subsequently, on August 3, Gomá, writing to his close friend Tomás Muniz, archbishop of Santiago, took credit for the appointment as a success and commented, "He is coming with two missions: one official, which is the repatriation of the Basque children; another unofficial, secret for now, which matches instructions that I am receiving directly from the Secretariat of State and which will probably end in the *de iure* recognition of the National Government within a short time. It appears that the mustard plasters I had sent there lately have had their effect."[29] In a letter to Gomá on July 24, Canon Despujol, his secretary, revealed his opinion, identical to Gomá's and repeatedly expressed to his intimates, that those at the Vatican had not understood the Spanish reality and the true character of the "crusade,"

---

27. See Ildebrando Antoniutti, *Memorie autobiografiche* (Udine: Arti Grafiche Friulane, 1975); Onaindia, *Hombre de paz en la guerra*, 271–302; Raguer, *La pólvora y el incienso*, 247–51.

28. Gomá y Tomás, *Archivo Gomá*, vol. 6, 529–30.

29. Granados, *El cardenal Gomá, primado de España*, 103.

and that this incomprehension was due to the nefarious influence wielded at the Vatican by some Basque and Catalan elements:

Permit me now to say frankly what I think, with all bluntness and freedom. This is another play by all the rabble that hangs around that holy house. They have realized that Your Reverend Excellency describes things as they are, and when you do, it goes against the grain, since it is in their interest to believe the exact opposite. For the same reason, they are sending a man who, however much he might like to tell the truth, will not do so, because he will be eager to stay here as N[uncio], and naturally all his efforts have to be to please his "*padrone*" [patron], alias Msgr. P[izzardo]. In addition, be sure that those of the brand-new ex-Republic [Euskadi] will do everything possible to monopolize him and have him dance to their tune. And here's the whole enormous danger: all the crowd going around in B[ilbao] will see in that traveler an element of defense and accusation: of defense against overseas [Rome]; of accusation against F[ranco] on the same point. All the more given that the motive, besides being offensive to F[ranco], is completely ridiculous, since [the evacuated children] don't have to do anything more than set out on the return trip: nobody needs to put any difficulties in their way to return to their homes.[30]

For his part, Antoniutti in his memoirs explains the charge he received from Pizzardo on July 23 this way: "In the Basque territory, I was to concern myself with the prisoners of war and the return of the children sent abroad because of the conflict that raged in that region."[31] Take good note: first, the prisoners. This is confirmed by the examination I have been able to make of the Antoniutti archival collection in the Archivio Segreto Vaticano: the expatriate children barely appear, and almost all the voluminous documentation consists of communications with the authorities of Franco's regime in defense of the Basque clergy. Pacelli's July 23 telegram to Gomá announcing Antoniutti's arrival also said that he would be occupied with the return of the Basque children "and other similar charitable works."[32]

But let us return to Antoniutti's arrival. Having been issued a visa by Churruca, he went to Paris, where Nuncio Valeri gave him extremely useful information about both zones, and then traveled

---

30. Gomá y Tomás, *Archivo Gomá*, vol. 6, 546–48. We have spelled out in square brackets the words that Despujol shortened to their first letters.
31. Antoniutti, *Memorie autobiografiche*, 29.
32. Gomá y Tomás, *Archivo Gomá*, vol. 6, 538–39.

by train to Hendaye. However, those in the National zone had the same misgivings that Despujol expressed. They did not want an apostolic delegate for the Basque Country who would reside there, but rather a nuncio of full rank in Salamanca. The head of the border police, Commander Troncoso, did not permit him to enter the country. Some journalists, whom someone had told that a nuncio was arriving, were there. Antoniutti was wearing a simple priest's cassock without any mark of his position, and for this reason they failed to identify him. Antoniutti suggested to the police officer who did not let him enter that those journalists would surely be interested in the news that an archbishop representing the pope was unable to enter Spain. Cardinal Gomá was in Santiago, where he was to preside at the reestablished ceremony of offering to the Apostle on July 25. His secretary, Despujol, sent to receive the apostolic delegate, informed him of the incident, and Gomá hurried to resolve it. The not very plausible excuse that was later given was that Churruca's telegram had been misfiled. Despujol appealed to the secretary of foreign relations, Sangróniz, and they found the telegram misfiled. Sangróniz went personally to deliver humble apologies to Antoniutti, but he did not fail to tell him that he should go directly to Pamplona, or in other words, that it would not be tolerated if he established himself in the Basque Country strictly speaking. Gomá was resident in Pamplona, even after the liberation of Toledo, and he was the "provisional unofficial chargé d'affaires" to Franco, for which reason Pamplona was the ecclesiastical capital until the end of the war.

Upon returning from Santiago, Gomá met Antoniutti in Valladolid, and they traveled together to Salamanca, where they were received by Franco. Antoniutti remembered his first contact with the heart of Franco's Spain this way: "I had the impression then that I found myself on top of a volcano that was spewing lava, sulfur, and rocks. From the stories I was told, I could imagine the aggressive violence that dominated Spain at that time and the repugnant atrocities that saddened the atmosphere."[33] Despite the stumble at his entry, Antoniutti immediately won the confidence and esteem both of the civil authorities and of the episcopate. They rejoiced when he was promoted to chargé d'affaires in September, and the presentation of his credentials was organized as if he were a nuncio, complete with the Caudillo's Moorish Guard.

---

33. Antoniutti, *Memorie autobiografiche*, 36.

Everyone was happy, except the Basques, who were supposed to be the chief targets of his mission. In August 1938, Antoniutti visited the colony of Basque children in Saint-Jean-Pied-de-Port (Donibane Garazi) and criticized the nationalists. He joined in the calumny of Franco's propaganda about an alleged theft of jewels and crowns belonging to the Child Jesus and Our Lady of Begoña. When the Vatican elevated its representation to the highest level in May 1938, both the government and the episcopate strongly desired and requested that Antoniutti should be the nuncio, but Pius XI named Gaetano Cicognani, who had been the nuncio in Vienna and was left without a post by Hitler's *Anschluss*.

Conclusion: "With Immense Joy"

On February 10, 1939, Pius XI, the friend of the Basques, died, and on March 2, as everyone expected, Pacelli was elected, taking the name of Pius XII. On March 5, Segismundo Casado, giving up the war as lost and hoping to obtain from Franco favorable terms of surrender, launched his coup d'état against Juan Negrín. In vain: Franco would only accept an unconditional surrender, leaving his hands free for repression, and on April 1 he was able to compose in his own hand the message of victory: "The war has ended." The brand-new pope hurried to send him a telegram of congratulations for the "Catholic victory in Spain," and he drove the point home on April 16 with a radio address that began with the words "With immense joy." It was a carefully prepared document. The project had been entrusted to a Jesuit educated in Germany, a professor at the Gregorian University, Fr. Joaquín Salaverri, who worked in contact with Fr. Gutiérrez del Olmo, the Father-General's assistant for the Spanish provinces. On the afternoon of April 12, Pius XII received Fr. Salaverri to comment on and revise the proposed text. They spoke in German. Pius XII commented on the draft and made changes to five phrases. He had noted in the margin, "Soften in order not to irritate and rather to express trust," and he introduced the phrase, "May those who seek as prodigal sons to return to the Father's house be received with benevolence and love." As late as April 14, the pope sent word to Fr. Salaverri to suppress a reference to the Protestant Reformation and, above all, to suppress the word "victory" in the opening paragraph. Salaverri considered this suppression "extremely painful" and wrote a letter to the pope respectfully insisting on maintaining the word, and the pope gave in. The speech was broadcast by Vatican Radio on the afternoon of April 16. However, the following day, Fr. Leiber, another Jesuit, a historian, and an advisor to the pope, told Salaverri that the Basques had been displeased to see themselves alluded to in what was said about "those deceived ones, whom a lying and perverse propaganda succeeded in seducing with flattery and promises," and about the (Basque) children "torn from their homes" and placed in danger of apostasy. Salaverri defended the text, saying that once it had been publicly read by His Holiness, it would be disrespectful to modify it, but three modifications were made, and it was in this form that the text was published in *L'osservatore romano* on April 17 and in *La croix* and other newspapers that reproduced it.[34]

Pius XII proclaimed his joy at the victory, which was—he said—"undoubtedly the fruit of that fecund blessing that [Pius XI] sent at the very dawn of the conflict to 'all those who had set themselves the difficult task of defending and restoring the rights of God and of religion," words taken from Pius XI's speech at Castelgandolfo on September 14, 1936, but of which we have already seen the nuanced reach, combined as they were with a condemnation of the excesses of religion's defenders. He called for upholding "justice for crime and generosity for the mistaken," and it was at this point that the previously noted phrases about the Basque children came.

Consequently, the Basque Catholic nationalists had to acknowledge that they had been mistaken, deceived, "those whom a lying and perverse propaganda succeeded in seducing with flattery and promises [of autonomy]," and "prodigal sons who try to return to the Father's house." His Holiness affirmed that if they returned to Franco, "they will be received with benevolence and love."

Every June 15, the "liberation" of Bilbao was celebrated. In the clandestine bulletin *Euzko Deya,* some Basque priests lamented the sight of their bishop on the dais celebrating the anniversary of their defeat alongside the military and civil authorities.

The exiled Basque priests set an excellent example in their ministry. Those held in the Carmona prison (which they shared with Julián Besteiro) were exemplary priests. Bishop Olaechea (the first bishop who spoke of a "crusade," but also the one who had called

---

34. The laborious process of composition of the message "With immense joy" has been carefully researched, on the basis of the documentation of the Curia generalicia of the Society of Jesus, by Alfonso Álvarez Bolado, S. J.; see Álvarez Bolado, *Para ganar la guerra, para ganar la paz*, 430–45.

for "no more blood," against the custom of shooting a few local Reds when burying a *requeté* who had fallen at the front) had been promoted to archbishop of Valencia. He was a good orator, much in demand for weddings and other solemn celebrations. On one occasion, he asked Cardinal Segura, then archbishop of Seville, for permission to celebrate a wedding in Seville. The far-right cardinal answered that he could not deny him permission, but that he was scandalized that he was going to a society wedding instead of going to visit the exemplary priests from his region who were prisoners in Carmona.

Upon the conclusion of the war, the Basque Church was harshly punished with the imposition of outsider bishops. Antoniutti, the former apostolic delegate, who had returned as nuncio, preached the Basque clergy's duty of obedience to their prelates. That exemplary diocese of Vitoria-Gasteiz, about which we spoke in the introduction, was torn to pieces. By a bull of November 2, 1949, the new dioceses of Bilbao and Donostia-San Sebastián were carved out of Vitoria-Gasteiz, and what was worse, the two new dioceses were attached to the ecclesiastical province of Pamplona, elevated to an archbishopric in 1956, while Vitoria-Gasteiz continued to be a suffragan of Burgos.

Franco had made the Catholic Church and its doctrine one of the basic pillars of his regime. It was one of the Movement's Fundamental Principles. It seemed that this situation would last forever, since Franco left everything "tied up and well tied up," and for twenty years, it did not go badly for him. However, something happened that he had not foreseen: the Church and its doctrine changed. The story goes that when Prince Metternich, by then in retirement, received the news in 1846 of the election of Cardinal Mastai Ferretti, who had a reputation as a liberal, he exclaimed, "I had foreseen everything at the Congress of Vienna, except the election of a liberal pope." The new pope, Pius IX, turned out not to be a liberal, rather the complete opposite, and Metternich could calm down, but Franco could not do the same after the election of John XXIII (1958) and the celebration of the Second Vatican Council (1962–65). He was disconcerted.

After announcing the council, John XXIII consulted the world's bishops about the topics to be discussed. The Spaniards, almost all named by Franco, either did not answer or limited themselves to requesting the solemn condemnation of Communism and the multiplication of more dogmas about and titles for the Virgin Mary.

An interesting exception is the bishop of Gran Canaria, Antonio Pildain Zapiain, whom we have already mentioned because Magaz tried in vain to prevent him from being consecrated bishop. As a good Basque priest educated at the exemplary Vitoria-Gasteiz seminary, he was very traditional in dogmatic matters and was consequently one of the most decided adversaries of religious freedom, but he was at the same time advanced on political and social issues, and he asked that the announced council condemn liberalism, totalitarianism, both absolute and mitigated; statism, which does without the principle of subsidiarity and absorbs many things that do not belong to it; the idolatrous nationalism of the large nations, which criminally tramples the natural rights of the small nationalities and regions; laicism, Communism, but also 'Mammonism', which denies what is due to workers and the poor in order to seek economic success alone, principally by means of what are known as corporations [*las sociedades llamadas anónimas*], in the unjust successes of which no few Catholics are collaborators.[35]

In recent years, books, articles, and conferences on Catholic opposition to Franco have multiplied. When Johann Baptist Metz directed Antonio Murcia Santos's thesis, "Obreros y obispos en el franquismo" (Workers and bishops under Franco)[36] at the University of Munster, he was astonished to see the outburst of violence that Vatican II provoked in Spanish Catholicism, even though he was familiar with the council's political repercussions. There was probably no other country in which the council's political impact was so considerable. Franco had used the Church politically, and now the opposition sought the Church's protection for its calls for freedom. It was like someone who stretches a rubber band but loses hold of it, and it bounces back and hits him in the face.

Toward the end of the first session, a group of Catalan Catholics distributed to all the council's bishops, *periti,* observers, and auditors a document opposing Franco's regime, on account of its dictatorial nature and the repression of the nationalities. The document "horribly upset"—according to Martín Descalzo—the large majority of the Spanish bishops, especially Morcillo and Cantero Cuadrado, who composed a very harsh reply and gave it

---

35. See Hilari Raguer, *Réquiem por la Cristiandad: El Concilio Vaticano II y su impacto en España* (Barcelona: Península, 2006), 60–64.

36. Published as *Obreros y obispos en el franquismo. Estudio sobre el significado eclesiológico de la crisis de la Acción Católica Española* (Madrid: Ediciones HOAC, 1995).

to Iribarren, the director of the council's Spanish press office, to be made public. Iribarren became alarmed upon reading the text and met with Montero and Martín Descalzo, who were also members of the council's Spanish information office. The three agreed that it would not be a good idea to publish that reply. They went to the residence of the cardinal primate of Toledo, Enrique Pla y Deniel, and asked him for advice. Pla, who was elderly and very ill, was one of the undersecretaries but did not attend the general congregations. With the energy that always distinguished him, he told them, on his responsibility, not to make that reply public, first of all because the Catalans' document was anonymous, and an anonymous text should never be answered, and also because the reply presented itself as coming from all the Spanish bishops, "and I am the primate," he said, "and they have not said anything to me."

More serious was the document, similarly anti-Franco in tone, circulated at the council the following year, this time not anonymous but signed by 339 Basque priests and a significant group of missionary bishops of Basque origin. The Spanish ambassador to the Holy See, Doussinague, discussed the matter with the bishops who were closest to Franco's regime and, with their agreement, suggested to the government to have the pope send an ecclesiastical visitor to the Basque Country to select those primarily responsible and punish them with exile, to which, he said, the Basque nationalists, who were sentimentalists, were very sensitive. Aware that the incident was only a prelude to the complications that Vatican II would bring in its train for Franco's regime, he concluded, "At the same time, the sanctions being very limited in number, international scandal will be avoided, the present case will be reduced in importance, and in sum, the foreseeable fire will be extinguished in its earliest stages."[37]

Yet the fire still has not been extinguished.

Bibliography

Aguirre y Lecube, José Antonio de. *De Guernica a Nueva York pasando por Berlín*. 3rd ed. Buenos Aires: Ekin, 1944.

Álvarez Bolado, Alfonso. *Para ganar la guerra, para ganar la paz.* Madrid: Universidad Pontificia de Comillas, 1995.

Antoniutti, Ildebrando. *Memorie autobiografiche.* Udine: Arti Grafiche Friulane, 1975.

---

37. Ibid., 149–50.

Bivort de la Saudée, J. "Les martyrs d'Espagne et l'alliance Basco-Communiste." *Revue des deux mondes* (February 15, 1940): 703–19.

Gomá y Tomás, Isidro. *Archivo Gomá. Documentos de la guerra civil*, vol. 6, *(Junio–Julio 1937)*, edited by José Andrés-Gallego and Antón M. Pazos. Madrid: CSIC, 2004.

Granados, Anastasio. *El cardenal Gomá, primado de España.* Madrid: Espasa-Calpe, 1969.

Iturralde, Juan de. *El catolicismo y la Cruzada de Franco.* Vol. 3. Toulouse: Egui-Indarra, 1965.

Lipuzcoa, Manu E. *La Iglesia como problema en el País Vasco.* Buenos Aires: Ekin, 1973.

Meer, Fernando de. *El Partido Nacionalista Vasco ante la guerra de España (1936–1937).* Pamplona: Eunsa, 1992.

Moriones, Ildefonso. *Euzkadi y el Vaticano 1935–1936. Documentación de un episodio presentada en edición crítica.* Rome: Tipogr. Orientale S. Nilo, 1917.

Murcia Santos, Antonio. *Obreros y obispos en el franquismo. Estudio sobre el significado eclesiológico de la crisis de la Acción Católica Española.* Madrid: Ediciones HOAC, 1995.

Onaindia, Alberto de. *Hombre de paz en la guerra.* Buenos Aires: Ekin, 1973.

Preston, Paul. *The Spanish Holocaust: Inquisition and Extermination in Twentieth-century Spain.* London: Harper Press, 2012.

Raguer, Hilari. *La pólvora y el incienso. La Iglesia y la Guerra Civil Española (1936–1939).* Barcelona: Península, 2001.

———. *Aita Patxi: Prisionero con los gudaris.* Barcelona: Claret, 2006.

———. *Réquiem por la Cristiandad: El Concilio Vaticano II y su impacto en España.* Barcelona: Península, 2006.

———. "Unas cartas de y al obispo Mugica sobre su expulsión y renuncia." *Scriptorium victoriense* 62, nos. 1–4 (2015): 67–75.

Rodríguez Aisa, María Luisa. *El cardenal Gomá y la guerra de España: Apectos de la gestión pública del Primado, 1936–1939.* Madrid: CSIC, 1981.

Tarragó, Josep M. *Le drame d'un peuple incompris: La guerre au pays basque.* Paris: H. G. Peyre, 1937.

7

How the British Administration Kept Franco Neutral in World War II

Angel Viñas

During most of World War II Spain remained in a rather unique position on the international scene. At the outbreak of hostilities in Europe, Franco decided upon a course of neutrality. Then in June 1940, Spain formally moved to a position of "non-belligerence." It returned to neutrality in October 1943. No other neutral in World War II varied its stance like this. Furthermore, up until the reorientation in June 1940, that neutrality was benevolent in its heavy bias toward the Axis. This reflected the fact that Nazi Germany and Fascist Italy had provided Franco with massive assistance during the Spanish Civil War. Without their help he would have found winning the war a much more difficult task.

Reasons for Spanish Neutrality

The reasons for benevolent neutrality are clear. First, neither the Fascists nor the Nazis had ever actually suggested an alliance with Franco. Second, Spain was economically very feeble and in no state to participate in a European war. Third, in the period September to October 1939 the Axis saw no need for Spain's assistance. Italy even invented a new position of "non-belligerency." Mussolini carefully abstained from joining the Third Reich in its attack on Poland.

This scenario changed dramatically in May 1940, when the Nazis put an end to the phony war in the West. The Wehrmacht occupied Norway, Denmark, the Netherlands, Belgium, and

Luxembourg in a very short space of time. France was invaded. The Panzer divisions began their unstoppable advance toward the English Channel. At the end of May, the British Expeditionary Force was evacuated to escape annihilation. The defeat of France was sealed in just a matter of weeks.

The rapid progress of the Nazi armies had two major consequences. First, it led Mussolini to declare war on France on June 10 and invade the French Midi. Second, it convinced Franco that a change in Spanish strategy might be to his benefit. He adopted a position of non-belligerency. The perception then arose that Spain might join the Axis. This had the potential to create a very nasty scenario for Britain, which now stood alone in the face of the German threat.

The response by the British government has been studied thoroughly in British, American, and Spanish historiography. *Diplomacy and Strategy of Survival* was the title Professor Denis Smyth gave to his ground-breaking research in 1986.[1] His doctoral dissertation was the first piece of academic work based on an in-depth study of the British records available at the time. To this he added a huge number of testimonies, diaries, and memoirs dealing with World War II. Foremost among them were the memoirs of Sir Samuel Hoare, later Viscount Templewood, recounting his time as Her Majesty's Ambassador in Madrid, from June 1940 to December 1944.[2] His memoirs were published in 1946 and led to a feeble riposte a year later by his antagonist Ramon Serrano Suñer, Franco's brother-in-law.[3] Serrano had been Hoare's principal adversary as Minister of the Interior and even more so as Foreign Minister, between 1940 and 1942. Serrano's counterattack became the bible in terms of explaining Franco's official posture in World War II to a Spanish public that was captive, subject to heavy censorship of all available media, and isolated from what was being written abroad.

---

1. Denis Smyth, *Diplomacy and Strategy of Survival: British Policy and Franco's Spain, 1940–41* (Cambridge: Cambridge University Press, 1986).

2. Sir Samuel Hoare, Viscount Templewood, *Ambassador on Special Mission* (London: Collins, 1946).

3. Ramón Serrano Suñer, *Entre Hendaya y Gibraltar* (Madrid: Ediciones y Publicaciones Españolas, 1947).

Historiography versus Myth

Smyth's work, which essentially covers the period from 1939 to 1941, established the framework for later research. He examined the formulation of British policy that combined diplomatic and political persuasion with economic and commercial pressure. He also examined military contingency plans to occupy the Canary Islands, although they were soon discarded. Smyth's contribution was, without a doubt, one of the greatest importance. He was followed, among others, by Professor Enrique Moradiellos in Spain, and Professor Paul Preston and Dr. Richards Wiggs in Britain. All three extended the analysis to the whole of World War II, on the basis of primary evidence kept in principally British archives, bolstered by some in Spain.

This research has influenced the way historians have approached Spanish neutrality in World War II. However, it made no great impact on public perception in Spain. Spaniards have remained in the thrall of Francoist propaganda and to selective memoirs by some of the Spanish protagonists. Foremost are Serrano Suñer's amended version (it turned out that his 1947 memoirs had been vastly doctored) and the diaries of his successor, General Francisco Gómez-Jordana Sousa.[4]

Both supported the myth spun by Franco (and maintained for over thirty years) that Spain's neutrality in World War II was preserved thanks to the supernatural cunning of the dictator himself. Franco was portrayed as the only man able to stand up to Hitler, making small concessions and playing with gestures of friendship so as to gain time and, by doing so, prevent the Nazi invasion of Spain. In short, Spain was friendly with Germany because otherwise Germany would have invaded Spain.

Furthermore, in maintaining Spanish non-belligerency, Franco rendered his most important service not only to Spaniards, but also to the Allies. It is therefore a pity that the latter never properly acknowledged the favor. Needless to say, Franco's court historians have been vociferous in articulating the dictator's cunning. In the case of Professor Luis Suarez, even as recently as a few months ago. They have been followed by flocks of journalists who resent the heavy criticism that "left-wing" historians have raised against the

---

4. Francisco Gómez-Jordana Sousa, *Milicia y diplomacia: Los diarios del Conde de Jordana 1936–1944* (Burgos: Editorial Dossoles, 2002).

Caudillo. In truth, critical historiography in Spain has long proved that Francoist assertions are purely mythical and have little basis in reality.

British Bribes

In this peculiar context, one particular allegation made by Professor Smyth deserves further consideration. He found tantalizing hints in the British National Archives concerning a covert operation launched by the British government in 1940. Apparently, generals close to Franco were given bribes, with the goal of influencing the dictator to keep Spain neutral.

Smyth's initial analysis was expanded upon in an article he published in French in 1991.[5] He named this operation "the charge of St. George's cavalry." The explanation of this name lies with a hint found in the diaries of the Minister of Economic Warfare, Hugh Dalton.[6] St. George was the figure depicted on the golden sovereigns that were allegedly used in the bribes. Not a single author dealing with Spain and Britain in World War II has failed to refer to this operation as being under the protection of the saint's cavalry.

However, the importance of the bribes has been summarily dismissed by later British historians, such as Professor David Stafford and Sir Max Hastings. My thesis to the contrary is that the bribes were the central operation in the effort to keep Franco neutral. I will share with you a few thoughts about the origins, implementation, and economic significance of the bribes.

A Declassification of Documents

In 2013 the British National Archives declassified a collection of documents from the holdings of the Permanent Undersecretary of State for Foreign Affairs, Sir Alexander Cadogan. Among these, one immediately drew the attention of Spanish newspapers. As a result of the impact this news caused in Spain, I was asked by a digital publication to provide some comments as a historian. I went to London, had a thorough look at the documents, and realized their

---

5. Denis Smyth, "Les Chevaliers de Saint-George: La Grand Bretagne et la corruption des généraux espagnols (1940–1942)," *Guerres mondiales et conflits contemporains* 162 (1991): 29–54.
6. Hugh Dalton, *The Fateful Years: Memoirs, 1931–1945* (London: Muller, 1957).

significance. Rapid analysis of a part of them led me to publish six articles in which I set out a very rough outline of the operation. Needless to say, the comments by readers were generally negative. I had dared question the probity of Spanish military heroes! I immediately saw that the bribes, if properly investigated, could shed new light on the corruption rampant in the dictatorship and the course of neutrality that was taken.

A number of trips to the British National Archives and others ensued. It emerged that the bribes were without doubt the basis of British policy toward Spain during World War II. Once one knew what to look for, it was only a matter of time before hints and veiled references became transparent. Political, diplomatic, economic, and espionage considerations were all subordinated to the bribery operation. The aim was not tactical but rather strategic: to buy time while Britain brought itself into a position to withstand the Nazi onslaught. Spain had to remain neutral during that period, initially estimated at some six months. This time was needed to make Gibraltar impregnable and reinforce British dispositions in the Mediterranean. This was an area in which British forces were engaging in direct combat with the Italians, and later the Germans.

The Two Main Originators

The origins of the bribery operation are to be found not in London but in Spain. Sir Samuel Hoare put its wheels in motion soon after his arrival in Madrid on June 1, 1940. The idea of bribery was transmitted to him the very next day by the Embassy's Naval Attaché, Captain Allan Hillgarth. This is well established. What was unknown were the circumstances in which the operation began.

In British historiography no author has denied Hillgarth's importance. He is generally portrayed as the originator of the bribes. This is not necessarily the case—there is another possible scenario. Note that both lack direct documentary support. However, we now know that the operation would have been impossible but for the cooperation and enthusiasm of a Spanish character who remains shrouded in mystery, the banker Juan March.

This gentleman was a prominent figure in Spanish political and economic life. He financed the acquisition of dozens of modern aircraft in Italy (bombers, fighters, transport planes, and hydroplanes) before the July 1936 coup. Obviously, they were intended not for a mere rebellion, but for a short civil war. Four contracts were signed on July 1, amounting to 39.3 million lire, equivalent to some 350 million euros today. March also contributed to the Francoist cause: 183.5 million dollars' worth of gold, plus 70 million in stocks and bonds. He was also instrumental in obtaining credit arrangements from banks in the UK, Portugal, and Switzerland for use by the Caudillo.

These staggering sums exceeded the value of the gold sold by the Bank of Spain to the Banque de France between the end of July 1936 and the end of January 1937, when sales were switched to the Soviet Union. In a word, Juan March's financial contribution to Franco in the Civil War was invaluable. March's entrée into the higher echelons of the dictatorship was, therefore, very easy. He knew from first-hand experience the cupidity of the new power holders. It is hard to imagine that he did *not* apprise Hillgarth of the possibility of influencing people close to Franco.

March could not have approached Hoare himself—there is no reason or documentary evidence to indicate that they had met previously. However, the new British Ambassador was open to Hillgarth's suggestion. There are two reasons for Hoare's quick acceptance of the proposal.

The first reason is that Hillgarth was no simple naval attaché. He had very high connections in London, and was well known to Prime Minister Churchill. They had met before the Civil War when Hillgarth, then retired in Mallorca as a former naval officer and honorary vice-consul, had hosted Churchill and his wife on one of their visits to the island. During the war Hillgarth had reported on the conditions of the area and the likelihood of the Balearics falling under Italian influence. Before the war was over he had been appointed honorary consul and became a mediator to the surrender of Republican forces in nearby Menorca.

At the end of the Civil War, Hillgarth was sent to the Embassy as an Assistant Naval Attaché. By the time the European conflict broke out he ranked as a fully-fledged Naval Attaché. As such, he was in contact with Churchill, then First Lord of the Admiralty. He was also the representative in Spain of the powerful Naval Intelligence Division. His entrée into Spanish naval circles encountered no obstacle. His knowledge of and familiarity with Spaniards, particularly the upper classes, was extensive. Under Hoare's predecessor, Sir Maurice Peterson, he had established a system of surveying Spanish harbors so as to detect any activity aimed at assisting the

Nazis. Hillgarth knew March, not only because the banker was a native of Mallorca, but also because he had offered his services to the Royal Navy in November 1939. Both had been to London together. However, March and Churchill never met themselves.

Sir Samuel Hoare

The second reason for Hoare's quick acceptance of the bribe idea relates to his own background. Hoare went to Madrid with a certain reluctance. He was the only one of Chamberlain's cabinet ministers not retained by Churchill upon taking over the premiership on May 10, 1940. They had fallen out in the past, for a number of reasons. As Secretary for India, Hoare's plans for the colony had been hotly contested by Churchill in 1934. As an appeaser of the Chamberlain school, Hoare had met with Churchill's indignation. This said, nobody could dispute Hoare's tenacity or his skills as a politician and administrator.

The Foreign Secretary Lord Halifax, like Hoare a fervid proponent of appeasement of the Fascist dictators, found a way to help his friend. He suggested he go to Portugal as a member of a British delegation and attend the tricentennial celebrations of Portugal's independence from Spain. He could then take advantage of the trip and continue on to Madrid to discuss commercial matters with Franco. Hoare, who dearly wished to be appointed Viceroy of India, followed his friend's suggestion.

Fate then chose to intervene. An official in the Foreign Office thought to put Hoare's visit to Spain to political use. The idea soon germinated that he could in fact be sent to Madrid as the next ambassador. The incumbent, one of Hoare's officials at the Foreign Office during his time as Foreign Secretary in 1935, was due to leave the Embassy.

To cut a long story short, Halifax submitted this possibility to Hoare, who accepted. As an MP for the London Borough of Chelsea, for legal and financial reasons he would have to go not as a regular ambassador but as an Ambassador on Special Mission. For similar reasons, that same status was also to be given to Stafford Cripps, for the Moscow post. However, the Soviets did not accept the suggestion and Cripps came as a regular ambassador.

Franco failed to fully appreciate the subtleties at play here and accepted Hoare's appointment without any trouble. This episode has, incidentally, led many historians into believing that the Court of St. James made an exception with Hoare so as to emphasize the importance of the Madrid Embassy. This is incorrect.

Hoare was no ordinary politician *cum* ambassador. He had begun his career in government under quite unusual circumstances. In July 1916 he was selected to liaise with the Russian General Staff as head of the military intelligence mission there. In May 1917, he was transferred to Italy as head of special intelligence. His purpose was to counteract Italian tendencies to seek terms with the Austrians. To this end, Hoare bribed journalists of various political and ideological hues, among them a young Socialist by the name of Benito Mussolini. In short, Hoare was no stranger to intelligence work. Quite the contrary.

An Expanding Operation

The bribes therefore started due to a happy coincidence of personalities, backgrounds, and needs. On June 3, Hoare wrote to Lord Halifax announcing that to ensure the success of his mission, he would need operational *carte blanche*. The following day he sent a highly confidential telegram. There existed the very real risk that Franco might bring Spanish neutrality to an end. However, a well-placed cabinet minister was in a position to intervene and help maintain it. Half a million pounds were needed. There would be no connection whatsoever with the embassy.

Although the minister's name was obviously not disclosed, I can make an educated guess as to his identity: the Minister of the Army, a crony of Franco's, named José Enrique Varela. On June 5, Churchill gave the green light. All this happened in a very short space of time: no more than twenty-four hours.

This speed can be explained by the dangerous situation Britain found itself in at the start of June 1940. However, I tend to think that the idea also found favor with Churchill because it was consistent with an established British practice about which the prime minister used to wax lyrical.

Britain had used enormous quantities of money to maintain the equilibrium in Europe ever since the eighteenth century at least, and even more so during the Napoleonic Wars. It had done the same in the Middle East during the Great War, supporting the Arabs against their Ottoman rulers. As far as Spain was concerned, the Central Powers and the Entente had also subsidized Spanish politicians. However, in 1940 the ambition was clearly higher: to bribe a cabinet minister so as to prevent Franco sliding away from neutrality.

At the time, Franco was indeed very tempted to join the Axis. On June 13, Franco formally moved from neutrality to non-belligerency. This was widely seen as a sign that the Caudillo might follow the Duce's example. Hoare did not take it as such. From the very beginning, based on his own experience and intuition, he maintained that Franco had not definitively decided to join the Axis. He was correct.

A telegram on June 12 announced that Hoare had been obliged to promise a greater sum if within the next three to four months the results of the initial bribe justified it. We can surmise that he made such promises through an intermediary. This could be no one but March.

Hoare could not do more. There was absolutely no question of actually handing over any money. It was not cash on delivery but cash *after* delivery (with delivery being Spain's continued non-participation in the war). No money could be wasted in buying foreigners' goodwill. The British foreign exchange position precluded it.

In any case, half a million pounds was a very respectable sum for the time. It was the same amount cashed out by March when he contributed to the funding of the rebellion of July 1936. It far exceeded the puny 20,000 pounds the British granted De Gaulle in his first two months after breaking with the Vichy Government.

A Top Secret Endeavor

Commander John Paul Furse, Hillgarth's Assistant Naval Attaché, was sent to London on June 21. The Embassy was going to require further funds. The circle of people to be bribed had grown. Furse brought a memorandum with him. This was one of the documents declassified in 2013. It was, in essence, a project—not yet a reality. However, it remains extremely important. It is the only available evidence with names listed along with the sums provisionally allocated to them. It was compiled, I believe, in haste, as befitted the urgency of the situation. Some of the names were literally absurd.

When Furse went to England the bribery operation had already amounted 3 million pounds' worth of promises. Frantic discussions ensued in London. Hoare received the green light on June 27.

From that point on, the Ambassador subordinated his diplomatic mission to three major considerations:

1. The need to not unduly upset Franco
2. The need to very carefully calibrate the political and economic measures to be taken. Disagreements with the Board of Trade and the Ministry of Economic Warfare became commonplace.
3. The need to support the recipients of the bribes and to make good on their payment after the danger of Spain joining the Axis had subsided.

The operation was absolutely top secret. Cadogan, who received most of Hoare's telegrams and communications on the subject, did not mention it in his diaries even once.[7] Churchill and his ministers kept quiet.

Details were restricted to a very small, select group of high officials in the Foreign Office, the Exchequer, and the Prime Minister's Office. Only months later were some of the heads of the Special Operations Executive (SOE) given information. In Madrid, except Hoare and Hillgarth, only the Australian-born counsellor, Arthur Yencken, and the Military Attaché, Brigadier Wyndham Torr, were in the know. Later on, the representative of the Ministry of Economic Warfare was also brought into the fold.

Hoare endeavored to bring all of the British secret services' activities in Spain under his control. No actions were to be taken without his consent. He delegated most of the supervision to Hillgarth. Only MI6 (the Secret Intelligence Service, SIS) escaped Hillgarth's oversight, although not Hoare's. However, the SIS was mainly conducting the gathering of information. Any true operational action was the purview of the SOE.

It is natural that this situation gave rise to confusion and downright resentment among those excluded. The relevant files are full of complaints. The operation itself, however, was never affected. On an occasion when Hillgarth reported to one of the War Cabinet subcommittees, no minutes were taken. On another occasion, he reported to the Joint Chiefs of Staff. Again no minutes were taken. What Hoare said about the operation in London remains shrouded in secrecy.

---

7. Sir Alexander Cadogan, *The Diaries of Sir Alexander Cadogan, O.M., 1938–1945,* edited by David Dilks (London : Cassell 1971).

Churchill himself went to great lengths to ensure the operation ran as smoothly as possible. Anthony Eden, who as Secretary for War had known nothing, was brought into the loop by Hoare as soon as he took the helm at the Foreign Office at the end of 1940. Hillgarth paid him a personal visit to apprise him of details that could not be put down on paper. Eden wavered only once in his support of the operation, and in fact became the main advocate for its extension.

The bribes were deemed so important that the initial period that was considered critical—six months—came and went, yet the operation held its course. This was due to three major factors:

1. It enabled the British to keep the bribed military figures sweet as they were not paid on the spot.
2. Army minister Varela's pro-neutrality stance was bolstered by a bribed ally: Colonel Valentin Galarza—another of Franco's trustworthy minions, who in May 1941 became minister of the Interior.
3. The need to defuse the potentially dangerous situation if Germany invaded Spain as a response to the Allied disembarkation in Northern Africa in November 1942.

Discord with the Americans

The money used for the bribes was never physically moved. It was mobilized via bank transfers. Extreme care was taken so that its origin was not revealed. The first half million pounds was credited in Lisbon to March's agents. A Bank of Portugal account in their names received another 2 million dollars in New York City. At a time when exchange controls were ubiquitous, many technical problems had to be solved. Eventually, new accounts were opened in New York City at the Swiss Bank Corporation, where March had significant financial interests, became the alleged source of funds. The aim was to complicate matters as much as possible while leaving no trace.

Soon a technical—but nevertheless major—obstacle arose. In mid-1941 the U.S. Treasury began requesting specific licenses to operate nonresident accounts. Clarification as to the origin and use of the funds was required. This meant that the recipients of the bribes were not able to instruct March to move the funds out of the United States. Much hand wringing ensued in London, followed by extensive perusal of the options. Eventually Churchill decided to approach the U.S. Secretary of the Treasury, Henry Morgenthau, and confide in him a part of the story.

What was essentially a technical issue then evolved into a highly politicized problem that took almost five months to solve. As the bribed Spaniards became increasingly concerned about how and when they could access their ill-gotten gains, a solution was absolutely necessary. The Americans gained more insight into this most secret of British operations when Hillgarth gave information to one of his U.S. counterparts, whose reports were read by Morgenthau.

Even Franco himself encountered problems with the new U.S. regulations. His account with the Portuguese Banco Spirito Santo was prevented from being used until World War II was over. Foreign exchange controls were thus a very serious matter.

The importance of this operation can be assessed in different ways. Firstly, by examining the amount of money involved.

The Financial Significance of the Bribes

Historians have, in general, underestimated the money mobilized by the Exchequer to fund the bribes. The two phases of the operation, after the extension required by TORCH, consumed 6.5 million pounds. Relative to the money spent by the British on the war this is, of course, a microdot in an immense ocean, however it should still not be underestimated. It was, for instance, the same amount the British government gave De Gaulle's Free French Movement up until the end of 1941. It was, therefore, not a small sum.

Rendering today's equivalent of 6.5 million pounds is a difficult task. Several methods can be used, with wildly diverging outcomes that range from 235 million to 1.2 billion pounds. However, this range is too wide to mean anything substantive in operational terms. The method that is technically most accurate places this equivalent at a maximum of 899 million, which I would take as the upper limit.

For the recipients of the bribes, their value in pounds (or dollars) did not have much meaning. They wanted to either have the money in pesetas or to keep it abroad in foreign exchange. Both gave rise to serious obstacles. To receive the money in pesetas the foreign exchange had to be imported. This could not be done through official channels. The Francoist monetary authorities would inquire as to the origin of the funds. If the beneficiaries kept the money abroad, this only postponed the problem. Foreign exchange controls were not only there to stay, but intensified in the years later.

I tend to believe that the beneficiaries would have been tempted to import the money. To express the amount involved in pesetas, the official exchange rate—44 pesetas to the pound—is of no use. The unofficial exchange rate in the Tangiers market was far more attuned to the economic and political realities of the time. This rate, which the British intelligence and security services occasionally used to fund some of their covert operations, was 49.60 pesetas to the pound. Therefore 6.5 million pounds would be equal to at least 322.4 million pesetas. According to the calculations of Professor Jose Angel Sanchez Asiain, this sum would mean 1.2 billion euros today. A staggering number.

That easily acquired money would most likely have been imported in 1944. By looking at some sums of money that carried considerable meaning in that year, we find yet another means of comparison.

The budget for certain government departments in 1944 was as follows:

- 100 million pesetas for the Ministry of Foreign Affairs
- 283 million pesetas for the Ministry of Justice and the Ministry of the Interior together
- 487 million pesetas for the Air Ministry

Either way, the outcome is the same: 322.4 million pesetas was not an inconsiderable sum. The Ministries of Justice and Interior were the departments that handled the workings of the judicial, internal security, and prison apparatuses and provided crucial support to an embattled dictatorship.

The above comparisons are, within their limitations, objective ones. There is, however, another possibility. These comparisons assume that March would have helped the beneficiaries by importing their money the easy way, namely by selling pounds in Tangiers, in exchange for pesetas. However, there is no documentation to prove that this would have been the case. The British were obviously not interested in operational details solely of importance to the beneficiaries.

However, I have documented an instance in which March helped the British in another covert operation, by buying old ships so as to prevent them falling into Nazi hands. This was done under the guise of a purely commercial operation with other aims. The money for this transaction (which in reality came from the SOE budget) was supposedly made available to March by a group of South American financiers. The aim was to export foreign goods to Spain without the Spaniards having to deplete foreign exchange reserves or use the bilateral clearing arrangement.

The alleged commercial operation was deemed so important that it was authorized by General Franco himself, upon recommendation of the Minister of Industry and Commerce, Demetrio Carceller, who was in good standing with the British.

March would have learned a valuable lesson in how to import goods outside the bilateral clearing agreement, provided he had foreign financing available. To do so, he would have to invent another financial group (namely, the beneficiaries), who were willing to fund the export of British goods to Spain. Two possibilities would then arise: The first being to sell a portion of the goods at government-fixed prices, along with a mark-up; the second being to channel other portions of the goods into the black market.

In both cases, the effective exchange rate of the bribes is likely to have been much higher than the Tangiers rate. The beneficiaries would have received even more in pesetas than our earlier calculations provide for.

Of considerable significance is the fact that this money would have been "earned" in three and a half years, at most, simply by preventing Franco from veering too close to the Axis, and helping maintain what was, after all, the official policy—that is, non-belligerency. What would be fascinating to know is just how many Spanish military and political fortunes were linked to these bribes.

Existing Lacunae

For reasons that are unclear, British official publications have never mentioned the bribery operation. Nor have the National Archives released documents that could fill in some of the lacunae in the primary sources available.

First, the actual list of beneficiaries remains unknown. There are indications that Hillgarth may have given Churchill a copy. If this is so, it has not been made available at either the National Archives or Churchill's own collection. Nor is there any hint whatsoever that it even arrived there in the first place.

Second, we also know nothing of the operational documentation generated by the British Embassy in Madrid. In all likelihood, Juan March would have very rarely visited the Embassy, given that it was carefully guarded by Spanish security. There is not much primary evidence available containing written communication with Juan March.

The idea that the Embassy produced no records is implausible, as well as absolutely impossible. A number of them were declassified in 2013. Moreover, there is a clear commonality to all covert SOE operations in Spain for which evidence still survives: the proper and accurate justification of the uses to which funds were put. This was the case even when the amounts involved were very small.

It might be argued that these operational details would reveal too much about the true nature of such a secret operation. If this were so, then I find it doubtful that such documentation could be of any use in today's vastly different economic, financial, and political circumstances. After all, plenty of material relating to the Bletchley Park operation and the XXX Committee has been released. British SIGINT, HUMINT, and counterespionage are now well-trodden grounds.

Furthermore, some of the names of the recipients of the bribes can be known without a shadow of a doubt. At the head of them, none other than Nicolás Franco, the dictator's own brother. At the time, he was Ambassador to Lisbon. He was in frequent contact with his brother and went to Madrid often to exchange information and provide advice. Needless to say, the content of these conversations is entirely unknown. Most likely no notes were taken at all.

Among the beneficiaries there are two ministers who stand out: Varela and Galarza. Three eminent generals are also identified: Luis Orgaz, Antonio Aranda, and Alfredo Kindelan. Some not so pleasant information has been released by the British authorities regarding the first of these generals.

Orgaz was reported by the British consul in Tetuan to be corrupt to his very core. At the time, he held the sought after and incredibly lucrative post of High Commissioner in Spanish Morocco. Incidentally, Franco's intelligence sources also alerted him to the general's financially dubious activities. No action was taken against him, for reasons which remain unknown. However, it is highly likely that Orgaz was privy to some murky details of Franco's rebellion in Las Palmas on July 18, 1936. One of the points that still raises controversy is the alleged accident that led to the death of the garrison's commander. In my opinion, General Amado Balmes was killed on Franco's orders.

Aranda, the second of these three eminent generals, was known to be a confidante of the British. Reputedly a freemason, Franco never dared take any punitive action against him. This is remarkable given Franco's well-known hatred of Freemasonry. A great number of officers in Franco's army fell victim to this hatred, with Freemasonry outlawed in 1940.

Kindelan, the third general, was one of the principal actors in the preparation that took place in advance of the July 18 rebellion. He is likely to have been involved in the secret communication with the Italian Fascists that led to the contracts of July 1. Kindelan was instrumental in making Franco Generalissimus and Head of State at the end of September 1936.

All three were rabid Monarchists and had difficulties stomaching Franco's policies to neither condone the return of the pretender to the Crown, nor restore the Monarchy. In all likelihood, many of the military individuals involved in the bribery operation were monarchists. March was as well.

It may be surprising to be told Varela was among the beneficiaries. He had managed to marry into a very wealthy Basque family (but not before 1940) and one might surmise that he would not have been so interested in March's money. However, it was reported to Franco that after Varela left the government, Orgaz had become very critical of his membership of the boards of numerous companies. Obviously, he did not say no to a good business proposition.

How much the aforementioned generals received is also unknown. In the documents declassified in 2013, it appears that Kindelan got at least four million pesetas, equivalent to 34.8 million euros today, that is, ten percent of the estimated total. It is public knowledge that the Kindelan family owned property in London. Given this sum, the amount provisionally allocated to him in June 1940 was far exceeded. This may be a consequence of adjustments to the beneficiaries' allocations, or because the total amount involved in the operation overtook the initial sums.

Other well-known names within the Spanish military are also likely to have been bribed. At the head of these was Carlos Martínez de Campos, who allegedly received German money as well. He was a frequent associate of Brigadier Torr, as was Kindelan, and their meetings could be explained easily as part of official business.

Martínez de Campos went on to become, by the way, one of King Juan Carlos' teachers in his youth.

We cannot say whether the bribed individuals were aware that the money March promised them was:

- The banker's own money
- Money given to him by wealthy Spaniards who were against Franco throwing his (and Spain's) lot in with the Third Reich
- Money originating from British sources

It was widely believed that, as a financier, March had worldwide interests. In truth, it did not take a genius to think that he was likely to be in contact with the British. As with so many elements of this nebulous and murky story, that hypothesis has yet to be conclusively proved. Strong hints point to at least Galarza knowing about the British connection.

Conclusion

There are number of reasons why Franco remained in a state of neutrality/non-belligerence/neutrality during World War II. In my view, two are especially prominent. First, the state of economic prostration Spain was experiencing and the minimal interest that Hitler took in a possible Spanish entry into the war. This assertion may be hotly contested, but it can be proved by taking a fresh look at well-known German documents and the results of German historiography.

Second, the Allies helped maintain Spain on this course. The British were the first to take conventional, as well as non-conventional, measures. Among the former measures, political and diplomatic action went hand in hand with hard-headed, precisely calibrated economic and commercial pressure. The Americans played second fiddle here.

Foremost among the non-conventional measures was the bribery operation. It is difficult to assess its real impact as many of the beneficiaries were in official or semi-official contact with the embassy and as such their information also traveled via mainstream channels.

One can quite easily imagine Hoare, Hillgarth, Yencken, or Torr speaking with Kindelan, Orgaz, Aranda, and various others, knowing full well they were in March's pocket. Admirable British sangfroid helped disguise their awareness of the corrupt nature of their Spanish interlocutors. But such is the way with covert operations. There is nothing new under the sun.

Bibliography

Cadogan, Sir Alexander. *The Diaries of Sir Alexander Cadogan, O.M., 1938–1945*, edited by David Dilks. London : Cassell 1971.

Dalton, Hugh. *The Fateful Years: Memoirs, 1931–1945*. London: Muller, 1957.

Gómez-Jordana Sousa, Francisco. *Milicia y diplomacia: Los diarios del Conde de Jordana 1936–1944*. Burgos: Editorial Dossoles, 2002.

Hoare, Viscount Templewood, Sir Samuel. *Ambassador on Special Mission*. London: Collins, 1946.

Serrano Suñer, Ramón. *Entre Hendaya y Gibraltar*. Madrid: Ediciones y Publicaciones Españolas, 1947.

Smyth, Denis. *Diplomacy and Strategy of Survival: British Policy and Franco's Spain, 1940–41*. Cambridge: Cambridge University Press, 1986.

———. "Les Chevaliers de Saint-George: La Grand Bretagne et la corruption des généraux espagnols (1940–1942)." *Guerres mondiales et conflits contemporains* 162 (1991): 29–54.

8

Transnational Nationalism: The Basque Exile in Barcelona-Paris-New York (1936–1946)

Ludger Mees

The Paradoxes of Nationalism

Nationalism is probably one of the most complex and intricate subjects of research in the social sciences. This is mainly as a result of its enormous malleability. In fact, nationalism is—as John Hall puts it—"essentially labile, characteristically absorbing the flavours of the historical forces with which it interacts."[1] Consequently, throughout its long history nationalism has adopted many, frequently contradicting faces. It can be considered an amalgam of paradoxes, which do not only surface when comparing different nationalist movements. They can also develop within one single movement over different historical phases, or even during the lifetime of particular nationalist leaders. These paradoxes may be related to the ideology (traditionalist versus liberal; democratic versus imperialist or fascist; ethnic versus civic), to the social composition (bourgeois versus cross-class), to its relation to other cultural markers (secular versus religious), or its goals (cultural versus political; state-reinforcing, -creating, -subverting, or -reforming). Inspired by the recent emergence of global and transnational

* This article is a result of a broader research project carried out thanks to the support provided by the University of the Basque Country (GIU 14/30), the Spanish Ministry of Economy and Competitiveness (HAR2015-64920-P) and the European Regional Development Fund.

1. See John A. Hall, "Conditions for National Homogenizers," in *Nationalism and Its Futures*, ed. Umut Özkirimli (Houndmills and New York: Palgrave-Macmillan, 2003), 15–16.

approaches to history, we might add another paradox to this long, but not exhaustive list, distinguishing an exclusive, local, and parochial pattern of nationalism and an inclusive, transnational, and cosmopolitan one.

This new methodological and conceptual approach in the scholarly debate on nationalism has been mostly applied in the fields of migration and diaspora studies.[2] Focusing on the Basque nationalist exile after the defeat in the Spanish Civil War, this chapter aims to make a contribution to this debate. Therefore the analytical scope will be broadened from a more classical inner history of nationalism (ideology, program, organization, and so on) to an investigation of its transnational or even cosmopolitan strategy between 1937 (conquest of the Basque Country by the Francoist troops) and 1946 (settlement of the Basque government in Paris). The Basque example shows that nationalist ideology and transnational praxis were not mutually exclusive. Being able to become a player within a transnational context and taking advantage of the transnational network was, without any doubt, an asset for the nationalist leaders, but on occasions, it could also become a liability. Defining Basque nationalists, and particularly Jose Antonio Agirre, the president of the Basque government-in-exile, as transnational players, does not imply any renouncement of their nationalist claims (Basque self-government). On the contrary, the term "transnational" refers here to a particular political strategy. This included "sustained and regular contact across borders over time;"[3] while also establishing "multiple ties or interactions linking people or institutions across the borders of nation-states [in this case: national communities like the Basque one]."[4]

---

2. Alejandro Portes, "Globalization from Below: The Rise of Transnational Communities," in *Latin America in the World Economy*, ed. William C. Smith and Roberto Patricio Korczenwicz (Westport: Greenwood Press, 1996), 151–68; Alejandro Portes, Luis E. Guarnizo , and Patricia Landholt, "The Study of Transnationalism: Pitfalls and Promises of an Emergent Research Field," *Ethnic and Racial Studies* 22, no. 2 (1999), 217–37; Zlatko Skrbis, *Long-Distance Nationalism: Diasporas, Homelands and Identities* (Oxford: Routledge, 1999); Kim Knott and Sean McLoughlin, eds., *Diasporas: Concepts, Identities, Intersections* (London: Zed Books, 2010).

3. Portes, Guarnizo, Landolt, "The Study of Transnationalism," 218.

4. Steven Vertovec, "Conceiving and Researching Transnationalism," *Ethnic and Racial Studies* 22, no. 2 (1999), 447.

Other scholars refer to this pattern of nationalism as "cosmopolitan nationalism."[5] This label is more problematic since, *sensu stricto*, it is linked not only to the conviction that "all human beings share the capacity for reason and are therefore, by nature, members of a universal community." For cosmopolitans this assessment is also the main argument for the claim that "political boundaries and national identities are morally arbitrary, and that all human beings should be held as the primary units of moral worth, as if they were equal citizens of a universal political community."[6] Obviously, this claim is to a large extent incompatible with any nationalism and its final goal of transforming a certain ethnic community into a political entity with a high level of self-government. However, as the history of liberal nationalism demonstrates, and organizations like Mazzini's Young Europe League symbolize, nationalism and cosmopolitanism are not necessarily contradictory phenomena. Instead, they can cohabit within one single national movement, whose members believe—like Mazzini did—in the common destiny of humanity and the happiness of all citizens in the world, while considering that the precondition for this happiness is the free and democratic constitution of each nation into a nation-state. In the case of the Basque nationalists and their leaders in exile, their strong attachment to a transnational belief system like Catholicism, together with their cross-border networking, nationalist thought went hand in hand with cosmopolitan experiences and convictions. Instead of categorically opposing nationalist parochial segregation to cosmopolitan projection and openness, and following Gerard Delanty, it would probably be more realistic to consider that "the ideas of cosmopolitanism and nationalism have been linked" in a tense relationship.[7]

As in other cases, it was the necessity of tackling the complicated situation of exile that pushed the Basque nationalists after 1937 to overcome the temptation of parochial closure by choosing

5. See Susanne Lachenicht and Kirsten Heinsohn, eds., *Diaspora Identities: Exile, Nationalism and Cosmopolitanism in Past and Present* (Frankfurt and New York: Campus, 2009).

6. See Garrett Wallace Brown, "Cosmopolitanism," in *The Concise Oxford Dictionary of Politics* [original: 2009; online version: 2016], ed. Iain McLean and Alistair McMillan, at http://www.oxfordreference.com/view (accessed 6.5.2016).

7. Gerard Delanty, "Nationalism and Cosmopolitanism: The Paradox of Modernity," in *The Sage Handbook of Nations and Nationalism*, ed. Gerard Delanty and Krishan Kumar (London: Sage, 2006), 358, 361.

"survival strategies which are both nationalist and cosmopolitan," strategies that are "in situations of exile or diaspora, necessarily complementary."[8]

In the Basque case, this paradox of parochial closure and transnational or even cosmopolitan performance and strategies has been evident from the very beginnings of modern nationalism. Basque nationalism rose as a traditionalist, clerical, and racial protest against the new industrial and capitalist modernity, rejecting any external influence on Basque society due to its destructive consequences for local morality and customs. Yet, this defensive, traditionalist, and parochial nature of early Basque nationalism stood in evident contrast to the transnational and cosmopolitan projection of Basque collectives ever since the age of Spanish colonial conquest. Many Basques participated in prominent and leading positions both in the area of business and trade, and served the Spanish Crown in many of the new colonial administrations in the countries of the New World.[9] During the nineteenth century, these first Basque settlements in Latin America expanded due to the massive influx of thousands of immigrants from the Basque territories in Spain and France, who left their homeland escaping permanent warfare (the War of Independence against Napoleon; two Carlist Wars; the Spanish-American War) and from military conscription, but also from the economic stagnation of an underdeveloped agriculture. When the Spanish Civil War and the Francoist dictatorship produced a new wave of political emigration, these Basque nationalist and republican refugees could take advantage of the social and cultural networks established over decades by their countrymen in the various communities of the Basque Diaspora.

This chapter aims to analyze the relation between Basque ethnic nationalism and the appeal of a broader transnational context

---

8. Lachenicht and Heinsohn, *Diaspora Identities*, 9, 13.

9. See William A. Douglass and Jon Bilbao, *Amerikanuak: Basques in the New World* (Reno: University of Nevada Press, 1975); William A. Douglass, *La Vasconia Global. Ensayos sobre las diásporas vascas* (Vitoria-Gasteiz: Gobierno Vasco, 2003); Gloria Totoricagüena, *Diáspora vasca comparada. Etnicidad, cultura y política en las colectividades vascas* (Vitoria-Gasteiz: Gobierno Vasco, 2003); and Oscar Álvarez Gila, ed., *Organización, identidad e imagen de las colectividades vascas de la emigración (siglos XVI–XXI)* (Bilbao: Universidad del País Vasco, 2010).

in which it was forced to act after the conquest of Bilbao by the Francoist army in June 1937 and the escape of Basque democrats into exile. Having lost the homeland, the Basque government was hosted subsequently in three huge metropolises: moving from Bilbao to Barcelona; from Barcelona to Paris; from Paris to New York; and from the US once again to the French capital. In each of these cities, the particular context had an important influence on the politics of the government-in-exile. After summarizing the main features of Basque ethnic nationalism prior to the Civil War, attention will be placed on the question as to how far these changing transnational contextual frameworks were of advantage for the exiled political body; or, on the contrary, whether, when, and why they became a liability. Before continuing, however, two methodological explanations should be added. First, this analysis will not be focused on the Basque Nationalist Party (PNV), but rather the Basque government, which was created after the beginning of the Civil War in 1936. The reason for this focus is that, even though the government was a multi-party coalition of nationalists, republicans, socialists, and communists, the PNV was the hegemonic party that controlled the most important departments; yet, the party itself was heavily weakened by repression and the dispersion of its leaders across the world. Secondly, if the government-in-exile was the real leader of ethnic nationalism and of all Basque anti-Franco democrats in general, this was to a large extent the consequence of the personal leadership of its charismatic President Jose Antonio Agirre. From the point of view of comparative history, it can be stated that neither the Catalans, nor the Galicians, or the Spanish republicans had anything similar to the leading personality of Agirre, who was not venerated as a hero solely by his nationalist followers. Instead, his charisma penetrated into nearly all communities of democrats across political boundaries. The history of Basque nationalism in exile cannot be correctly understood without paying a certain tribute to Agirre's biography and his particular leadership.[10]

---

10. A recent and detailed analysis of Agirre's political biography can be found in Ludger Mees, José Luis de la Granja, Santiago de Pablo, and José Antonio Rodríguez Ranz, *La política como pasión. El lehendakari José Antonio Aguirre (1904–1960)* (Madrid: Tecnos, 2014).

Basque Ethnic Nationalism until the Civil War

Basque nationalism as a sociopolitical movement was created at the end of the nineteenth century.[11] In 1895, Sabino Arana Goiri founded the first cell of what later would be the Partido Nacionalista Vasco, the Basque Nationalist Party. Arana was a thirty-year-old former law student, and son of a well-off, Catholic family with Carlist leanings from Bilbao. The early PNV was a small semi-legal party with a rank-and-file membership that came from an urban petty-bourgeois background. The party's ideology was a mix of traditionalist anti-liberalism, anti-socialism with xenophobic tendencies toward immigrant workers, severe criticism of the corrupt political system of the Restoration Monarchy, and the desire for Basque independence. Yet, the incorporation of significant sectors of the Basque urban middle and upper-classes contributed to smooth the early PNV's ideological and political radicalism by designing a more moderate and gradual program that set the achievement of regional autonomy as its principal political aim. Ever since, this duality and the pendulous swing between ideological radicalism and realistic pragmatism, between separatism and autonomy, has been one of the outstanding features of Basque majority nationalism.

In the context of the acute social and political crisis in fin-de-siècle Spain[12] Basque nationalism was shaped as a sort of "reactive

11. For what follows see Santiago de Pablo, Ludger Mees, and José Antonio Rodríguez Ranz, *El péndulo patriótico. Historia del Partido Nacionalista Vasco*, vol. 1 (Barcelona: Crítica, 1999); Ludger Mees, "Der 'spanische Sonderweg': Staat und Nation(en) im Spanien des 19. und 20. Jahrhunderts," *Archiv für Sozialgeschichte* 40, (2000), 29–66; Javier Corcuera, *La patria de los vascos. Orígenes, ideología y organización del nacionalismo vasco, 1876–1903* (Madrid: Taurus, 2001); Ludger Mees, *Nationalism, Violence and Democracy: The Basque Clash of Identities* (Houndmills and New York: Palgrave-Macmillan, 2003), 5–31; and José Luis de la Granja, *Ángel o demonio: Sabino Arana. El patriarca del nacionalismo vasco* (Madrid: Tecnos, 2015).

12. See Juan Linz, "Early State-Building and Late Peripheral Nationalisms Against the State: the Case of Spain," in *Building States and Nations*, vol. 2, ed. Shmuel N. Eisenstadt and Stein Rokkan (Beverly Hills: SAGE, 1973), 32–116; An overview on the scholarly debate about the (relative) weakness of the Spanish nation building in Ludger Mees, "Rückständiges Zentrum, moderne Peripherie. Probleme des spanischen Nation Building im 19. und 20. Jahrhundert," in *Ränder der Moderne. Neue Perspektiven auf die Europäische Geschichte (1800–1930)*, ed. Christof Dejung and Martin Lengwiler (Köln: Böhlau, 2016), 221–45.

collective action . . . against someone who had unjustly deprived, or tried to deprive, a local population of a precious resource."[13] The targets of nationalism were the Spanish state, the socialist labor movement, and the industrial and financial bourgeoisie. The "deprived resources" in the nationalist discourse were independence, morality and customs, religion, and language. Even if Basque nationalism quickly penetrated into other sectors of society and after World War I became a popular cross-class social movement, for a long time it was not able to overcome its reactive, defensive, and relatively fragile character.

The Civil War and the subsequent dictatorship supposed the beginning of a long period of unrest for Basque nationalism. The Statute of Regional Autonomy, which after a long struggle had finally been passed and come into effect in October 1936, was abolished and all political parties were banned. As terror and repression against political enemies and indeed against all expressions of Basque cultural particularism became a daily experience in the Francoist Basque Country, the members of the first regional Basque government under the nationalist President Jose Antonio Agirre had to escape. The Basque Country had been conquered in June 1937, but the Civil War was still going on in other regions.[14] In this context, at the end of October 1937 Agirre decided to establish the headquarters of his government in Barcelona. This first crossing of the Basque border would not be the last.

Barcelona

The migration to Barcelona was decided on for three reasons, one strategical, one humanitarian, and another one political and ideological. First of all, Barcelona and the Catalan surroundings still remained within the Republican sector. It was the ideal place to symbolize the Basque government's commitment to the defense of the Republic and, at the same time, facilitate a fluid communication with those of the political leadership who remained in

---

13. Charles Tilly, *From Mobilization to Revolution* (New York: McGraw-Hill), 146.
14. See Santiago de Pablo, Ludger Mees, and José Antonio Rodríguez Ranz, *El Péndulo Patriótico.Historia del Partido Nacionalista Vasco*, vol. 2, *1936–1979* (Barcelona: Crítica, 2001); and José Luis de la Granja, *El oasis vasco. El nacimiento de Euskadi en la República y la Guerra Civil* (Madrid: Tecnos, 2007).

French exile. Second, after the conquest of Bilbao, Barcelona, and in general Catalonia, had become the destination for thousands of Basque exiles, particularly after the decision taken in October of 1937 by the French government to expel all Spanish refugees from the French territory. The calculations of historians fix the number of Basque exiles in Catalonia between 50,000 and 100,000 by the beginning of 1938. With all of these people to be attended to, the organization of humanitarian aid became one of the most important issues for the Basque government during its time in Barcelona.[15] Finally, a third argument was the necessity of being close to the heart of political decision-making. In fact, in 1938 Barcelona was the capital of three governments: the central government of the Spanish Republic, the Catalan regional government (Generalitat), and the Basque government. For the Basque nationalists, the proximity of the Generalitat, which was also directed by a Catalan nationalist, had a special relevance, since the PNV had always considered Catalan nationalism as its closest ally in the struggle against the Spanish centralist state.

When the Basque government settled in Barcelona, Agirre and his ministers started working in a friendly environment facilitated by the first Basque Diaspora, which had been made up by the first refugees who had arrived after the Francoist conquest of Navarre, Araba, and Gipuzkoa during the summer of 1936. In close coordination with the Catalan nationalist Esquerra party, in October of that year a Basque Secretariat was set up, to be followed one month later by the "General Delegation of Euzkadi in Catalonia," which started to work predominantly in the field of humanitarian aid. The weekly paper *Euzkadi* was published with the function of establishing communication among the different collectives of exiles and between the exiles and the Basque administration. The celebration of a "Pro-Euzkadi Week" tightened the bonds of political and economic solidarity between the Basques and the Catalans.

Agirre and his government, however, only had sixteen months to take advantage of this positive environment. In synthesis, a few conclusions concerning the government's activity during this period might be considered.[16] First, in the field of humanitarian

---

15. Gregorio Arrien and Iñaki Goiogana, *El primer exilio de los vascos: Cataluña 1936–1939* (Barcelona: Fundación Ramón Trias Fargas; Fundación Sabino Arana, 2002), 123; Joan Serrallonga I Urquidi, *Refugiats i desplaçats dins la Catalunya en guerra 1936–1939* (Barcelona: Ed. Base, 2004), 152.

16. Ludger Mees, "Tan lejos, tan cerca. El Gobierno Vasco en Barcelona y las

assistance to the thousands of refugees, the government performed a commendable task in spite of the shortage in economic resources. Second, by displaying an active strategy of communication and propaganda (publication of a daily newspaper, radio programs), it helped to foster a sense of solidarity and identity among Basque refugees. Yet, and this is the third conclusion, in terms of political and military success, the summary is not exactly positive. The Basque Brigade set up by the government never became the strong military unit at the service of the Basques interests Agirre had imagined. Instead, it ended up integrated into the Spanish Republican army. The incompatibility of Spanish centralist politics and the Basque and Catalan search for higher levels of self-government weakened the anti-Francoist alliance. Thus, the proximity of the three governments, instead of consolidating the common struggle against Spanish fascism, shaped a latent conflict between two of the governments with the third, a conflict that finally exploded by the withdrawal of the Basque and Catalan nationalist ministers from the central Republican government presided over by the socialist Juan Negrín in August 1938. Finally, the various attempts at secret negotiations with the British Foreign Office aimed at a British mediation in the Civil War and the granting of Basque and Catalan self-government in a new postwar Spain were not successful and, after becoming public, contributed even more to the deterioration of the already tense relations between the partners of the Republican front. In the meantime, Franco's army, efficiently supported by Hitler and Mussolini, reached the Mediterranean and continued their offensive until the conquest of Barcelona on January 26, 1939. A few days later, the Basque President Agirre accompanied his Catalan homologue Lluís Companys in crossing the Spanish-French border in the Pyrenees. Exile in Barcelona was followed by exile in Paris and a new transnational challenge began.

Paris

The transfer from Barcelona to Paris did not alter most of the circumstances that Agirre and his government had to face in the Catalan capital. The Francoist victory in Catalonia, and then, by the end of March, in Madrid and the rest of the Republican enclaves,

---

complejas relaciones entre el nacionalismo vasco y el catalán," *Historia Contemporánea* 37 (2008), 557–91.

produced a new wave of refugees from Catalonia to France who all had to be attended to. On the other hand, there was no doubt that Paris was a new exile, although the French Basque Country was not so far away. Agirre and his ministers frequently traveled to Bayonne (Baiona) or Saint-Jean-de-Luz (Donibane Lohizune) to be with their people and give an impulse to inner-Basque solidarity while raising the morale of Basques citizens on either side of the border. Although the government was in exile, it was, at the same time, in a region of the homeland that all nationalists considered part of the Basque nation and that, according to the nationalist program, was to join the other Basque territories on the Spanish side of the border in a unified *Euskadi* or *Euskal Herria* in the future. Yet, despite this advantage, there remained two unresolved problems for nationalist politics. First, in the French part of the Basque Country nationalist ideology was clearly a minority phenomenon within a mostly agrarian and highly religious society, which usually voted for French conservative parties.[17] Second, the Basque government and its activities depended on the maintenance of good relations with the French central government. Active nationalist propaganda in the French Basque Country would have jeopardized this relationship and that is why Agirre and his men pursued a strategy based mostly on humanitarian issues and characterized by a self-imposed abstinence in nationalist doctrine, at least in all those aspects in which it might have touched French national interests. Nationalism was subordinated to transnationalism. In this sense, the International League of Friends of the Basques, founded in December 1938 in Paris, was an important aid to this strategy. As a transnational network, it had the dual purpose of organizing assistance for Basques refugees and, at the same time, mobilizing influential French politicians, intellectuals, and clergymen to support the Basque cause as members of the League without touching the complicated issue of the French Basque Country.[18]

Furthermore, there were two major differences between the exile in Paris and the previous one in Barcelona. The first was that now the Spanish Republic, for whose defense Agirre had moved to Barcelona, had ceased to exist. Not only had all the republican

17. James Edwin Jacob, *Hills of Conflict: Basque Nationalism in France* (Reno: University of Nevada Press, 1994).
18. Jean-Claude Larronde, *Exilio y Solidaridad. La Liga Internacional de Amigos de los Vascos* (Villefranque: Bidasoa, 1997).

institutions been banned by Franco, but, moreover, as if the Spanish republican forces had wanted to make a special contribution to the debacle, their crude confrontations against each other made survival of the institutions in exile impossible. Agirre and the other leaders of the PNV drew an important conclusion out of this new situation: if the Republic was buried and there was no longer any constitution or government, all the commitments to the Spanish state that the nationalists had undertaken when accepting regional autonomy within the state had to be canceled. Once all those restrictive bonds with the state were eliminated, the door was open for a more radical nationalist strategy. In 1939, and within a context of transnational lobbying, nationalist ideology surfaced in the PNV and the Basque government. The most important consequence of this strategic turn was Agirre's requirement, communicated to all the Basque parties that intended to continue in his government, which was to invite them to break their organic relations with Spanish parties and adopt a clearly Basque national program. This requirement produced the severest crisis of the Basque government-in-exile, as an important sector of the Basque socialist party led by the former minister Indalecio Prieto rejected this pretension and threatened to leave the Basque government. It took years to surmount this crisis and to deactivate the danger of an immediate collapse of the multiparty coalition, which since October 1936 had become the symbol for the indestructible union of all Basques democrats in their fight against fascism.

After September 1939, there was another major difference between the Catalan and the French exile of the Basque nationalists. The outbreak of World War II after the German aggression against Poland had changed the geopolitical situation. Due to the treaties of mutual assistance in the event of a military invasion signed with the Polish government, France and Great Britain had to abandon their strategy of appeasement and enter the war. President Agirre immediately published a manifesto in which he offered the French government the support of the Basques in the fight for democracy. The Basque delegation in London did the same thing through their contacts with the Foreign Office. This offer of support produced two tangible consequences during the war: the first was the collaboration of the Basque intelligence services with the French and the British governments; and the second the constitution of a Basque military unit that during the final months of the war fought the

German troops near Bordeaux.[19] However, all attempts of extracting a political pay-off for this solidarity from the European allies, in terms of a formal guarantee for Basque self-government and sovereignty in the postwar Europe, failed. Thus, the Basque government's transnational strategy turned out to be rather unilateral, and not reciprocal.

This unconditional commitment to the cause of Western democracy was nothing more than a confirmation of the decision taken in the Spanish Civil War, but it was at the same time a dangerous strategic gamble, since it made the Basque nationalists not only declared enemies of the Franco dictatorship, but also of the Caudillo's powerful fascist allies. Agirre himself had to suffer the consequences of this new situation in May 1940 on a family visit to Belgium, when he was surprised by the invasion of the country by the German Wehrmacht. Since he did not manage to return to Paris, he was forced to go underground and to start his particular dangerous odyssey through Hitler's Europe.[20] With the help of a new passport facilitated by a Panamanian diplomat José Antonio Aguirre became José Andrés Álvarez Lastra, who now usually wore glasses and had a moustache. With this new identity, Agirre decided that the safest place to hide was probably where nobody would expect him to be, and that was in the heart of Nazi Germany, in Berlin. In the German capital he had the confidence and the help of other South American diplomats, which proved to be a necessary condition for survival, but also could have turned out to be a fatal death sentence in the event of any leak to the Gestapo. This danger was not at all exaggerated as the case of the Catalan President Companys proved: Companys was caught in France by the Gestapo, delivered to the Spanish police, sentenced to death, and executed in October 1940. Fortunately, Agirre was lucky and managed to escape together with his wife, son, and daughter from Berlin to the Swedish town of Gothenburg and from there, after

---

19. Juan Carlos Jiménez de Aberásturi, *De la derrota a la esperanza: políticas vascas durante la Segunda Guerra Mundial (1937–1947)* (Bilbao: IVAP, 1999); Pablo, Mees, and Rodríguez Ranz, *El Péndulo Patriótico*, vol. 2, 75–142; Juan Carlos Jiménez de Aberásturi and Rafael Moreno Izquierdo, *Al servicio del extranjero. Historia del servicio vasco de información (1936–1943)* (Madrid: Machado Libros, 2009).

20. See José Antonio Aguirre, *Escape via Berlin* (New York: Macmillan, 1944); José Antonio Aguirre, *Diario 1941–1942* (Bilbao: Fundación Sabino Arana, 2010).

fifteen months of living covertly underground, to Latin America, where he reappeared in August 1941.

During the long period of his odyssey, the Basque president was able to maintain contact with several of his political friends and advisers. Among them the most important and decisive one was probably his contact with the Philippine multimillion-aire of Basque origin and US American passport holder Manuel Ynchausti. Apart from sending money to Agirre, Ynchausti managed to obtain the help of the State Department to facilitate travel and visa requirements for Agirre and his family. These contacts between the magnate Ynchausti and the Roosevelt administration predetermined the decision of Agirre and his government in relation to their third exile, as they obviously could not return to Paris, which had been occupied by the Germans. The former seat of the Basque government at the Avenue Marceau was handed over to the Spanish government together with all the documents that the Basques had not taken away or burned before the occupation by the Nazis. One of these documents contained a list of all members of a nationalist network of resistance operating in the Spanish Basque Country. Its members were immediately jailed and their leader Luis Alava executed after being sentenced to death by a military tribunal. After the loss of Barcelona and Paris, New York became the new host for the Basque government-in-exile. Basque transnationalism was no longer European, but worldwide.

New York

The United States was not a strange or remote place for the Basques when Agirre and his government arrived. Basque immigration to the US started later than that to Latin America and was initially in the indirect form of Basque migrants who had previously settled in one of the Latin American countries. It was at the time of the California Gold Rush in the mid-nineteenth century that the pull of making money attracted Basques from Latin America who decided to sail into San Francisco Bay. The Basques soon reached the conclusion that it was easier to make money by utilizing the livestock skills they learned in Latin America to feed the mining camps, and so they began raising cattle and especially sheep in California, Idaho, and Nevada. The transformation of the informal ethnic networks into formal ethnonational institutions also began later than in Latin America. Whereas in Montevideo the Laurac Bat, the first Basque

Center, had already been founded in 1876, to be followed one year later by that of Buenos Aires, the first Basque Mutual Aid Society, based in Boise, capital of Idaho, was not created until 1908.[21]

The other focus of Basque immigration to the US from the mid-nineteenth century was New York. Its huge port was a great attraction for a people such as the Basques who throughout their history had accumulated rich labor experience in all kinds of work related to the sea. One of them who made fortune as a businessman and owner of a travel agency, a hotel, and a famous restaurant was Valentín Aguirre. In 1913, Aguirre was also one of the prominent promoters of the Centro Vasco-Americano, which in 1928 moved to a new building in the nearby Cherry Street. From this moment, he was one of the most important sponsors of all the ethnocultural initiatives organized around the Basque Center.

He also maintained a close relationship to the Delegation of the Basque government that was established in 1938, first in the New Weston and Elysée hotels, and later in an elegant apartment on the Fifth Avenue in the center of Manhattan. The first delegates were Anton Irala, the General Secretary of the Department of Presidency, Ramón de la Sota MacMahon, and his uncle Manu de la Sota y Aburto, both members of the family of the nationalist industrial magnate Ramón de la Sota y Llano, whose enterprises had been expropriated and nationalized by Franco. From the very beginning of the Delegation's activity, its principal aim was not only to gain support for the Basque and the Republican cause in the Civil War, but also to establish relations with the US government. Therefore, the personal contacts with different members of the Roosevelt administration cultivated by Ramón de la Sota from his university studies in Cambridge were very helpful.[22]

This was the prevailing context of the Basque communities in the US when President Agirre was on his way to Brazil after escaping from Sweden. Most of the approximately 40,000 Basques lived in California (25,000) and in Idaho (8,000), the rest in other places like Nevada, Oregon, or New York.[23] In several of these places

21. See Gloria Totoricagüena, *The Basques of New York: A Cosmopolitan Experience* (Vitoria-Gasteiz: Gobierno Vasco, 2003), 99.

22. Koldo San Sebastián, *El exilio vasco en América. 1936/1946. Acción del gobierno* (San Sebastián: Txertoa, 1988), 56; David Mota, Un sueño americano: el Gobierno Vasco en el exilio y Estados Unidos (1937-1979), (Oñati: IVAP, 2016)

23. San Sebastián, 61.

there were ethnocultural networks that had been formalized by creating Basque Centers or similar institutions. The Delegation of the Basque government in New York was working successfully in establishing direct links with the US government and several Basques who had made money and were well related to the US establishment provided their financial and personal help.

One of the latter was the aforementioned Manuel Ynchausti. When Agirre arrived in Brazil, Ynchausti had started negotiations with Carlton Hayes, head of the History Department at Columbia University and a friend of President Roosevelt, in order to contract the Basque President as a history lecturer. This contract was necessary to obtain a visa and a permission of residence in the US. Ynchausti realized his aim after making clear that he himself would sponsor the contract by making regular donations to the university. Previously he had negotiated this issue with high-ranking officials in the government. When the Basque president and his family arrived in New York on November 6, 1941, and even if the Roosevelt administration took care that this arrival was conducted without major publicity, there were strong reasons that made the presence of Agirre in the United States interesting for the US government. Most of them had to do with the Basque transnational appeal. First, Agirre was a member of a group of democratic, Catholic, and anti-fascist intellectuals and politicians who, thanks to the mediation of the Rockefeller Foundation, had been granted asylum in the US. Among these Catholic intellectuals we find leading personalities such as Luigi Sturzo, Heinrich Brüning, Frans Van Cauwelaert, Jacques Maritain, and others. These were all leaders supposed to play an important role in the political reconstruction of postwar Europe. Second, Agirre and the Basque nationalists controlled broad ethnopolitical networks in Latin America and their influence on those predominantly Catholic societies and governments could produce a counterbalance to the impact of conservative and clerical pro-Axis propaganda. Finally, Agirre's profile as a Catholic democrat who during the Spanish Civil War had fought against Spanish fascism and had offered the Basques' active support to the Western democracies after the beginning of World War II, might be of use for Roosevelt. The president had to struggle against a mostly pacifist and isolationist public opinion that had to be convinced about the necessity of US military engagement in the war against Hitler. The Japanese aggression on Pearl Harbor one month after

the arrival of Agirre accelerated this process and led to the declaration of war on Japan and, subsequently, that of Germany on
the US.[24]

Besides his lectures at Columbia, during his years in New York
the Basque President developed a frenetic activity, which covered
various areas. The first was the area of propaganda in favor of the
Basque question and against international fascism. He repeated
this message in public talks, articles in the papers, manifestos published together with other European Catholic leaders, and in the
publication of a newsletter under the name of "Basques."

A second, even more important area of activity was the
strengthening of transnational ties. The Basque president continued on with the work that the delegates of his government had
already advanced before his arrival and deepened and consolidated
relations with different leading officials of the State Department.
Agirre did not manage to personally meet President Roosevelt nor
was he able to talk to the Secretary of State Cordell Hull. But he
did have a personal lunch with Vice President Wallace. The fruit of
all these intense relations with officials of the Roosevelt administration was a secret agreement of cooperation between the Basque
and the US government. Even if the original document—if there
is any—has not yet been found by historians who have been working on this issue, its content is more or less known.[25] The Basques
committed themselves to organize a campaign of propaganda in
several countries in Latin America and to use their network of
secret services and espionage against German interests in favor of
the allies, but also against communist groups. In return, they were
granted a preferential relationship with the American government, other infrastructure facilities (such as the use of diplomatic
bags for confidential communications), and funding. Among the

---

24. See William L. Langer and S. Everett Gleason, *1940–1941: The Undeclared War* (New York: Harper & Brothers, 1953); Ian Kershaw, *Wendepunkte.
Schlüsselentscheidungen im Zweiten Weltkrieg.* 2nd ed., (München: DVA, 2008),
375–415 [original English edition: *Fateful Choices: The Decisions That Changed
the World, 1940–1941* (London: Allen Lane 2007)]; Iñaki Goiogana, "José Antonio Aguirre, profesor en la Columbia University," in *Exilio y universidad (1936–
1955). Presencia y realidades*, ed. José Angel Asunce, Mónica Jato, and María
Luisa San Miguel (San Sebastián: Ed. Saturrraran, 2008), 599–643.

25. Xabier Irujo, *Expelled from the Motherland. The Government of President
José Antonio Agirre in Exile, 1937–1960*, trans. Cameron Watson and Jennifer
Ottman (Reno: Center for Basque Studies, University of Nevada, 2012), 123–25.

important achievements of the Basque spies during World War II, two shall be mentioned here: the obtainment of the secret instruction given by the Franco government to the captains of the Spanish sea cargoes in case of Spanish military involvement in the war and the robbery of the secret communication codes from the safe of the Spanish Embassy in Washington.[26] Several leading nationalist politicians such as, for instance, Anton Irala and Jesús Galíndez, were directly contracted as secret agents for US intelligence. What they did not know was that, just in case, the FBI was also spying on several Basque government officials.

Agirre himself did not hesitate to fulfill his propaganda commitment. Between August and October of 1942, he went on tour to visit ten Latin American countries. This trip had been funded by the American government, particularly by the Office of Panamerican Affairs headed by the millionaire Nelson Rockefeller, who was a friend of Ynchausti. In a letter to the President of the Columbia University, the Basque president asked to excuse the impossibility of continuing with his lectures during his absence. He argued that he had been invited by different Latin American universities and, as he wrote to Columbia president Mr. Murray Butler, "this is confidential, that I am going on a mission that an agency of the U.S. government has entrusted to me."[27] This trip to Latin America was to be the most successful of all the international engagements performed by Agirre, who gave twenty-three lectures in different universities, as well as more than a hundred public talks, many of which were broadcast live on local radio stations. Agirre was also received by the presidents of Mexico, Panama, Colombia, Chile, Peru, Uruguay, and Cuba.[28]

At the end of the war, Agirre and his delegates continued their work of propaganda and transnational relations, now directly targeting the Franco regime within the new organization set up in the aftermath of the Conference of San Francisco in April 1945: the United Nations Organization.

It goes without saying that the final horizon of all political activities carried out by Agirre and the Basque nationalists was the

---

26. Jiménez de Aberásturi and Moreno, *Al servicio del extranjero*, 457–513.
27. Letter from Jose Antonio Agirre to Nicholas Murray Butler, New York, August 15, 1942. Copy of the document facilitated by the Archivo del Nacionalismo, Artea.
28. Ludger Mees, *El profeta pragmático. Aguirre, el primer lehendakari (1939-1960)*, (Irún: Alberdania, 2006), 75–76.

abolition of the Spanish dictatorship and the recovery of Basque self-government. Therefore, it was necessary to strengthen the government, which was supposed to seize power and guarantee a peaceful transition to democracy in the Basque Country when the moment of the dictator's displacement was to come. Due to Agirre's odyssey and the exile of several of his ministers, the Basque government had practically disappeared, even if the former minister of the Republican government, Manuel Irujo, tried to assure political continuity by creating the Basque National Council in London. After his arrival in New York, Agirre ordered the dissolution of the Council. In February 1945, he called several of his ministers to discuss the reorganization of the government. The results of these meetings were published in a communiqué, which recovered the requirement formulated previously in 1940 that all ministers of the government had to be members of "Basque organizations without any dependence on non-Basque disciplines and political parties."[29] The immediate protest of the non-nationalist parties, especially that of the Basques socialists, forced the president to drop this demand and to moderate the political strategy of the government.

This shift toward pragmatism and moderation was necessary as a condition for the implementation of another important aim pursued by Agirre in the last sphere of his activities carried out during his stay in New York. Thanks to his multiple international contacts, Agirre had concluded that Washington, London, and Paris did not really care about what was happening in Bilbao. Instead, the western democracies needed to know what was happening at the center of political power in Spain. The Basque president was convinced that none of the democratic powers would lift a finger to help overthrow the Spanish dictatorship without having a well-defined and strong political alternative that was able to maintain the social order and impede a new civil war. Since the Basque president was probably the only politician who was respected by any of the different sectors of Spanish republicanism, he used this privilege and his presence at the Conference of San Francisco to start a process of mediation among these Republican forces, who since the end of the Civil War and the breakdown of the Second Republic had been at odds. Finally, Agirre managed to convince all of them that the reestablishment of democracy required the union of the democrats and the constitution of a strong government. In August 1945,

---

29. Jiménez de Aberásturi, *De la derrota a la esperanza*, 614.

this Spanish government-in-exile, presided over by the republican José Giral, was constituted in Mexico, and the leader of the Basque nationalists had been its principal promoter. Over the next two years, Agirre and Manuel Irujo, his nationalist minister in the Republican government, *de facto* controlled to a great extent the political strategy as well as the budget of this government.[30] This was mainly conducted from Paris, as in June 1946 Agirre had left New York in order to establish his government-in-exile once again in the French capital, which also hosted the Spanish Republican government-in-exile. However, it is well known that neither this cooperation with the Spanish democrats, nor the rich network of multiple international relations, were able to set in train an end to Francoism and return self-government to the Basques. In the context of the Cold War, for the Basques' US American partners and friends Franco became clearly more important than Agirre had ever been. What once had been considered one of the politically most promising advantages for Basque politics in the New York exile now became a liability for the struggle against Franco. The unrealistic, even blind confidence in "American friends," who were eventually supposed to pay in return for the Basques' support during the war, over the years turned out to be a strategic dead end. In 1960, Agirre died in his last exile at the age of fifty-six after suffering a heart attack. Franco and his dictatorship lived on for another fifteen years.

Conclusions

When in June 1937 the Basque government was forced into exile, the response given to this new situation was the pursuit of a survival strategy that aimed at building a transnational network of cooperation and support in the struggle against Franco and for Basque self-government, once the dictatorship had been abolished. The setting up of this transnational strategy was initially not at all an easy task, because it was conditioned by two important obstacles: first of all, Agirre's government could not claim to represent a state. It only administered a small region within the Spanish state that, in 1936, had attained a certain level of regional autonomy. Hence, as many records in the Archives of the American

---

30. Mees, *Profeta*, 95–158.

government during the years of World War II show,[31] formally there were doubts as to whether the Basque could be treated as a government like so many other governments-in-exile and whether it was possible to sign any kind of agreement with it. Furthermore, Agirre and his government, unlike for instance the Polish or the Czechoslovakian governments-in-exile, did not figure militarily with an army comparable to the units under control by the two aforementioned governments. Given these remarkable disadvantages, from a historical point of view, Agirre's and his government's success in introducing the Basque question into the transnational arena can be considered astonishing. This success was only possible because the Basques did indeed have something to offer their partners: a government that was the only politically solid Republican institution still alive and active after the collapse of the Spanish Republic; political influence among nearly all sectors of the Spanish exile; a well-organized and highly reputable diaspora in most Latin American countries; an efficient broad network of espionage within Spain and abroad willing to supply information in the fight against fascism; and, finally, Agirre's enormous personal charisma that made him probably the most popular and respected leader of the entire Spanish exile.

However, while Agirre and his colleagues were successful in building up an important transnational network, they failed to make any tangible political capital out of it. This was basically a consequence of two facts. First, their transnationalism was not a relation between equal partners. Instead, it was a temporal and fragile relation marked by an obvious imbalance of power, especially after the end of World War II, when the impending Cold War helped Franco to mutate from being an ally of fascism to a partner of the Western democracies in their fight against Soviet communism. And second, in Agirre's particular personality the evident success in becoming a well-related transnational player in the end became a liability, because it triggered an exaggerated optimism about his personal and his government's influence all over the world that would seriously compromise his capacity to analyze and interpret the political process more realistically. In the middle of this transnational artificial bubble, the Basque president was unable—or unwilling—to recognize that his great ease in developing contacts with high ranking politicians in the US (and

---

31. Mees et alii, *Política como pasión*, 442–55.

in Europe) was not necessarily an indication of the level of empathy, active involvement, and decisive support of the American (and European) "friends" toward the Basque question.

Thus, at the end, the great gamble on transnationalism as a political survival strategy did not produce any tangible result. The Basque president, who had been the most active promoter of this strategy, died. Franco remained in power, the Basque Country continued being a part of the Spanish state without any kind of self-government, and the Basque issue simply disappeared from the agenda of the western democracies. Not even the decisive impulse to Agirre's cosmopolitanism through his active involvement in the process of European unification at the end of his life brought any benefit. Nevertheless, despite frustration and failure, the history of Basque nationalist cosmopolitanism in exile also has a clear projection into the globalized world of the twenty-first century, in which traditional concepts and notions like sovereignty, nation, and state have become more and more jeopardized. As the German sociologist Ulrich Beck has pointed out, cosmopolitanism means the end of the idea of the nation and the nation-state as "closed societies." Cosmopolitanism is not the new paradigm of the postnational era. It does not substitute the idea of the nation. Instead, it may form a complex amalgam with the nation as a "rooted cosmopolitanism."[32] Or, in the words of Gerard Delanty: "Cosmopolitanism is no longer an individualistic disposition but has been incorporated into the cultural horizon of modernity and into the imaginaries of many nations. It is thus possible to see the nation as a vehicle for cosmopolitanism which is not disembodied and rootless."[33]

Would it be a great ahistorical exaggeration to label President Agirre's nationalism in exile as a unique, imperfect, and contradictory, but yet real pattern of "rooted cosmopolitanism" *avant la lettre* in contrast to the exclusive, parochial, and xenophobic nationalism that is celebrating a powerful revival across Europe and the US at the beginning of the twenty-first century?

---

32. Ulrich Beck, *The Cosmopolitan Vision*, trans. Ciaran Cronin (Cambridge: Polity Press, 2006); Ulrich Beck and Edgar Grande, *Cosmopolitan Europe*, trans. Ciaran Cronin (Cambirdge: Polity Press, 2006).
33. Delanty, "Nationalism and Cosmopolitanism," 366.

Bibliography

Aguirre, José Antonio. *Escape via Berlin.* New York: Macmillan, 1944.
————. *Diario 1941-1942.* Bilbao: Fundación Sabino Arana, 2010.
Álvarez Gila, Oscar, ed., *Organización, identidad e imagen de las colectividades vascas de la emigración (siglos XVI-XXI).* Bilbao: Universidad del País Vasco, 2010.
Arrien, Gregorio, and Iñaki Goiogana, *El primer exilio de los vascos. Cataluña 1936-1939.* Barcelona: Fundación Ramón Trias Fargas; Fundación Sabino Arana, 2002.
Beck, Ulrich, *The Cosmopolitan Vision.* Translated by Ciaran Cronin. Cambridge: Polity Press, 2006.
Beck, Ulrich, and Edgar Grande, *Cosmopolitan Europe.* Translated by Ciaran Cronin. Cambirdge: Polity Press, 2006.
Corcuera, Javier, *La patria de los vascos. Orígenes, ideología y organización del nacionalismo vasco, 1876-1903.* Madrid: Taurus, 2001. English: *The Origins, Ideology, and Organization of Basque Nationalism, 1876-1903.* Translated by Albert Bork and Cameron J. Watson. Reno: Center for Basque Studies, University of Nevada, Reno, 2006.
Delanty, Gerard. "Nationalism and Cosmopolitanism: The Paradox of Modernity." In *The Sage Handbook of Nations and Nationalism*, edited by Gerard Delanty and Krishnan Kumar. London: Sage, 2006.
Douglass, William A. *La Vasconia Global. Ensayos sobre las diásporas vascas.* Vitoria-Gasteiz: Gobierno Vasco, 2003. English: *Global Vasconia: Essays on the Basque Diaspora.* Reno: Center for Basque Studies, University of Nevada, Reno, 2006.
Douglass, William A., and Jon Bilbao. *Amerikanuak: Basques in the New World.* Reno: University of Nevada Press, 1975.
Gal, Allon, Athena S. Leoussi, and Anthony D. Smith, eds. *The Call of the Homeland: Diaspora Nationalisms, Past and Present.* Leiden and Boston: Brill, 2010.
Goiogana, Iñaki. "José Antonio Aguirre, profesor en la Columbia University." In *Exilio y universidad (1936-1955). Presencia y realidades*, coordinated by José Angel Asunce, Mónica Jato, and María Luisa San Miguel. San Sebastián: Ed. Saturraran, 2008.
Granja, José Luis de la. *El oasis vasco. El nacimiento de Euskadi en la República y la Guerra Civil.* Madrid: Tecnos, 2007.
————. *Ángel o demonio: Sabino Arana. El patriarca del nacionalismo vasco.* Madrid: Tecnos, 2015.

Hall, John A. "Conditions for National Homogenizers." In *Nationalism and its Futures*, edited by Umut Özkirimli. Houndmills and New York: Palgrave-Macmillan, 2003.

Irujo, Xabier. *Expelled from the Motherland: The Government of President José Antonio Agirre in Exile, 1937-1960.* Translated by Cameron Watson and Jennifer Ottman. Reno: Center for Basque Studies, University of Nevada, Reno, 2012.

Jacob, James Edwin. *Hills of Conflict: Basque Nationalism in France.* Reno: University of Nevada Press, 1994.

Jiménez de Aberásturi, Juan Carlos. *De la derrota a la esperanza: políticas vascas durante la Segunda Guerra Mundial (1937–1947).* Bilbao: IVAP, 1999.

Jiménez de Aberásturi, Juan Carlos, and Rafael Moreno Izquierdo. *Al servicio del extranjero. Historia del servicio vasco de información (1936–1943).* Madrid: Machado Libros, 2009.

Kershaw, Ian. *Wendepunkte. Schlüsselentscheidungen im Zweiten Weltkrieg.* 2nd ed. München: DVA , 2008. Original English edition: *Fateful Choices: The Decisions That Changed the World, 1940–1941.* London: Allen Lane 2007.

Knott, Kim, and Sean McLoughlin, eds. *Diasporas: Concepts, Identities, Intersections.* London: Zed Books, 2010.

Lachenicht, Susanne, and Kirsten Heinsohn, eds. *Diaspora Identities: Exile, Nationalism and Cosmopolitanism in Past and Present.* Frankfurt and New York: Campus, 2009.

Langer, William L., and S. Everett Gleason, *1940–1941: The Undeclared War.* New York: Harper & Brothers, 1953.

Larronde, Jean-Claude. *Exilio y Solidaridad. La Liga Internacional de Amigos de los Vascos.* Villefranque: Bidasoa, 1997.

Linz, Juan. "Early State-Building and Late Peripheral Nationalisms Against the State: The Case of Spain." In *Building States and Nations*, vol. 2, edited by Shmuel N. Eisenstadt and Stein Rokkan. Beverly Hills: Sage, 1973.

Mees, Ludger. "Der, spanische Sonderweg': Staat und Nation(en) im Spanien des 19. und 20. Jahrhunderts." *Archiv für Sozialgeschichte* 40 (2000): 29–66.

———. *Nationalism, Violence and Democracy: The Basque Clash of Identities.* New York: Palgrave-Macmillan, 2003.

———. *El profeta pragmático. Aguirre, el primer lehendakari (1939–1960).* Irún: Alberdania, 2006.

———. "Tan lejos, tan cerca. El Gobierno Vasco en Barcelona y las complejas relaciones entre el nacionalismo vasco y el catalán." *Historia Contemporánea* 37 (2008): 557–91.

————. "Rückständiges Zentrum, moderne Peripherie. Probleme des spanischen Nation Building im 19. und 20. Jahrhundert." In *Ränder der Moderne. Neue Perspektiven auf die Europäische Geschichte (1800-1930)*, edited by Christof Dejung and Martin Lengwiler. Köln: Böhlau, 2016.

Mota, David. *Un sueño americano: el Gobierno Vasco en el exilio y Estados Unidos (1937-1979)*. Oñati: IVAP, 2016.

Pablo, Santiago de, Ludger Mees, and José Antonio Rodríguez Ranz. *El péndulo patriótico. Historia del Partido Nacionalista Vasco*, vol. 1. Barcelona: Crítica, 1999.

————. *El Péndulo Patriótico. Historia del Partido Nacionalista Vasco*, vol. 2. Barcelona: Crítica, 2001.

Portes, Alejandro. "Globalization from Below: The Rise of Transnational Communities." In *Latin America in the World Economy*, edited by William C. Smith and Roberto Patricio Korczenwicz. Westport: Greenwood Press, 1996.

Portes, Alejandro, Luis E. Guarnizo, and Patricia Landholt. "The Study of Transnationalism: Pitfalls and Promises of an Emergent Research Field." *Ethnic and Racial Studies* 22, no. 2 (1999): 217–37.

San Sebastián, Koldo. *El exilio vasco en América. 1936/1946. Acción del gobierno*. San Sebastián: Txertoa, 1988.

Serrallonga I Urquidi, Joan. *Refugiats i desplaçats dins la Catalunya en guerra 1936–1939*. Barcelona: Ed. Base, 2004.

Tilly, Charles. *From Mobilization to Revolution*. New York: McGraw-Hill, 1978.

Totoricagüena, Gloria. *Diáspora vasca comparada. Etnicidad, cultura y política en las colectividades vascas*. Vitoria-Gasteiz: Gobierno Vasco, 2003.

————. *The Basques of New York: A Cosmopolitan Experience*. Vitoria-Gasteiz: Gobierno Vasco, 2003.

Vertovec, Steven. "Conceiving and Researching Transnationalism." *Ethnic and Racial Studies* 22, no. 2 (1999): 447–62.

Wallace Brown, Garrett. "Cosmopolitanism." In *The Concise Oxford Dictionary of Politics*, edited by Iain McLean and Alistair McMillan. 3rd ed. Oxford : Oxford University Press, 2009. Online at http://www.oxfordreference.com/view (accessed May 6, 2016).

9

Agirre's Goverment and Europe's Political Construction

Leyre Arrieta

Antecedents (1895–1945)

Sabino Arana, the founder of Basque nationalism, and the early leaders of the PNV gave almost no attention to Europe and continental issues. However, interest in Europe increased over the years, especially after World War I and articles and references relevant to European matters began to appear in the nationalist press. Basque nationalists became aware of the demands of other European minorities and stateless nations, and those demands became part of their own thinking. The PNV shared this growing interest in Europe, which for these nations represented progress, democracy, plurality, and diversity of languages and cultures, along with new political hopes and possibilities. Europeanism in the PNV, and later in other Basque nationalist groups, was always linked to the issues of national minorities. After 1915, Europe came to be seen as a platform for broadcasting national demands and an adequate arena for internationalizing the "Basque national question." The nationalist press reflected this growing interest in European events and nationalist politicians attended the Third Conference of the Union of European Nationalities in Lausanne, Switzerland, in 1916, along with several other Conferences of European Nationalities.[1]

---

1. The following articles and books are of interest for a deeper understanding of the external action of Basque nationalism in its early years: Xosé Manoel Núñez-Seixas, "¿Protodiplomacia exterior o ilusiones ópticas? El nacionalismo vasco, el contexto internacional y el Congreso de Nacionali-

During the 1920s and 1930s, interest in international and especially European themes steadily increased. Europe became more
central to nationalist proposals, basically for three reasons. First, a
new generation of nationalist leaders, led by Agirre and destined
to bring about the ideological renewal of the party and the government, embraced the "Paneurope" concept of Austrian aristocrat
Richard Coudenhove-Kalergi, founder of the Paneuropean Union.
This Union was a political concept of a Europe built around politics rather than geography.[2]

Second, these men read and were sympathetic to the person-
alist approach that later involved integral federalism. In fact, the
central element of integral federalism was unity in diversity. Even
though there are no explicit references to these ideas in the writings of Agirre, his lexical constructions clearly reflect the personal-
ist texts of authors such as Alexandre Marc, Emmanuele Mounier,
and Denis de Rougemont, with many references to human beings,
humanity, and the family.[3]

The reflections of Agirre regarding human beings and nationalities are completed in the following works: *Cinco conferencias pronunciadas en un viaje por América* (Five Speeches Given
during a Trip to the Americas, 1944) and *De Guernica a Nueva
York pasando por Berlín* (From Guernica to New York by Means of
Berlin, 1943). In these publications there are frequent references to
the fact that,

---

dades Europeas (1914–1917)," *Cuadernos de Sección. Historia-Geografía. Eusko
Ikaskuntza-Sociedad de Estudios Vascos* 23 (1995), 243–75 and *Entre Ginebra y
Berlín* (Madrid: Akal, 2001); Xosé Estévez, "El nacionalismo vasco y los Con-
gresos de Minorías Nacionales de la Sociedad de Naciones (1916–1936)," in *XI
Congreso de Estudios Vascos. Nuevas formulaciones culturales: Euskal Herria y
Europa* (Donostia-San Sebastián: Eusko Ikaskuntza/Sociedad de Estudios Vas-
cos, 1992), 312–22; Alexander Ugalde, *La Acción Exterior del Nacionalismo
Vasco (1890–1939): Historia, Pensamiento y Relaciones internacionales* (Oñati:
HAEE/IVAP, 1996) and "Entrada del nacionalismo vasco en el Congreso de
Nacionalidades Europeas, 1929–30: siguiendo la documentación del Fondo
Apraiz," *Revista Internacional de Estudios Vascos* 42, no. 2 (1997), 403–421.

2. The proposals of this visionary Europeanist have been compiled in two books
by Richard Coudenhove-Kalergi, *Una bandera llamada Europa* (Barcelona: Argos, 1961) and *Paneuropea. Dedicado a la juventud de Europa* (Madrid: Tecnos,
2011).

3. These ideas can be found in the works of Denis de Rougemont, Guy Héraud,
Emmanuel Mounier, and Alexandre Marc (see references).

> Christianity, with its doctrines of fraternity and equality among
> all men and all peoples, offered a key doctrinal base that fit with
> an international organization that was built on mutual respect
> and an agreement among equals. For me as a Christian, ladies
> and gentlemen, it is clear that the doctrine of Christ established
> the foundation for the human order, both at an individual and a
> collective level.[4]

Also that,

> Europe is again the scenario of the rise of nationalities, as the
> birthplace and seat of different peoples and civilizations. Indi-
> vidual and social liberty were insufficient if the national soul of
> peoples was not being treated with respect . . . State and Nation
> are not the same thing . . . What matters for the peace of the
> world is the problem of the Nations, as these were made by God,
> and States are more or less just political creations, as is every-
> thing made by men.[5]

The third and maybe the main reason why Europe became
more central was that these young politicians established contact
with prominent representatives of Christian Democracy, like Luigi
Sturzo and Jacques Maritain. These connections were later reinforced and consolidated during World War II.

This younger generation would also be the most fervent in
defending the Europeanist project. A significant and much trum-
peted example of the deep-rooted Europeanism of the Basque
nationalists was the celebration of the second *Aberri Eguna*, or
Basque Homeland Day in Donostia-San Sebastián in 1933, under
the slogan "Euskadi–Europa" (Basque Country-Europe). This
event was attended by more than 5,000 followers. Moreover, the
International League of Friends of the Basques (Liga Internacional
de Amigos de los Vascos, LIAV) was created in Paris in 1938. The
League was established with the objective of helping Basque refugees in France, and as an organ to inform the public regarding the
problems faced by the Basques as a people. It received the support
of prominent French individuals.[6] Mainly thanks to the efforts of

---

4. José Antonio Aguirre, *Cinco conferencias pronunciadas en un viaje por
América* (Buenos Aires: Ekin, 1944), 168.
5. José Antonio Aguirre, *De Guernica a Nueva York pasando por Berlín* (Buenos
Aires: Ekin, 1943), 364.
6. Such as cardinal Jean Verdier, Archbishop of Paris; monsignor Clement

journalist Pierre Dumas, the League was able to carry on an intense level of activity and, due to the well-known figures involved, was for several years a valuable instrument for direct influence upon the French government.[7]

Consequently, during World War II, nationalist politicians were very active internationally, participating in the Cultural Union of Western European Countries, in the Federal Union, and in the International Christian Democratic Union, all of which were deeply Europeanist. As the outcome of the war became favorable to the Allies, initiatives and proposals for unity in Europe were launched en masse, many seeking the construction of a Europe built on bases other than states. Basque nationalist hopes for a future in that Europe increased accordingly.

Basque Government Activity in Different Europeanist Movements and Organizations (1945–1950)

Let us now see how the Basque government took an active part in several Europeanist initiatives in immediate post-World War II period, arguably the most promising moment for nationalist hopes at this time.

Golden years (1945–1948)

After World War II, many movements and organizations emerged seeking a united Europe capable of recovering its past prominence and that saw itself overshadowed by two international giants: the United States and the USSR. Europeanist initiatives that were initially private in nature began to enjoy popular support, which spread to political leaders and eventually governments. Basque nationalists interpreted this as an extremely advantageous panorama. After two painful and cruel wars in quick succession, Basques imagined that in reconstructing the continent, European countries would give the nationalities within their borders due consideration as a way to ward off future conflict.

Mathieu, Bishop of Aire et Dax; George Rivollet, former minister and Secretary General of the Confederation Nationale des Anciens Combattants; François Mauriac, member of the French Academie, and so on.

7. Jean Claude Larronde, *Exilio y Solidaridad. La Liga Internacional de Amigos de los Vascos* (Bilbao: Bidasoa, 1988).

Moreover, Agirre and his colleagues had another, external reason for optimism: the excellent relations that they developed in the United States.[8] During his years in exile in New York, Lehendakari (President) Agirre had established close links with prominent European and North American politicians and intellectuals who were living there, such the aforementioned Sturzo and Maritain. For these reasons, the second half of the 1940s was the period of greatest expectation for Agirre's Government.

During these years, optimism permeated the Basque government's membership. Though in hindsight it may appear exaggerated and illusory, Basques at that time were being invited to many international events. Lehendakari Agirre was a gifted and charismatic leader whose fame had spread in tandem with the story of his dramatic escape from Europe to the United States, and Basque representatives were very active between 1945 and 1948, when the Basque Nationalist Party (Partido Nacionalista Vasco, PNV) and the Basque government achieved their highest level of recognition in Europe and enjoyed successes that further fueled their confidence.

Although the Basque Europeanist program was neither explicit nor well-defined until Javier Landaburu published *La Causa del pueblo vasco* (The Cause of the Basque People, 1956), it was in the years immediately following World War II when the cardinal points of this discourse about Europe were established. The basis of this discourse was the Agirre Doctrine, arguing for the full recognition and participation of the Basque Country in Europe as a member nation. The Agirre plan was based on a supposed crisis of the nation-state and foresaw a federal configuration of Europe based on peoples or infra-state entities, rather than states. It defended the right for the freedom of peoples with enough political will and capacity to be autonomous. This perspective had already been expressed by Agirre in 1945 in an article

---

8. On relations in the United States, see David Mota Zurdo, *Un sueño americano. El Gobierno Vasco en el exilio y Estados Unidos (1937–1979)* (Oñati: IVAP, 2016); Juan Carlos Jiménez de Aberásturi and Rafael Moreno Izquierdo, *Al servicio del extranjero. Historia del Servicio Vasco de Información (1936–43)* (Madrid: Antonio Machado Libros, 2008); José Félix Azurmendi, *Vascos en la Guerra Fría. ¿Víctimas o cómplices? Gudaris en el juego de los espías* (Donostia: Ttarttalo, 2013), and also Koldo San Sebastián, "J. A. Aguirre: Democracia cristiana y europeísmo en EEUU," *Hermes. Revista de Pensamiento e Historia* 34 (2010): 2–81.

titled "L'homme et la Nationalité. Bases de la Paix future" ("Man and Nationality. Bases of the Future Peace").[9]

The name of this doctrinal approach, the Agirre Doctrine, comes from the fact that Agirre was one of its most fervent defenders. But, he was not the only one. Input from Jose María Lasarte, Manuel Irujo, Jesús María Leizola, Jesús Galíndez, and, above all, the abovementioned Landaburu, enriched and completed this theoretical base.

They thought that the Europeanist project could be inserted seamlessly into the doctrinal framework of Basque nationalism, since a federal Europe would provide a natural solution to the "Basque national question." In their opinion, a reduction in the sovereignty of the states might offer new opportunities for stateless nations such as the Basque Country. This was the ideal framework for constructing and consolidating Basque identity and the ideal platform for broadcasting the demands of the Basque people. It also circumvented the stereotypical accusations levelled against Basque nationalism that it was consciously isolationist. The following significant comments were pronounced by Iñaki Unceta, Secretary of the National Council of the Basque Nationalist Party (Euzkadi Buru Batzarra, EBB):

> Those who think we want to close ourselves in our own world of songs and dances are not well informed. What we want is to retain and love what is ours, protecting our essence and our full personality, while openly showing it to others and learning whatever we should learn, without ever forgetting who we are. We are an old tree that grows new and robust young branches, a tree that must not and will not break loose of its roots, because then it would die.[10]

Besides being a platform to show the Basque situation and avoid the accusations of isolationism, Europe also created a context for encouraging political hostility toward the Franco regime among European and American states.

---

9. *Euzko-Deya* (Paris) 211, March 31, 1945, 1–2. It can also be found in José Antonio Agirre, "El problema de las nacionalidades ante la Federación Europea," in *Obras Completas*, vol. 2 (San Sebastian: Sendoa, 1981).

10. Letter from Iñaki Unceta to Francisco Javier Landaburu, Bayonne (Baiona), October 14, 1949, AN (PNV Archives in the Sabino Arana Foundation), EBB, 120–3.

In sum, Agirre and his government saw Europe as an open door to new political aspirations and possibilities. They had arrived at this door by two separate but not divergent paths: the Christian Democratic movement and federalism. The Basques' involvement in these two frameworks was not at all contrived. Alignment with these doctrinal bases provided the Basques with two practical paths toward Europe and gave them access to the European Movement—the main promotor of Europe's political construction—and, in turn, to the European construction process. If it had not been for the relations the Basque nationalists had developed in earlier years, they would never have been allowed to take part in the process of European integration.

So, on the one hand, we have the Christian Democracy. As I said previously, the contacts with those groups and personalities were not artificial at all. On the contrary, they were a natural consequence of their own convictions and the development of Basque nationalism. Beforehand, in 1942, on his American trip, Agirre had proposed the idea of celebrating a South American Catholic personalities' Congress. In addition, in December, the *lehendakari* signed a manifesto with another forty-three Catholic intellectuals who lived in the United States. This manifesto dealt with the Christian values on which any society must be founded in the future.

In this Christian Democratic sphere, the PNV maintained relations with other parties, principally the French MRP (Mouvement Republicain Populaire, Popular Republican Movement), the Italian DC (Democrazia Cristiana, Christian Democracy), and the German CDU (Christlich Demokratische Union, Christian Democratic Union). Some of these parties were led by charismatic pro-European politicians like George Bidault, Alcide De Gasperi, and Konrad Adenauer.[11] And this fact contributed to the development of Christian Democracy and, definitely, to the promotion of Europeanism. The PNV and the Basque government had close relationships with some of them, above all with the French and Italian parties. Basque nationalists were in several MRP congresses. Agirre, together with Landaburu and other colleagues, participated, for example, in MRP national congresses in 1949, 1951, 1954, and 1959, and was always received with warm applause.

---

11. See Michael Gehler and Wolfram Kaiser, eds., *Christian Democracy in Europe since 1945*, vol. 2 (New York: Routledge, 2004).

Actually, in 1947 the PNV was a founding member of the New International Teams (Nouvelles Équipes Internationales, NEI), the most important Christian Democratic organization in Europe. In fact, some of its meetings were even held at 11 Avenue Marceau, the Parisian seat of the Basque government-in-exile. For the PNV, the NEI was the most important way to enter into the Christian Democratic sphere: First, because this organization was a cornerstone within this framework in Europe and in the world as well; and second, since the PNV participated in it as an autonomous rather than as a Spanish group.[12] And this condition provided the PNV with some privileges that were maintained until 1960, when a Spanish party (DSC, Democracia Social Cristiana, Christian Social Democracy) asked to join the NEI. Basques participated in almost all the congresses of this body. From 1947 to 1958, Agirre took part in all except those of 1949 and 1957. Moreover, Agirre was a member of the Honorary Committee of the NEI and Landaburu was a member of its first Executive Committee. In the meetings and congresses of this body, Basques took advantage of the opportunity to interview important political figures like Luigi Sturzo, Alcide de Gasperi, and so on.

At the global level, Basque representatives also participated in the American Christian Democratic Organization, and took part in some of its congresses (for example, in Santiago de Chile and in New York in 1955, in Paris in 1956, and in Brussels in 1958).

On the other hand, we find federalism, the second door that Basques used to join European organizations. That door was opened when Landaburu and Juan Carlos Basterra (a politician of another nationalist party, the ANV, Acción Nacionalista Vasca, Basque Nationalist Action), took part in the Federalist World Conference held in Luxemburg in October 1946. Following Agirre's orders, Basterra and Landaburu traveled there exclusively as representatives of the Basque government. When they signed the minutes of the conference as representatives of the inexistent Basque Federalist Movement (Movimiento Federalista Vasco, MFV), both of them became, informally and unknowingly, the founders of that movement. Officially, this Basque federalist organization was founded in March 1947. Besides Basque nationalists, Basque

---

12. On this seat's symbolism, see Leyre Arrieta, "El simbolismo poliédrico del nº 11 de la Avenue Marceau de París," in *La celebración de la nación. Símbolos, mitos y lugares de memoria*, ed. Ludger Mees (Granada: Comares, 2012), 117–34.

republicans and socialists joined the new organization as well. At the Spanish level, the PNV participated actively in the constitution of the Federalist Spanish Council of the European Movement (Consejo Federal Español del Movimiento Europeo, CFEME) in 1949. At the Basque level, another federalist body was founded in 1951: the European Federalist Basque Council (Consejo Vasco por la Federación Europea, CVFE, today Eurobask).[13]

The foundation of the Basque Federalist Movement enabled the Basques to join the most important federal body in Europe: the Union of European Federalists (UEF). It was constituted in a congress held in Montreux (Switzerland) in 1947. This Union defended an integral federalist program and was born with an absolutely European vocation. Moreover, it was the link between several federalist tendencies. Through this body Basques could also participate in the aforementioned and very important European Movement.

After the inaugural congress, the next meeting of the UEF was the really famous congress in The Hague, held in May 1948. Three Basques, President Agirre, Landaburu, and Basterra, participated in this significant event. At the beginning, they were forbidden to join it, apparently, because of pressure from Salvador de Madariaga, a Spanish writer and president of the Cultural Committee of the European Movement. However, in the end, thanks to the help of the French and the Dutch, they were able to participate as onlookers, not as official participants. But, anyway, I would like to underline the fact that these three men were there, in the conference that has been considered the beginning of the process of building a United Europe.

In this same year, 1948, the Basque Federalist Movement participated in another UEF congress, held in Rome in November. The last UEF congress that decade took place in Strasbourg in 1950.

In the next few paragraphs, the frictions between two groups within the PNV will be explained. The people who represented the Basque government and Basque Nationalist Party in all those meetings and organizations were called "the Paris group." It was a group made up of the generation of young politicians I mentioned

---

13. Landaburu described the founding of the MFV in the article "De Luxemburgo a Estrasburgo," *Alderdi* 32 (November 1949), 13. On the CVFE, see Alexander Ugalde, *El Consejo Vasco del Movimiento Europeo (1951–2001)* (Vitoria-Gasteiz: Consejo Vasco del Movimiento Europeo, 2001).

before. Led by Agirre, they represented the most modern, democratic, and Europeanist contingent of the PNV. The most noteworthy of these was the previously mentioned Landaburu, the main
representative of the Basque government in Europe. Alongside
him were *Lehendakari* Agirre, Manuel Irujo, Jesús María Leizola,
and José María Lasarte. Also prominent were Iñaki Rentería and
Iñaki Agirre, members of the PNV youth organization.

These men were in Paris working in principle only for the government and the PNV's governing body, the aforementioned EBB,
was based in Iparralde, the Basque territory in France, hundreds of
kilometers away. But, since these individuals were in Paris, where
important matters were decided on, and because they really were
a small group, they ended up representing both the Basque government and the PNV in European bodies and forums. Ultimately,
it was this that caused the conflict of interest. The occasional disagreements between the "Paris group" and the PNV leadership
had to do with this double role: who were Landaburu and his colleagues representing, the government or the party?

And it so happened that, as the Paris group assimilated the
idea of a united Europe and began to comprehend the reality of
the situation, their pragmatism increased, their position became
more moderate, and the initial demands of Basque nationalism
faded into the background. Familiarity with day-to-day Europeanist politics and feasible possibilities distanced them intellec-
tually from classical concepts of sovereignty and independence
as they sought other ways of articulating their demands in Spain
and Europe. This created distrust among the non-Parisian leaders, who were under constant pressure from the Arana wing, the
most radical wing of the party. Divergent paths became apparent in 1949 over the creation of the Federalist Spanish Council of
the European Movement. Agirre, along with the abovementioned
Spanish writer Salvador Madariaga, had promoted this council
and logically pushed for PNV participation; and it is significant
that the organization was officially launched at the seat of the
Basque government-in-exile.

Though the EBB did not reject PNV collaboration with other
Spanish political forces and representatives, as expected, the Arana
wing criticized it openly. This wing was more orthodox and sought
to uphold the tenets of the founder, never renouncing independence for the Basque Country. In practice, this meant avoiding any
actual commitment to Spain or Spanish political forces.

Another troubling source of friction for the party leadership was that the Parisian contingent was not always eager to comply with its orders. The desire to be everywhere, shake every hand, and take advantage of every opportunity provided by context, chance, or contact, led to many occasions on which the Parisian-based politicians had to improvise. They had to make spontaneous decisions without waiting for instructions from afar.

Lehendakari Agirre was the nexus between the two currents, maybe the only leader capable of reconciling opposing positions. And he achieved it. But Agirre died in 1960. In the decade following his unexpected death, and especially after 1970, the fracture deepened between those in Paris and PNV members based in the Basque provinces.

Major Change in 1948

But now let us go back to 1948. At this stage, the Basque government and the men in Paris were determined to participate in everything possible. These were difficult times for them; so it was hoped that taking advantage of every opportunity would serve as a magic wand to guarantee a dignified existence or even recognition in the European arena. Significantly, until 1948 the PNV was the only democratic "Spanish" contingent in European bodies. However, with the onset of the Cold War in 1947, Franco's Spain began to be perceived on both sides of the Atlantic as a valuable geostrategic asset in the fight against communism. Western European countries stopped condemning the Franco regime and initiated bilateral relations. The 1948 Congress of The Hague, whose central objective was to create a united Europe, reinforced a state-based Europe and thwarted the aspirations of federalist currents and, of course, of the Basque nationalists.

Though disappointed, the Basque nationalists continued to look to Europe. Landaburu expressed the fact that they remained confident in a federal Europe, "in spite of disappointments and obstacles," because "if the heart is missing, Europe will only be an abstract concept for sociologists and politicians but indifferent for the masses."[14] Moreover, Europe was the only viable option for

---

14. The first quote is from Francisco Javier Landaburu, "Nacimiento de Europa," OPE (the Basque government bulletin), no. 574 (1949), 1–2, published in "Ante el resurgir de Europa," *Euzko Deya* (Buenos Aires) 366 (1949), 1. The second quote is from Francisco Javier Landaburu, "L'Ame populaire de l'Europe,"

toppling the Franco regime, after the Basques had been "abandoned" by the United States and the monarchical-socialist plan of Prieto had failed. In his book *La Causa del pueblo vasco* (The Cause of the Basque People), Landaburu justified this choice and explained that accepting the Europe of the states was the lesser evil on the road to a better Europe. He states:

> Today the Europe of the States is being constructed because it is the easiest and fastest to make and because one of the stimuli for organizing Europe is fear. When this fear subsides and doctrine matures, it will be possible to build a Europe of the Peoples. In that Europe, no one will be able to deny us our place as a federalist and pacifist people, since Europe will have no other finality than peace.[15]

Years later, another of the main Basque nationalist leaders, Manuel Irujo, explained this decision clearly: "[in The Hague] Basques had in their hearts and minds a Europe of the Peoples. What was born instead was the Europe of the States. Agirre and company had to choose between a Europe of the States or no Europe at all; not different versions of Europe. They accepted the Europe of the States."[16]

Disillusion and Resignation (1950–1970)

A transcendental decade in the process of European integration, and a truly critical period for the Basque government, began in 1950. European countries overcame internal political instability and consolidated their political and economic situations. Gigantic steps were taken toward European integration with the creation of the European Coal and Steel Community, the Common Market, and the Euratom. As the links between countries grew stronger, transatlantic relations and anti-communism thrived in Western democracies. This also led to improved relations with the Franco regime, which was useful as another shield against communism.

Euzko Deya (Paris) 309 (1949), 3.

15. Francisco Javier Landaburu, *La causa del pueblo vasco* (Bilbao: Editorial Geu, 1977), 227.

16. Manuel Irujo, "Euzkadi–Europa I," *Alderdi* 274 (1972), 7–8. The dilemma Irujo described has not gone away, as we shall see in the various tendencies within Basque nationalism. The PNV decision to stay aboard the European train, though it was not going on the fast and direct track they had hoped for, is still valid today.

In turn, the Franco government reinforced its Europeanist tendencies and sought new connections with European institutions and organisms.[17] Though Spain was blocked from access to official bodies while under a dictatorship, the regime managed to join international cooperation networks. The gradual rehabilitation of the Franco regime and its increasingly open relations with the US government became two "evils" in this unhappy phase of history, from the Basque standpoint. It is important to note the blind faith placed in the US government by *Lehendakari* Agirre. The agreement signed in 1953 between Washington and General Franco only reinforced the fact that cooperation was now irreversible. Yet even in this context, Agirre predicted that this bilateral agreement would never actually have the significance expected of it. He continued to believe that US policy would necessarily seek out a fully democratic Europe.

This decade could not have begun on a worse footing for the Basque nationalists. In June 1951, the Basque government-in-exile was ordered by the French government to abandon its seat at 11 Avenue Marceau. The building had acquired enormous symbolic significance for Basque and Spanish democrats, as a center of democracy and European integration. Many years later, Mari Zabala, Agirre's widow, said that rarely had she seen her husband so sad as in that moment. As well as this, financial difficulties led to the departure a number of PNV members, leaving the party and the government in crisis and totally unable to react to the emergence in 1959 of ETA (Euskadi ta Askatasuna, the Basque Country and Freedom organization). ETA was born as a cultural group against the Franco regime, but later it embraced the armed struggle. It committed its first murder in 1968.

Given these tribulations, or perhaps it was because there was no other option, the Basque government continued to see Europe as a viable alternative and a last hope for overthrowing the Franco regime. Nationalists focused their efforts on nurturing the good foreign relations that had been cultivated after the World War II and preventing Franco's Spain from participating in European bodies or frontline European politics.

---

17. For further reading on the strategy of diminishing the gap between the Franco regime and Europe, see Antonio Moreno Juste, *Franquismo y construcción europea* (Madrid: Tecnos/Movimiento Europeo, 1998) and Julio Crespo MacLennan, *España en Europa (1945–2000). Del ostracismo a la modernidad* (Madrid: Marcial Pons, 2004).

But in the 1950s their presence in European forums diminished. And, in addition, there was a willingness to cooperate with Spanish institutions as a means of participating in Europe: a position that in previous years had created serious concern in the most extreme wing of the PNV. The relevant European bodies were designed around party participation on a state level; so when other Spanish political parties began to seek involvement in these entities, the PNV was obliged to capitulate and join in with these other parties in order to avoid exclusion. Theoretically, the PNV did not renounce separatism or independence, but the context forced a strategic and transitory suppression of these demands.

The unexpected death of Agirre in March 1960 marked the end of this critical stage and the beginning of a new phase in Basque exile history, which lasted until 1977. During this time the Common Market managed to attract new members. Meanwhile, encouraged by the economic growth of the 1960s, the Franco regime began to try to develop relations with Europe and managed to sign several commercial treaties.

And, maintaining the prior decade's tendency, the PNV joined forces with other Spanish democratic groups in an attempt to prevent any potential participation of the Franco government in Europe; even though this approach had previously been criticized by the less pragmatic sector of the party. This strategy was adopted with the long-term goal of being well-positioned for the transition period that would follow the death of the dictator. The Basques also took advantage of the European trend in the 1960s and further repeated its discourse, favoring a "Europe of the Peoples." Integral federalist currents enjoyed a revival in the 1960s, protected by official policies favoring regions. "Europe of the Regions" and "Europe of the Ethnicities" became popular terms. However, these fell short of the Basque nationalist vision for a "Europe of the Peoples," in which the Basque Country figured as a nation, not a region.[18]

Early in this phase, new Basque nationalist groups emerged that also considered themselves Europeanist, such as ETA and the French Basque nationalist group Enbata. With the double objective of countering the potential allure of these groups in

---

18. These ideas are found in press articles such as: "¿Por qué luchamos los vascos? Por la integración europea," *Alderdi* 186 (October 1962), 19–20. They can also be seen in AN, EBB, 15-1; and "Al pueblo Vasco," *Alderdi* 226–227 (February–March 1966), 3–6.

Europeanist circles and in order to reaffirm their hard-earned position in Europe, the PNV organized the 1968 Aberri Eguna or Basque Homeland Day in Donostia-San Sebastián under the same "Euskadi–Europe" slogan that had been used in 1933. This was a way of clearly indicating that the PNV had been the elder statesman in pro-European matters.

Conclusion: The Symbolic Dimension of Europe

From its founding in 1895 through the end of Franco's dictatorship, several phases can be identified that led to the evolution of the Agirre government's Europeanist project. These reflect the varying attitudes, areas of focus, international contexts, and political moments in the history of Basque nationalism. The first phase extends from 1895 until the end of World War II, a period in which foreign involvement, and especially issues regarding Europe, gradually gained in importance in party plans. The second phase (1945–1950) was one of great expectation that began with the Allied victory in World War II. These early postwar years were the "golden age" of Basque nationalist involvement in Europe and were marked by the rise of its Europeanist discourse and the establishment of a rich network of links between Basque leaders and European bodies or parties. Never before had Basque nationalists relied so much on Europe. Previously unimaginable doors were opened in the infancy of European construction. However, the outcome of European integration was radically different from that which Agirre and his colleagues had hoped for. The 1950s was a phase of disillusion, when hopes in the opportunities Europe might offer the Basque Country turned into disappointment in the face of the political reality. This was followed by a phase of resignation extending from 1960 until 1977, which was characterized by resigned but voluntary participation in Spanish bodies. During this period Basque nationalists adopted the then-fashionable term "Europe of the Peoples." This concept is still operative, and remains the leitmotiv of the Europeanist discourse of the PNV and other Basque nationalist parties, whose discourse is based on the concept of European construction as an unfinished process and has remained almost unchanged since 1977.

At this point, we must wonder if Basque nationalist European politics in exile was a success or a failure. The answer must be double and ambiguous. On the one hand, the presence of the Basque nationalists in the NEI or in The Hague Congress, or their participation in bodies like the European Movement that influenced European Political construction, must be considered successful, without any doubt. However, the Basques' representation in these European bodies was not autonomous, with the exception of the NEI. The Basques' aspiration to have direct representations in European bodies, not through the Spanish groups, was not possible. In addition, the entities in which Basques took part had no official character. They were private.

On the other hand, regarding the consequences of the Basques' European politics, we can consider them disappointing, and even more so if we take into account the Basques' initial claims, which saw Europe as one of the best allies to finish with the Franco regime. The simple truth is that, apart from continuous demonstrations of sympathy and one or another statement against the Franco regime, little else was what Basques got at those events. Many years later, a journalist asked Irujo: "What did you do in those European forums?" And Irujo, with his usual honesty, answered: "What did we do? We made fools of ourselves. But if we had to do it for the Basque Country, we just did it."

Nevertheless, the politics that I termed the "politics of the presence," of being in all the events and at all the meetings they could, enabled the nationalists' claims to be listened to in European forums and they made contacts with representatives of other stateless nations. In addition, these forums served to spread and make known the Basque situation, and, principally, to denounce the Franco regime's atrocities.

Finally, to conclude, I would like to underline the symbolism of Europe for the Basque nationalists. The symbolic dimension of Europe was even greater during the long exile of the Basque government. It was the ideal playing field and the privileged podium from which to broadcast issues involved in the "Basque national question." Postwar Europe was a beacon of democracy and the best antidote to totalitarian regimes such as Francoism. The common Europeanist sentiment even became a critical link between Spanish democratic forces and Basque nationalists. Authoritarian regimes such as the one led by General Franco had no place in the framework of democratic Europe. Consequently, support for a united Europe was also a fight for freedom and a struggle against Franco. In the eyes of Basque nationalists, Europe represented *askatasunaren itxaropena* ("the hope of freedom" in Euskara, the Basque language).

So, since the Basque nationalists first envisioned the possibility of the Basque Country fitting into a broader context, Europe has been present in nationalist thinking as a place of opportunity and a final horizon for articulating a future in which Euskadi, the Basque Country, could control its own destiny.

Bibliography

Aguirre, José Antonio. *De Guernica a Nueva York pasando por Berlín*. Buenos Aires: Ekin, 1943.

———. *Cinco conferencias pronunciadas en un viaje por América*. Buenos Aires: Ekin, 1944.

———. *Obras Completas*. 2 vols. San Sebastián: Sendoa, 1981.

Arrieta, Leyre. *Estación Europa. La política europeísta del PNV en el exilio (1945–1977)*. Madrid: Tecnos, 2007.

———. "El simbolismo poliédrico del n° 11 de la Avenue Marceau de París." *In La celebración de la nación. Símbolos, mitos y lugares de memoria*, edited by Ludger Mees (Granada: Comares, 2012).

Azurmendi, José Félix. *Vascos en la Guerra Fría. ¿Víctimas o cómplices? Gudaris en el juego de los espías*. Donostia: Ttarttalo, 2013.

Coudenhove-Kalergi, Richard. *Una bandera llamada Europa*. Barcelona: Argos, 1961.

———. *Paneuropea. Dedicado a la juventud de Europa*. Madrid: Tecnos, 2011.

Crespo MacLennan, Julio. *España en Europa (1945–2000). Del ostraciscmo a la modernidad*. Madrid: Marcial Pons, 2004.

Estévez, Xosé. "El nacionalismo vasco y los Congresos de Minorías Nacionales de la Sociedad de Naciones (1916–1936)." In *XI Congreso de Estudios Vascos. Nuevas formulaciones culturales: Euskal Herria y Europa*. Donostia-San Sebastián: Eusko Ikaskuntza/Sociedad de Estudios Vascos, 1992.

Galeote, Geraldine. "La temática europea en el discurso del Partido Nacionalista Vasco (PNV)." *Revista de Estudios Políticos* 103 (1999): 259–78.

Gehler, Michael, and Wolfram Kaiser, eds. *Christian Democracy in Europe since 1945*. Vol. 2. New York: Routledge, 2004.

Granja, José Luis de la, Jesús Casquete, Santiago de Pablo, and Ludger Mees, coords. *Diccionario ilustrado de símbolos del nacionalismo vasco*. Madrid: Tecnos, 2012.

Granja, José Luis de la, Ludger Mees, Santiago de Pablo, and José Antonio Rodríguez Ranz. *La política como pasión. El lehendakari José Antonio Aguirre (1904–1960).* Madrid: Tecnos, 2014.

Héraud, Guy. *Les principes du fédéralisme et la Fédération européenne.* Paris: Presses d'Europe, 1968.

———. "Pour une Europe des Ethnies." In *La crisis del Estado y Europa.* Oñati: HAEE/IVAP, 1988.

Jansen, Thomas. *The European People's Party: Origins and Development.* Basingstoke: Macmillan, 1998.

Jiménez de Aberásturi, Juan Carlos, and Rafael Moreno Izquierdo. *Al servicio del extranjero. Historia del Servicio Vasco de Información (1936–43).* Madrid: Antonio Machado Libros, 2008.

Landaburu, Francisco Javier. *La causa del pueblo vasco.* Bilbao: Editorial Geu, 1977.

———. *Obras completas.* Bilbao; Idatz Ekintza, 1982–1984.

Larronde, Jean Claude. *Exilio y Solidaridad. La Liga Internacional de Amigos de los Vascos.* Bilbao: Bidasoa, 1988.

Marc, Alexandre. "Historia de las ideas y de los movimientos federalistas desde la Primera Guerra Mundial." In Gastón Berger et al. *El federalismo.* Madrid: Tecnos, 1965.

———. "La révolution personnaliste." In *Du personnalisme au fédéralisme européen. En hommage à Denis de Rougemont.* Genève: Centre Européen de la Culture, 1989.

Mees, Ludger. *El profeta pragmático. Aguirre, el primer lehendakari (1936–1960).* Irún: Alberdania, 2006.

———. "Aguirre, Europa y el Partido Nacionalista Vasco." *Hermes. Revista de Pensamiento e Historia* 35 (2011): 58–72.

Moreno Juste, Antonio. *Franquismo y construcción europea.* Madrid: Tecnos/Movimiento Europeo, 1998.

Mota Zurdo, David. *Un sueño americano. El Gobierno Vasco en el exilio y Estados Unidos (1937–1979).* Oñati: IVAP, 2016.

Mounier, Emmanuel. *Qué es el personalismo.* Buenos Aires: Criterio, 1956.

———. *Manifiesto al servicio del Personalismo. Personalismo y cristianismo.* Madrid: Taurus, 1972.

———. *El personalismo: antología esencial.* Salamanca: Sígueme, 2002.

Mouvement Enbata. *Fédéralisme basque et européen.* Bayona: Mouvement Enbata, 1965.

Nagel, Klaus-Jürgen. "Entre la 'independencia en Europa', una 'Europa con cien banderas' y una 'Europa de' o 'con las regiones'." *Hermes. Revista de Pensamiento e Historia* 35 (2011): 4–22.

Núñez-Seixas, Xosé Manoel. "¿Protodiplomacia exterior o ilusiones ópticas? El nacionalismo vasco, el contexto internacional y el Congreso de Nacionalidades Europeas (1914-1917)." *Cuadernos de Sección. Historia-Geografía. Eusko Ikaskuntza-Sociedad de Estudios Vascos* 23 (1995): 243–75.

———. *Entre Ginebra y Berlín*. Madrid: Akal, 2001.

———. "Sobre la idea de la Europa de los Pueblos. En el período de entreguerras (1918–1939)." *Hermes. Revista de Pensamiento e Historia* 35 (2011): 32–44.

Pablo, Santiago de, Ludger Mees, and José Antonio Rodríguez Ranz. *El Péndulo Patriótico. Historia del Partido Nacionalista Vasco*. 2 vols. Barcelona: Crítica, 1999–2001.

Rougemont, Denis de. *Tres milenios de Europa. La conciencia europea a través de los textos. De Hesíodo a nuestro tiempo.* N.p.: Revista de Occidente, 1963.

———. *Lettre ouverte aux Européens*. Paris: Albin Michel, 1970.

———. "Un autre modèle de civilisation." *L'Europe en formation* 278 (1990).

San Sebastián, Koldo. "J. A. Aguirre: Democracia cristiana y europeísmo en EEUU." *Hermes. Revista de Pensamiento e Historia* 34 (2010): 2–81.

Ugalde, Alexander. *La Acción Exterior del Nacionalismo Vasco (1890–1939): Historia, Pensamiento y Relaciones internacionales.* Oñati: HAEE/IVAP, 1996.

———. "Entrada del nacionalismo vasco en el Congreso de Nacionalidades Europeas, 1929–30: siguiendo la documentación del Fondo Apraiz." *Revista Internacional de Estudios Vascos* 4, no. 2 (1997): 403–21.

———. *El Consejo Vasco del Movimiento Europeo (1951–2001).* Vitoria-Gasteiz: Consejo Vasco del Movimiento Europeo, 2001.

———. "La participación vasca en el movimiento europeísta y federalista." In *Los vascos y Europa*, edited by Víctor Manuel Amado Castro and Santiago de Pablo. Vitoria-Gasteiz: Sancho el Sabio, 2001.

10

Basque Fashion in Exile: Creativity and Innovation, from Balenciaga to Rabanne

Miren Arzalluz

This chapter aims to explore the way in which war and exile impacted the work of two of the most influential fashion designers of the twentieth century, Cristobal Balenciaga and Paco Rabanne. Forced by the Spanish Civil War to leave their native Basque Country, and compelled to confront further hardships and uncertainties during World War II in France, they overcame adversity and stood out in the challenging scene of Paris fashion through unprecedented creativity, rigor, and innovation. Resourcefulness, adaptability, resilience, and rebelliousness forged in hardship and struggle were at the heart of some of the most iconic creations of the history of fashion design.

Cristóbal Balenciaga

Balenciaga's professional journey can be traced back to 1917, the year he founded his first fashion establishment in San Sebastián,[1] a spa town par excellence on the Spanish Basque coast. After beginning dressmaking under his mother's wing while still a child in his native Getaria, Balenciaga became a tailor's apprentice in 1907 at one of San Sebastián's renowned tailoring establishments, thanks to a recommendation from the elegant Marquesa de Casa Torres. The marquise, an aristocrat and a loyal customer of Paris's best

---

1. Today the official name of the city, Donostia-San Sebastián, includes both the Basque and the Spanish names. For purposes of clarity and in keeping with the conventions of the time, the name San Sebastián will be used in this article.

couturiers, allowed Balenciaga to pour over her impressive wardrobe during her long summer stays at the villa in Getaria owned by her family.[2] From that moment on, Balenciaga's life would be inexorably linked to Parisian couture and to the work of its leading exponents. After rigorous technical training, Balenciaga began working as a tailor in the new San Sebastián branch of the Parisian department store Au Louvre, which opened in 1911, where his outstanding talent for dressmaking soon earned him the position of head tailor of the ladies' dressmaking workshop.[3] Aside from getting to know the ins and outs of the not-so-exclusive world of ready-to-wear dressmaking, his new job would give him the opportunity to visit Paris at last and in turn become acquainted with the world of haute couture that he so aspired to join.

World War I gave rise to a microcosm of luxury, consumerism, and fashion on the so-called Côte Basque. Added to the intensive tourism activities in San Sebastián and Biarritz, spurred largely by the most important royal houses and aristocratic families of Europe from the late nineteenth century on, was the golden exile of entrepreneurs, artists, writers, and all manner of celebrities escaping the horrors of war in a brazen attempt to avoid reality by dedicating their lives to leisure, amusement, and above all, unlimited spending. The Bilbao and San Sebastián bourgeoisie, whose buoyant economic situation allowed them to emulate the trendsetters, participated to a moderate degree in a lifestyle in which fashion played a fundamental part. The unexpected conditions created by World War I on the Basque coast made it the perfect time for the fashion enterprise. Encouraged by this extraordinary atmosphere, Balenciaga opened his first couture establishment in San Sebastián in 1917.

Between 1917 and 1936, Balenciaga opened seven establishments, five in San Sebastián, one branch in Madrid (1933), and another in Barcelona (1935). Over the years he dressed the Spanish royal family and court, European high society, and the upper-middle classes of the Basque cities of Bilbao and San Sebastián, and of Madrid and Barcelona. Before relocating to Paris,

---

2. Based on Cristóbal Balenciaga's own testimony from an interview for *Paris Match* magazine following the closure of Maison Balenciaga in 1968. Virginie Merlin, "Balenciaga devient un visage," *Paris Match*, no. 1005, August 10, 1968.
3. For the early personal and professional development of Cristóbal Balenciaga, see Miren Arzalluz, *Cristóbal Balenciaga: The Making of a Master (1895–1936)* (London: V&A Publishing, 2011).

Balenciaga had overcome all manner of obstacles related to the changing sociopolitical climate, such as the disastrous effects on San Sebastián tourism of General Primo de Rivera's ban on gambling, or the forced exile of his most valued clients (mainly royals and members of the aristocracy) following the 1931 proclamation of the Second Spanish Republic. Moreover, during these years Balenciaga got to know the ins and outs of Paris haute couture and the particulars of couturiers, suppliers, buyers, and clients, with the invaluable help of his Parisian associate and partner in life, Wladzio d'Attainville. The 1936 Spanish Civil War came when Balenciaga was at one of his finest hours, just when his interest prompted him to expand his business and show his work to larger audiences in other cities. Once again, Balenciaga knew how to turn problems into opportunities, establishing himself in Paris while keeping a close watch on the developments of the war, waiting for the right time to restart activities in his San Sebastián, Madrid, and Barcelona houses. Success probably caught him by surprise and forced him to confront the biggest professional challenge of his life to date.

The Outbreak of War in San Sebastián

A number of accounts attribute Balenciaga's departure from San Sebastián to the outbreak of the Civil War in 1936, but the exact date is unknown. Bettina Ballard (correspondent and fashion editor for American *Vogue* between 1935 and 1942 as well as 1945 and 1956 respectively) places Balenciaga in San Sebastián when the city was ravaged by bombs in August 1936 and adds that it was while he was taking refuge from one of the bombardments that he met Nicolás Bizcarrondo, one of his future partners in his Paris enterprise.[4] It is more likely, however, that the two knew each other before the war. After all, they had lived in the same building on Avenida de la Libertad number 2, so it would be perfectly conceivable for them to have shared a bomb shelter during one of the raids.

The adjacent apartment had been occupied since 1926 by Víctor Mendizábal, his wife, Catalina Coyos, and their daughters, Simona and Virgilia, a wealthy family of independent means.[5] Virgilia was

---

4. Bettina Ballard, *In My Fashion* (London: Secker & Warburg, 1960), 115.

5. Archivo Municipal de San Sebastián, Sección B, Negociado 10, Serie II, Libro 1181, Expediente 1, 1926.

a schoolteacher who, in 1920, married an engineer by the name of Nicolás Bizcarrondo Gorosábel.[6] The couple moved in with the girl's parents, who spent long periods of time in Argentina, where they had both lived years earlier. Nicolás Bizcarrondo, grandson of the beloved San Sebastián poet, Indalecio Bizcarrondo (fondly known as Bilintx), ran his engineering practice from his home on Avenida de la Libertad.[7] Virgilia and Simona's sister, Claudia, lived in Paris with her husband, Nemesio Sangrador, and their daughters, María Isabel and Carmen, and would often visit the family residence in San Sebastián.[8] Over the course of these visits, Claudia must have noticed the quality of Balenciaga's designs, and she soon became a regular customer. Maritxu Esnal (a relative of Balenciaga and employee at the House of Balenciaga since the early 1930s) clearly remembered Claudia and said that the "Señora de Sangrador" was the one who persuaded Virgilia and Nicolás to help Balenciaga establish himself in Paris.

Nicolás Bizcarrondo was a prominent Republican, who, alongside his brothers Antonio and Alfredo, became an active member of the Acción Republicana (Republican Action) party founded by (the first prime minister of the Second Spanish Republic) Manuel Azaña in 1930.[9] Bizcarrondo was a candidate on the Acción Republicana ticket in the neighboring town of Alza for the November 1933 general elections.[10] His political commitment forced him into exile after the fall of San Sebastián in September 1936, and he and Virgilia went to Paris, where they were supported by Claudia and her family.

Balenciaga and Wladzio also settled in Paris and soon afterward met with their exiled neighbors and devised an adventurous

---

6. Antonio Zavala, *Indalecio Bizcarrondo 'Bilintx', 1831–1876* (Donostia-San Sebastián: Caja de Ahorros Municipal de San Sebastián, 1978), 73.

7. Archivo Municipal de San Sebastián, Sección C, Negociado 4, Serie III, Libros 2365 (1928), 2367 (1929), 2366 (1930), 2371 (1934), 2372 (1935), 2339 (1936).

8. Sección B, Negociado 10, Serie II, Libro 1361, Expediente 1 (Padrón de habitantes, avenida de la Libertad, 2, 1935).

9. Antonio Elorza and Ander Elorza, "El linaje de Vilinch," *El Diario Vasco*, February 9, 2007.

10. In 1933, the neighborhood of Alza was an independent town located to the east of San Sebastián. In 1940, it was annexed into the city limits. See Aitor Cerezo, "II. Errepublika Altzan, udaletxeko akten bidez," in *Altza, Hautsa Kenduz-VIII* (Altza: Altzako Historia Mintegia, 2005), 83.

plan, bolstered by the enthusiasm and conviction of Claudia and Virgilia. On July 7, 1937, Cristóbal Balenciaga joined forces with Nicolás Bizcarrondo and Wladzio Jaworowski to create an haute couture house in Paris called Balenciaga, located at 10 Avenue George V, and Cristóbal presented his first collection there in August 1937. The reaction from the fashion press was immediate. The magazine *L'Officiel* described the House of Balenciaga collection as "full of taste and distinction;"[11] the *New York Herald Tribune* pointed out that the young designer remained faithful to his philosophy of simple lines and no unnecessary adornments;[12] and *Harper's Bazaar* declared that "Balenciaga projects a new quality into the couture, a definite personality into the fray."[13]

Infanta Dresses and Geneva Exhibition

After establishing himself in Paris in 1937 and presenting his first collection in August the same year, Balenciaga quickly earned a place among the most famous haute couture houses of the day. Critics were quick to pick up on the impeccable cut of his suits, the simple sophistication of his evening wear and what they perceived as references to Spanish culture.

In 1939, in the midst of the historicist craze that pervaded all Paris couture collections, Balenciaga was inspired by an international cultural event that was intimately connected to a most extraordinary episode of the Spanish Civil War, and which provided him with an excellent opportunity to step into the spotlight. That summer, the League of Nations in Geneva housed an anthological exhibition of some of the most emblematic works of Spanish art. The treasures had been evacuated from Spain after the fall of Catalonia in 1939 and moved to Geneva to avoid the risk of destruction in the war. In Geneva they were delivered to the care of the League of Nations following an agreement between the Republican government and the International Committee for the Rescue of Spanish Art Treasures, an organization consisting of museum

---

11. *L'Officiel de la Couture et de la Mode de Paris*, Paris, no. 196 (December 1937).
12. *The New York Herald Tribune*, New York, August 6, 1937, in Pamela Golbin, *Balenciaga Paris* (Paris: Les Arts décoratifs, 2006), 32.
13. *Harper's Bazaar*, New York, October 1938.

directors and curators from around the world.[14] After making an inventory of all the works, the League of Nations officially handed the collection over to the Franco government at its headquarters in Burgos on March 30, 1939. However, in the interim, a number of the evacuated works were showcased in Geneva at the Musée d'Art et d'Histoire in an exhibition entitled Chefs d'Oeuvre du Musée du Prado (Masterpieces of the Prado Museum), on view from June to August 1939, and "unanimously hailed as Europe's most important cultural event of the year."[15] The poster used to promote the exhibition featured Velázquez's portrait of Doña Mariana de Austria, the much celebrated centerpiece of the exhibit.

On August 3, 1939, Balenciaga presented his new A/W collection in which a series of elaborate evening gowns became the inevitable stars of the show. Made in luxurious satin and velvet, they were very clearly reminiscent of seventeenth-century fashions, and more specifically of the magnificent gowns of the Habsburg court that Velázquez had so superbly represented. The enthusiastic fashion press named these gowns the "Infanta" dresses and was quick to establish a direct association between Balenciaga's latest collection and the masterpieces on display in Geneva since early June.

Balenciaga might have decided to overtly reference the Velázquez "Infantas" that had been salvaged from the destruction of the Spanish Civil War—a war from which he had only recently fled—as a means of pointing out the tragedy to the world. It could also be argued that, in doing so, he found an ingenious way of rapidly gaining the spotlight among an international audience historically fascinated with displays of Iberian exoticism. Whatever prompted the Basque couturier to create this tribute collection, the fashion world responded fervently and Balenciaga's "Infanta" dresses were featured widely in the international press and massively copied by the ready-to-wear industry on both sides of the Atlantic. Moreover, it triggered a renewed interest in the work of the Spanish masters, showing, once again, the mutual influence between art and fashion.

The dress editor at the *Tobé Report*—a weekly magazine published by one of the oldest American fashion forecasting companies

---

14. Isabel Argerich and Judith Ara, *Arte Protegido*, exhibition catalogue, Geneva, March–April 2005 (Madrid: Sociedad Estatal para la Acción Cultural Exterior; Museo Nacional del Prado and Instituto Histórico Español, 2005), 48.
15. Ibid.

and dedicated to fashion industry professionals—wrote in detail about the reaction of fashion editors, buyers, and professionals from around the world after attending Balenciaga's new show:[16]

> For Balenciaga, the young Spaniard who has climbed to the top ranks of the Paris couture with surprising rapidity in the past two years, drew the inspiration for his beautiful collection of evening clothes directly from the masterpieces of Spanish paintings with which he had lived in Madrid – particularly those of Velasquez [sic]. A ripple of excitement ran through the crowded salons as one after another of the lovely dresses that passed was recognized as coming directly from this or that familiar Velasquez or Goya painting.

By the next day even those who had never heard of Velasquez or Goya or Greco were talking about "the Prado paintings" with as glib a facility as if they had lived in Madrid all their lives and were used to visiting the Prado every day.[17]

The Basque Delegation in Paris

The pages of the local San Sebastián press were busy covering the war and made no mention of Balenciaga's Paris presentation. However, many of Balenciaga's customers who knew him from their trips to San Sebastián received the news with great enthusiasm and were thrilled at his success. Elvira and "Rafita" (Rafaela) Arocena, Mexican sisters of Basque descent, had visited the couturier's salon in San Sebastián and knew all about his designs by the time his first collection appeared in Paris. In a letter to her sister Elvira in Mexico, Rafita, now living in Paris, wrote of family matters, and added: "Balenciaga has opened a house here and it's a huge success. He opened here with Franco's permission because obviously he couldn't work there any more with no good Spanish cloth available."[18]

Elvira Arocena, to whom this letter was destined, was heiress, together with her sister, to the fortune of her Basque grandfather

---

16. *Tobé Report* (September 7, 1939), 1–3.
17. Ibid., 1.
18. Correspondence between Elvira and Rafaela Arocena, Centro de Investigaciones Históricas de la Universidad de La Laguna, Archivo Histórico Juan Agustín de Espinoza, S. J., Fondo Familiar Belausteguigoitia Arocena, no. FFAC5F10d472.

and cotton manufacturer Rafael Arocena Arbide, who emigrated to Mexico in 1867. Elvira had been born in Mexico and sent to the Basque Country as a child having lost her mother at a very early age. It was there where she met and married the prominent Bilbao-born doctor, Athletic de Bilbao soccer player, and Basque nationalist militant Francisco Belaustegigoitia, also known as Belauste III among his passionate soccer fans.[19] They both moved to Mexico in 1933, after the Mexican government had urged the great landowners to live in the country under threat of losing their extensive properties.[20] Francisco took charge of the family business while he continued his political commitment to the Basque national cause, actively engaging in the hosting and support of political refugees as president of the Basque Center in Mexico. Belaustegigoitia also donated the necessary funds to the EAJ-PNV (Euzko Alderdi Jeltzalea- Partido Nacionalista Vasco, Basque Nationalist Party) in order to acquire a building at number 11 Avenue Marceau in Paris.[21] Since the early days of 1937 this elegant mansion had become the headquarters of the delegation of the Basque government in the French capital thanks to arrangements made by Rafael Picavea, Basque delegate in Paris, who had rented it earlier from an American woman called Hélène Brawn.[22] Only a few months later, Belaustegigoitia's generous contribution (1,460,000 francs) made the purchase possible.[23]

The new Basque delegation was located very near Cristóbal Balenciaga's Paris residence at number 28–30 on the same street, and only a few blocks from the headquarters of the recently established Maison Balenciaga at number 10 Avenue George V. Moreover, Balenciaga was indirectly connected to Rafael Picavea, whose only daughter María was a loyal client of his house in San Sebastián, as well as Elvira and Rafita Arocena, wife and sister-in-law of Francisco Belaustegigoitia. These connections, together with Nicolás Bizcarrondo's Republican militancy and the aforementioned physical proximity, would have facilitated the establishment

19. Francisco J. Illarramendi Lizaso, "Francisco Belausteguigoitia, el patrón," *IZAR, 100 años de innovación industrial en Bizkaia* (IZAR, 2010), 34.

20. Ibid., 37.

21. Ibid.

22. Eduardo Jauregi, "Historias de los Vascos: 11, Avenue Marceau," *Deia*, at http://blogs.deia.com/historiasdelosvascos/2012/07/06/11-avenue-marceau/#.V5CY70BHaCE.google (accessed March 2016).

23. Ibid.

of some kind of relationship between Cristóbal Balenciaga and the Basque delegation in Paris.

The historical archive of the Basque government holds documental evidence of the relationship between the House of Balenciaga and the Basque delegation in Paris, which in the years after World War II had also become the headquarters of the Basque government-in-exile. In a letter dated February 13, 1947,[24] sent by Basque delegation treasurer Agustín Alberro to Nicolás Bizcarrondo, the former asks Balenciaga's associate to intercede with the chancellor at the Spanish Consulate in Paris on behalf of Ignacio Leizaola, resident in Bilbao and brother of Jesús María Leizaola, Minister of Justice and Culture in the government of José Antonio Agirre, and future president of the Basque government himself after Agirre's death in 1960. Leizaola was in need of an official translation and legalization of his birth certificate, and Alberro turned to Bizcarrondo in the knowledge that Balenciaga and his partners maintained a cordial and formal relationship with the representatives of the Spanish Franco regime in Paris. Bizcarrondo must have handled the delicate issue successfully since only a few weeks later he himself requested a favor from the Basque government. A new missive from Alberro to Bizcarrondo, dated March 3, 1947,[25] tells us about a money delivery made by Iñaki de Lizaso, Basque delegate in London, to José Balenciaga, nephew of Cristóbal, following a request made by Bizcarrondo to the representatives of the Basque government in London. The delivery was successful and Bizcarrondo would settle his 61,600-franc debt with Alberro in Paris.

Nazi Occupation and the Hat Controversy

Agustín Alberro's conviction of Balenciaga and his partner's connection to the Franco authorities might have been motivated by an extraordinary event that took place some years earlier during the Nazi occupation of Paris and the rule of the Vichy government. This event is reproduced in detail in various documents archived in the Spanish Embassy during this period.

---

24. Letter from Agustín Alberro to Nicolás Bizcarrondo, February 13, 1947, EAH-AHE, Archivo Histórico del Gobierno Vasco, Departamento de Hacienda, Legajo 763-01.
25. Ibid., March 3, 1947.

The outbreak of the war and the occupation of Paris in June 1940 had imposed a drastic change of rhythm upon Parisian fashion. The privations of the occupied city and the severe restrictions on materials that the authorities imposed on the diminished haute couture industry played a decisive role in the development of couture collections from 1940 onward. However, whereas clothing was closely rationed and accessories like footwear and bags, belts, and gloves were subject to regulations, headgear witnessed an explosion of shapes and colors and a riot of materials: tulle, veils, lace, feathers, artificial flowers, grosgrain, felt ribbon, straw, and so on. As Dominique Veillon would state in her masterpiece *Fashion Under the Occupation* (2002), "never before had so many bizarre ideas and preposterous creations burst forth as between 1940 and 1944."[26] As difficulties in renewing one's wardrobe grew in parallel to restrictions and ration cards, clothes first assumed a practical and utilitarian aspect, which each individual tried to embellish in his or her own way. The only exception was that of hats, which took on an unexpected prominence, as if they were the last refuge on unbridled fantasy. Hats may possibly have symbolized the wish to flee from the difficulties of daily life, but they were also a demonstration of insolence, a means of mocking the occupier, a sort of provocation[27] that did not go unnoticed by the Germans.

The reduced number of couture houses that was authorized to operate during the occupation led the trend for extravagant hats, limited as they were by severe restrictions on the use of materials and strict regulation of the composition and presentation of their collections. As regulations and controls reached unbearable heights in 1943, so did hats, literally. The Autumn–Winter 1943 collection at the House of Balenciaga presented the most extraordinary designs including gigantic turbans, historically inspired large feathered hats, and oversized geometric forms that resulted in rather abstract creations. Did this hat galore respond to necessity? Was it the result of creative resourcefulness in the face of scarcity? Or was it pure defiance? Whatever Balenciaga's intentions, his audacious collection provoked a conflict with the governing authorities that could have devastating consequences for his enterprise.

---

26. Dominique Veillon, *Fashion Under the Occupation*, trans. Miriam Kochan (Oxford and New York: Berg, 2002), 61.

27. Ibid., 66.

In a letter dated January 21, 1944, Balenciaga's associate and partner in life Wladzio d'Attainville wrote to his friend Juan Ranero, a diplomat at the Spanish Embassy in Vichy, in a state of agitation:

> My dear friend, if I may take the liberty to implore you to convey our request to the ambassador that he intercede (if possible) with the French Government (or the minister for Production), to try and solve a matter of great concern to us.
>
> We tried to phone you yesterday but you were not in the office, and Carmen Latorre very kindly spoke directly with Mr. Lequerica, asking that he recommend us to the German authorities, as we are told that they are the promoters in this case.
>
> The case is the following: a Decision (N V.A.I5) has been handed down from the Director in charge of the "Comité General d'Organisation de l'Habillement" limiting the use of fabrics subject to quotas for the manufacture of women's hats; we have recently been subject to this regulatory control, showing that more cloth has been used in some of the hats in our collection than the amount stipulated by the decision; the Director General of Textiles summoned us a few days ago to announce that we would be sanctioned, adding that this was suggested by the occupation authorities. We expressed our point of view, that is, we said that we considered our infringement of little significance (the entire excess, according to the control conducted, was 65 meters of cloth, a blend of silk and plant-based fibers, 0.90 in width; containing no wool), and that we were certain that the vast majority of fashion houses in Paris were making hats as large as ours; we were told that the gravity of the matter lay not exactly in the amount of cloth, but in the fact that we had created the fashion, and therefore are considered the sole offenders.[28]

Judging by the harsh verdict of the Director General of Textiles, Balenciaga was guilty, not so much of exceeding the amount of material allowed for the making of hats (since the infringement seemed to be minor after all); but he was responsible for leading fashion, for guiding and influencing others in producing and adopting the new trend for large and extravagant hats. However, d'Attainville was persuaded that other reasons lay behind the sanction, and so he confided in his friend: "As you can easily understand, under no circumstances can we use this argument, but we

---

28. Letter from Wladzio d'Attainville to Juan Ranero, January 21, 1944, AGA (10)97 54/11379.

are absolutely convinced that this and similar attacks we have had to deal with in the past are due to the apprehension that many people in Paris feel regarding the great success achieved by Balenciaga, a foreigner."[29]

Balenciaga's remarkable success since his establishment in Paris in 1937 might have caused jealousy and resentment among some of his fellow couturiers, who might have been all too willing to report him, a foreigner, to the controlling authorities. However, the Paris haute couture industry was no stranger to international couturiers and, since its emergence in the mid-nineteenth century, it had been largely made up of a force of designers and couture professionals from around the world. Moreover, as later developments would soon prove, the sanction had indeed been imposed at the suggestion of the German authorities, who must have interpreted Balenciaga's leading role in the new hat trend as an invitation to excess and disobedience. Such an irresponsible and dangerous act could only be punished severely:

> we would have quietly dropped the matter as we have done in the past if the sanction had been reasonably acceptable. But we have just received the aforementioned sanction, signed by the Minister for Production, Monsieur Bichelonne, which consists of nothing less than the total closure of our house for three months, as of tomorrow, February 22. The damage this causes us goes without saying, as does our indignation at being the only hat manufacturer receiving this punishment, and at the fact that the sanction affects not only our hat section but also our suits, which have nothing do to with the matter.[30]

Faced with a disastrous prospect, d'Attainville's anxiety was aggravated by the fact that Cristóbal was delayed in his return to Paris (possibly from a trip home to visit his mother in her house in Igeldo) and he was disconcertingly uninformed as to Balenciaga's whereabouts. What would have been a minor concern under normal circumstances acquired a completely different meaning in times of war in a country torn in two.

We were expecting Cristóbal to arrive today; he would surely have come to Vichy immediately upon learning about this matter to explain our situation to the ambassador and to you; but for

---

29. Ibid.
30. Ibid.

reasons unbeknownst to me, he has not arrived; and neither myself nor Bizcarrondo are able to travel under these circumstances.[31]

D'Attainville finished his missive with sincere gratitude from Bizcarrondo and himself, and his warmest regards to whom seemed to be a close friend.

Both Juan Ranero and the Spanish Ambassador to Vichy, the Basque politician and diplomat José Félix Lequerica, acted rapidly and with determination. Ranero was already coordinating a plan together with Ambassador Lequerica on January 24, the day he received the letter from d'Attainville, three days after it had been sent from Paris. As Ranero himself explained in a new missive to d'Attainville,[32] in addition to a first approach to the German Embassy in Vichy (which Ranero judged would be rather unfruitful), Lequerica had already arranged an urgent meeting with the Minister of Production Bichelonne in Paris on the following day, January 25, to persuade him to reconsider the severe sanction and close only the hat section of the House of Balenciaga and not the dressmaking section, which was the heart of Balenciaga's activity. Ranero also urged d'Attainville that either he or Bizcarrondo should meet with Minister Bichelonne in Paris after Lequerica had addressed the matter with him.

All of Ranero's and Lequerica's diplomatic efforts ultimately proved to be successful. In a letter to Lequerica from Gustav Struve, Counsellor of the German Legation in Vichy, dated February 29, the former confirmed a softening of the original sanction: "In response to his Excellency's petition regarding the closure of the Balenciaga House of Haute Couture, I have the honor to inform you after receiving news from the German Embassy in Paris that the firm will remain open; however, the hat section, of lesser importance, shall remain closed for 3 months."[33]

In a highly formal letter written by Nicolas Bizcarrondo to Ambassador Lequerica dated February 26, 1944,[34] he described the same outcome as it had been officially communicated to the House of Balenciaga by the Ministry of Production on that same day.

---

31. Ibid.

32. Letter from Juan Ranero to Wladzio d'Attainville, January 24, 1944, AGA (10)97 54/11379.

33. Letter from Gustav Struve to Spanish Ambassador José Félix Lequerica, February 29, 1944, AGA (10)97 54/11379.

34. Letter from Wladzio d'Attainville to Spanish Ambassador José Félix Lequerica, February 26, 1944, AGA (10)97 54/11379.

Sincere expressions of gratitude and respect followed for what had been a diplomatic intervention of vital importance for the survival of Balenciaga's enterprise in Paris. The survival and ultimate success of the house he had worked a lifetime to build was the utmost priority for Balenciaga. Nothing could hinder his sole dedication to his work, a métier he embraced wholeheartedly when he was barely a child.

Paco Rabanne

"I have always had the impression of being a time accelerator. Of going as far as is reasonable for one's time and not indulge in the morbid pleasure of the known things, which I view as decay. I talk of mutation, of the unquenchable thirst for novelty, and of permanent rupture. To be fixed in a concept is to become a living corpse."[35]

Paco Rabanne's words reflect his iconoclastic approach to fashion, a rebellious attitude that marked his work from the beginning to the end of his prolific career. His commitment to questioning established ideas about dress, his audacious experimentation with unconventional materials, and his informed architectural vision were at the heart of some of the most revolutionary designs of his career, beginning in the 1960s.

Rabanne's characteristic resilience and combative temperament were forged very early in his life. Born Francisco Rabaneda Cuervo on February 18, 1934, in Pasaia, a fishing village on the Spanish Basque coast, Paco was the son of an Andalusian military officer and a seamstress from Santander who built a home in the Basque Country where their four children were born. Rabanne's father, Francisco Rabaneda Postigo, had served under King Alfonso XIII, sworn his allegiance to the Second Spanish Republic in 1931, and volunteered to join the militias organized by the Communist Party—a party of which both he and his wife were prominent members—when Franco's military uprising took place in July 1936. He eventually joined the army of the Basque government as commander of the communist battalion, Larrañaga.[36] He was captured

---

35. Lydia Kamitsis, "Entretenien avec Paco Rabanne," *Paco Rabanne*, exhibition catalogue (Marseille: Musée de la Mode, 1995), 10.

36. Military card of Francisco Rabaneda Postigo, Departamento de Defensa del Gobierno de Euzkadi, Bilbao, February 18, 1937, GOAZ Museum-Museo del

by Italian forces in Santoña, together with around 15,000 *gudaris*, or Basque soldiers, the remains of the Basque army that had headed to Santander after the fall of Bilbao earlier in June. He was finally imprisoned and killed at the hands of Franco forces on October 15, 1937. This was a well-known exemplary execution in which fourteen gudaris were carefully chosen according to their political affiliation while they were being held at the prison of El Dueso;[37] they were six Basque nationalists, two republicans, two socialists, two anarchists and two communists, Francisco Rabaneda among the latter. They were gathered in two isolated cells located at the prison basement, where they wrote their letters to their families before being shot at a nearby beach.[38] These letters were handed to the prison chaplain, Jesús Moreno, who sent them to Francisco's mother in Melilla two days after the execution, asking her to take care of them and hand them over to María Luisa when she had the chance.[39] As Rabanne himself later confessed, he had been unable to read his father's last words to his family until very recently, at an homage to the men killed in El Dueso organized by the Sabino Arana Foundation in 1997.

Despite his youth during the development of the war, Paco Rabanne vividly recalls following his father wherever he went at the front, being protected by his mother during the bombings, his mother's desperation when losing track of her husband, and the horror and uncertainty that ruled his world when he was only a child. A number of documents gathered by the Sabino Arana Foundation from Rabanne's family (on the occasion of the aforementioned homage in 1997) enable us to partly reconstruct their steps during those terrible months. María Luisa Cuervo Fernandez, Paco Rabanne's mother, had worked as head seamstress at the House of Balenciaga in San Sebastián since the early 1930s. Traveling closely behind her husband at the front, she worked as a head seamstress in charge of a dressmaking workshop arranged by the Republican government in Bilbao as part of the war effort. The fall of Bilbao

---

Nacionalismo Vasco, K. 1194, Sig. RCO.

37. Luis de Guezala, "Historias de los Vascos: Santoña, catorce hombres fusilados al amanecer," *Deia*, at http://blogs.deia.com/historiasdelosvascos/2012/10/15/santona-catorce-hombres-fusilados-al-amanecer/#.V5C85TkZXr4.google (accessed March 2016).

38. Ibid.

39. Letter from Jesús Moreno to Dulce Postigo, 17 November 1937, GOAZ Museum – Museo del Nacionalismo Vasco, K. 1194, Sig. RCO.

in June 1937 forced the family to leave hastily, without news from Francisco, and establish themselves in Barcelona, the last Republican stronghold. María Luisa managed to find shelter for her young family in a refuge run by the PSUC (Partit Socialista Unificat de Catalunya, Unified Socialist Party of Catalonia), a Catalan party of communist ideology that welcomed comrades coming from places that had already fallen to the Franco forces or were in imminent danger of doing so.

On September 1, 1938, an intriguing telegram that mentioned María Luisa Cuervo was sent from Barcelona by Manuel de Irujo to José María Lasarte, head of the Basque intelligence service and working with his men from the Bayonne-based Villa Mimosas, in the French Basque Country. Irujo, who had just resigned as Minister of Justice in the Republican government of Juan Negrín, was working from the Basque General Delegation in Catalonia that he had been instrumental in creating in November 1936. Irujo told Lasarte the news about María Luisa's recent visit at the delegation in Barcelona with manifest urgency: "The wife of Francisco Rabaneda Postigo, head of the Basque Army First Brigade, who we had assumed shot on October 15, 1937, has reported to us, saying he is alive. Notify urgently. Irujo. September 1, 1938."

From Irujo's telegram we infer that, almost a year after the executions of Santoña, María Luisa must have received promising news about her husband's fate while in Barcelona. Hopeful and disoriented, she turned to the Basque delegation in Barcelona, where many Basques found help and assistance in such dramatic circumstances. It would not be long before she found out the painful truth.

A few months later the Rabaneda Cuervo family was on the move again forced by new developments in the war. The fall of Barcelona at the end of January 1939 provoked a massive exodus of Republican refugees who rushed desperately toward France and crossed the border in the early days of February. It is estimated that around 400,000 refugees walked across the Pyrenees in search of French shelter, 17,000 of whom were women and children, María Luisa Cuevo and her four children among them. The French authorities opened their borders reluctantly, forcing thousands of hopeless refugees to pile in improvised concentration camps in appalling conditions so they could be easily controlled. This heart-breaking scenario is all too familiar to us today. Years later Paco Rabanne would remember these tragic events, resenting

those French soldiers who took from his mother the few belong-
ings she brought with her, including the only photograph of her
husband she had managed to keep throughout the war. According
to Rabanne himself, his family was held in the camp of Argèles-
sur-mer, before heading north to a new home.[40] He would turn five
years old that month.

The rigorous controls undertaken by the Ministry of Interior
throughout the country recorded the name, date of birth, place of
residence in Spain, as well as the date and place of arrival in France,
for every single refugee. The records compiled by the authorities
at the department of Finistère reveal that María Luisa and her
four children, Olga, Pacífico, Francisco, and Dulce, had arrived in
Le Conquet on February 1, 1939, and they were joined by María
Luisa's mother, María Fernández Sierra, only two days later, on February 3.[41] As the documentation indicates, they were staying at an
old hotel called Beau Seajour, now owned by the Brest city council
and turned into a center for refugees, where they lived under strict
surveillance. However, another unfortunate turn of events was soon
to take place with the outbreak of World War II and the arrival in
Brittany of German forces in the summer of 1940.

All Republican refugees had to move quickly and with the
greatest caution as their situation turned critically dangerous. The
new German authorities, encouraged by the Franco regime and
with the connivance of the Vichy government, actively hunted
down all suspected political exiles to either deport them or intern
them in concentration camps both in France and Germany. A
known communist militant, María Luisa had every reason to fear
the worst for herself and her family. In September 1940 her mother-in-law, Dulce Postigo (Francisco's mother), presented an official
request at the Delegation of the Spanish Government in Melilla,
where she was living at the time, for an authorization for María
Luisa and her children to leave her current residence in Morlaix
and move to Melilla to join the rest of her family. To her despair,
the request was promptly turned down. María Luisa must have
cut off communication with her mother-in-law temporarily after
the failed attempt at leaving for Melilla; a few weeks later, the Red
Cross delegation at the Irun border sent a letter, dated October

---

40. "Le Finistère-Nord de Paco Rabanne," *Le Télégramme*, August 8, 2009.
41. Liste nominative et notices individuelles de réfugiés espagnols à Le Conquet,
Finistère, 23 Février 1939 (fol. 1270), F/7/14727, Archives Nationales.

24, to Dulce Postigo, informing her that María Luisa and her four children were perfectly safe at a new Morlaix address.

There followed long years of hardship and necessity, hard work and efforts to obtain the support of organizations such as *Solidarité* Espagnole (Spanish Solidarity). It was precisely thanks to a representative of this association in Morlaix that María Luisa Cuervo contacted the Delegation of the Basque Government in Paris and obtained a war widow's pension that would considerably ease the distressing situation of her family. The file of María Luisa Cuervo, archived by the Social Security Department of the Basque Government between September 1946 and December 1950, gives us details of the family's life and whereabouts, as well as the hardships young Paco had to endure while growing up in a country he must have perceived as hostile.[42] The last correspondence between the Rabaneda family and Laureano Lasa, Director General for Social Assistance, shows a heart-breaking situation, made ever more desperate by the government's exhaustion of funds, which made the family seriously consider the possibility of leaving France and emigrating to another country. In the last letter archived in the file, dated December 27, 1950, Dr. Lasa sent information and guidance about a potential move to Chile, the only country facilitating the reception of immigrants at the time. The family never left for Chile, moving to Paris instead, possibly around 1952. It was in Paris where Paco would finally start a new and promising life.

He initiated his studies in Architecture at the École Nationale Supérieure de Beaux-Arts under the guidance of Auguste Perret. For over ten years he combined his university studies with his work designing and crafting decorative accessories for reputed haute couture houses including Balenciaga, Courrèges, Pierre Cardin, and Givenchy. Despite his growing expertise and success, the young designer bitterly admitted in an early interview with the *New York Times* that, "except for Balenciaga and Givenchy, most couturiers gave me the boot."[43] Balenciaga might have decided to help the young designer, moved by memories of his early years in San Sebastián and by the precarious situation of Paco's mother, his former employee. However, it was Paco's determination and

---

42. Expediente de María Luisa Cuervo, EAH-AHE, Archivo Histórico del Gobierno Vasco, Departamento de Asistencia Social, Carpeta no 154, 1946–1949.
43. Gloria Emerson, "Paco's Sewing Kit: Pliers and Wires," *New York Times*, March 3, 1966.

creative use of materials that encouraged Balenciaga to incorporate Rabanne's designs into his couture creations of the late 1950s and early 1960s. Inspired by the work of the innovative architects that taught him at university (Auguste Perret and his use of reinforced concrete, Jean Prouvé's work in metal, and Jean-Louis Avril's cardboard furniture), Paco Rabanne took over Balenciaga's textile experimentation and investigated new materials, such as metal and plastic, in ways that no one had ever imagined could be applied to fashion. Balenciaga and Rabanne shared an avant-garde and architectural vision of dress, reinforced in the latter's case by his formal academic and professional training in the subject. As Rabanne himself admitted in a recent interview,

> During my architecture studies I learned about drawing, perspective, rigor, and the use of volume; and my mother, who had been head seamstress at Balenciaga's, taught me how to construct a garment, only by looking at it. This is how I went from architecture to fashion, making a synthesis of the two.[44]

Paco Rabanne has repeatedly acknowledged his admiration and creative debt to Balenciaga's extraordinary simplification and architectural vision, considering himself "one of his disciples" and "a member of his school, a school of rigor and exactitude."[45]

In 1959 the American magazine *Women's Wear Daily* published seven sketches of dresses designed by an unknown designer called Frank Rabanne, the name he temporarily adopted until the official launch of his brand in 1965. Although he had decided to slightly modify his name in order to make it sound more French, he finally opted for maintaining his first name in its original Spanish informal form, a way of acknowledging his background, his personal history, the origins that had caused his family so much trouble for all those years. Beyond a calculation in terms of marketing, it must have acquired a deeper meaning related to his pride and sense of dignity.

On February 1, 1966, Paco Rabanne presented at the Hôtel George V his first Manifesto Collection, "12 Unwearable Dresses in Contemporary Materials," in which twelve barefoot models paraded to the sound of Pierre Boulez's "Le marteau sans maître."

---

44. "Paco Rabanne. De la arquitectura a la moda," *De Punta Magazine*, July 26, 2011.
45. Kamitsis, "Entretien avec Paco Rabanne."

They were clad in scandalous outfits, made entirely of rhodoid sequins and plaques linked together with metallic rings, using the same techniques he had previously experimented with in his most daring accessories. The choice of such an ignoble and inappropriate material as rhodoid, used only occasionally for making plastic raincoats, was in line with the Dada and Panique movements favored by Rabanne in his early years. His penchant for the uncommon grew more radical in successive collections, especially from 1968 onward, with his unprecedented use of metal, the material of discomfort par excellence. His metallic dresses were viewed by many as being incompatible with the search for freedom of movement that characterized the concerns of some of the most avant-garde designers of the time. Paco Rabanne was forced to explain himself:

> In my view, fashion is a reflection of a political, social, and artistic moment. It is therefore linked to tastes of its epoch, in all their forms of expression. I was disheartened by the discrepancy between the innovations achieved by painters and sculptors and the incredible conformity which reigned within this métier. Therefore, I tried to bring in the modern elements that had not yet entered this art, which was self-contained and oblivious of its times. This is why I've worked with plastic, leather, metal.[46]

Paco Rabanne remained an irremediable iconoclast, loyal to the principles that guided his revolutionary work until his retirement in 1999. Fifty years after his first and outrageous presentation, his name still resonates with the architectural vision, experimental drive, and critical spirit of his seminal collection.

Conclusion

Rabanne's rebelliousness, his obsession with breaking with established canons of dress and beauty, his heated plea for freedom, and his provocative attitude stem from an extraordinary personality forged in struggle, an enduring battle against all imaginable odds, coupled with loss, violence, fear, rejection, and necessity. His was a survivor's soul, and a mind as creative as it was audacious. After all he had gone through, he was fearless, limitless. As with

---

46. *Le Fait Publique*, March 1969, cited in Lydia Kamitsis, "L'oeuvre hors norme," in *Paco Rabanne*, exhibition catalogue (Marseille: Musée de la Mode, 1995), 14.

all avant-garde artists, Rabanne's untamable spirit coexisted with a deep-rooted respect for traditional couture and dressmaking techniques, which he had learned from his mother at a very early age—just as Cristóbal Balenciaga had done.

Balenciaga had dedicated his life to his chosen métier, working indefatigably since his childhood, striving for perfection, overcoming political and economic obstacles, and developing an extraordinary ability to adjust in order to survive and succeed. And he did so with astounding professional integrity and creative excellence. It is no wonder that he triumphed, but also that he felt somehow drained at the end of his career. In an interview given to the British newspaper *The Times* three years after his retirement in 1968, Balenciaga meaningfully confessed: "Nobody knows what a hard métier it is, how killing is the work. Under all this luxury and glamour. The truth is, it's a dog's life!"

Paco Rabanne, on the other hand, wrote years later about his early and traumatic experiences with astonishing serenity. He recalled the minuscule bedroom he shared with his older brother in their new home in Ploujean and the insomnia that overcame him night after night for long months. Exhausted and equally determined, one day in 1941, when he was barely seven years old, Paco decided he had to put an end to the unbearable situation by literally stopping time. This strength of mind was to unleash what he believed to be one of the most extraordinary events of his life: his first out-of-body experience. Beyond our own views on such psychological or spiritual experiences, it is not difficult to understand that this intense episode, or his perception of it, must have helped the young Paco overcome the emotional and psychological trauma he had experienced since leaving the safety of his home in Pasaia back in 1936. As the Basque designer himself put it, "What an ineffable pleasure it was to float in total silence in that universe of peace and light as opposed to the noisy and furious world in which I lived at the time."[47]

Bibliography

Argerich, Isabel and Judith Ara. *Arte Protegido*. Exhibition Catalogue. Geneva, March–April 2005. Madrid: Sociedad

---

47. Paco Rabanne, *Journey: From One Life to Another* (Shaftesbury: Element Books, 1997), 2.

Estatal para la Acción Cultural Exterior; Museo Nacional del Prado and Instituto Histórico Español, 2005.

Arzalluz, Miren. *Cristóbal Balenciaga: The Making of a Master (1895–1936)*. London: V&A Publishing, 2011.

Ballard, Bettina. *In My Fashion*. London: Secker & Warburg, 1960.

Cerezo, Aitor. "II. Errepublika Altzan, udaletxeko akten bidez." In *Altza, Hautsa Kenduz-VIII*. Altza: Altzako Historia Mintegia, 2005.

Elorza, Antonio, and Ander Elorza. "El linaje de Vilinch." *El Diario Vasco*, February 9, 2007.

Emerson, Gloria. "Paco's Sewing Kit: Pliers and Wires." *New York Times*, March 3, 1966.

Golbin, Pamela. *Balenciaga Paris*. Paris: Les Arts décoratifs, 2006.

Harper's Bazaar, New York, October 1938.

Illarramendi Lizaso, Francisco J. "Francisco Belausteguigoitia, el patrón." In *IZAR, 100 años de innovación industrial en Bizkaia*. IZAR, 2010.

Kamitsis, Lydia. "Entretenien avec Paco Rabanne" and "L'oeuvre hors norme."*Paco Rabanne*. Exhibition Catalogue. Marseille: Musée de la Mode, 1995.

L'Officiel de la Couture et de la Mode de Paris, Paris, no. 196 (December 1937).

"Le Finistère-Nord de Paco Rabanne." *Le Télégramme*, August 8, 2009.

Merlin, Virginie. "Balenciaga devient un visage." *Paris Match*, August 10, 1968.

Miller, Lesley Ellis. *Cristóbal Balenciaga (1895–1972): The Couturier's Couturier*. London: V&A Publications, 2007.

"Paco Rabanne. De la arquitectura a la moda." *De Punta Magazine*, July 26, 2011.

Rabanne, Paco. *Journey: From One Life to Another*. Shaftesbury: Element Books, 1997.

Tobé Report, September 7, 1939.

Zavala, Antonio. *Indalecio Bizcarrondo 'Bilintx', 1831–1876*. Donostia-San Sebastián: Caja de Ahorros Municipal de San Sebastián, 1978.

Veillon, Dominique. *Fashion Under the Occupation*. Translated by Miriam Kochan. Oxford and New York: Berg, 2002.

Part 2

Legacy

11

Agirre at the Crossroads

Joseba Zulaika

"He is already in his casket, but you can go see him," François Mauriac was told. The French Nobel Prize winner could utter only "broken words" in the presence of his friend Agirre's corpse, dead in late March, 1960. Later he wrote, "The casket has a crystal peephole at the face's level. What a vision! . . . In this face, as if eaten away from inside, I cannot recognize the noble and frank face of Don José Antonio de Aguirre. . . . Who could have been the victim of a more unjust destiny than he?" Mauriac went on: "With the liberation [of Europe from fascism], José Antonio de Aguirre drank the chalice to the last dregs, when he understood that Franco would be respected and the apparent victory of the democracies covered up, concealed, at the very heart of the West, another very hidden victory: the one of the professional armies and policemen."[1] Mauriac saw in Aguirre's face the horror that had destroyed its nobility and that still haunts his legacy—the bitter truth of the century embodied in a man representing a small country in the midst of the twentieth century's political dilemmas and military atrocities.

The vision Mauriac contemplated in Aguirre's extinguished face reflected modernity's apocalyptic ending—not only the death of God, but the death of Democracy, Liberty, and Justice, values that Agirre had claimed axiomatic for his Basque nation and upon which he had wagered his life. If the Spanish Civil War "is like an

---

1. Quoted in Martin de Ugalde, "José Antonio de Aguirre y Lecube," in José Antonio de Aguirre y Lecube, *Obras Completas*, vol. 1 (Donostia: Sendoa, 1981), 58.

internal miniature of the entire century,"[2] the events of Gernika/
Bilbao over which Agirre presided are a miniature of the miniature—the inaugural quintessence of the horror that would soon
expand to the Holocaust. A study of Agirre's legacy brings to our
attention not only the century's global unfinished agenda, the one
Mauriac referred to as imposed by the victorious professional
armies and policemen, but also the obstinate persistence in Basque
politics of the impasses he struggled with.

Crossroad 1. Democracy/Fascism

The Spanish military uprising of July 18, 1936 presented Agirre with
an inaugural life-defining crossroad: the split within the Basque
Nationalist Party between the religious allegiance to the Church
that sided with Franco and the political allegiance to the Republic
that had promised them more political autonomy. The leaders of the
party met the very day of the uprising to reach a decision.

Jose Maria Areilza would write about that meeting while narrating his visual encounter with Agirre on the Sunday morning of
the 19th in Bilbao's Jardines de Albia. After a night listening to the
radio harangues, Areilza went to Sunday mass by 7 am to Saint
Vincent's church in Albia. Soon he saw that a group of sleepless
men who seemed to come from an all-night meeting entered the
church: they were the members of the executive committee of the
Basque Nationalist Party, including Agirre, who were coming from
the adjacent party headquarters in Sabin Etxea. As the mass was
over, Areilza bought the daily newspaper and found out that they
had taken the position of siding with the Republic. In the incoming
struggle "Between democracy and fascism," the nationalists said,
they would fight for the Republic to the end. Areilza read the text
in disbelief once and again at the very stairs of the church, "feeling
a shiver of emotion while realizing that something was being torn
apart at the entrails of our country."[3]

Agirre saw him reading the paper, greeted him from the distance, "and understood for sure my sorrow realizing that the die

---

2. Alain Badiou, *The Century*, trans. Alberto Toscano (Malden, MA: Polity
Press, 2007), 22.
3. Areilza, quoted in Jesús María Leizaola, *Conversaciones sobre Jose Antonio
Aguirre* (Bilbao: Idatz Ekintza, 1983), 138.

had been definitively cast."[4] From then on only weapons would do the talking. Areilza's perspective on the situation was fatalistic: "it seemed as if a superior, implacable, destiny was pushing men and groups to occupy positions that they had to maintain when the curtain would raise and begin the tragedy."[5] Their lives were being controlled by a destiny split between two nationalisms. Areilza himself would soon end up joining the victorious Francoists. "Until Fascism is defeated, Basque nationalism will remain at its post," Agirre would proclaim three months later in front of the Republican deputies at the Cortes of Valencia.

Areilza was born in Portugalete, on the Nervión's Left Bank, had studied engineering in Bilbao, and had been a neighbor of Agirre in Getxo since 1932. They would take the same train at the same station. When in October of 1934 the traditionalist Marcelino Oreja was assassinated by the separatist "reds," a much pained Agirre went to Areilza to express his horror at the murder. In February of 1936, as both men were competing in the elections from ideologically polar opposite positions, they stumbled on each other's path and greeted each other in a friendly manner while discussing the prospective results. As the military coup led by Franco was declared, each one chose to fight in his own military camp against the other to the end.

Crossroad 2. Christ/Lenin

Agirre and Areilza used to meet every Sunday at their parish church. In the important religious festivities of the Holy Week or Corpus Christi, when the procession would require the pallium held by six poles, the two men wearing the frontal ones used to be Agirre and Areilza—Agirre the left pole and Areilza the right one. Afterwards they would meet at the sacristy and chat and carry on a normal and friendly relationship among Christian neighbors despite their political differences. A key reason why Areilza was so taken aback by Agirre's decision to side with the secular Republic, responsible for so many violent excesses against the Church's temples and people, was that he knew about Agirre's deep religiosity. They had undergone the same religious education, received the sacraments, and prayed in the same parish. The decision to

---

4. Ibid., 138.
5. Ibid., 136.

back or oppose the Republic was, on first sight, tantamount to a declaration of what was most axiomatic in their lives: the priority of religion or politics.

Religion was pivotal to Agirre's personal belief and experience. But in the crossroads of Spanish politics, where the antagonism between Christianity and Marxist socialism represented a major cultural fault-line, Agirre's faith would be sorely tested as the Catholic Church openly sided with the fascists. So how could Agirre live with his decision to give priority to politics over religion? He had to learn that one thing is religious experience and quite another the institution of the Church.

The Basque Church was caught in the crossfire between its allegiance to the legitimately established autonomous government and the Vatican's blunt pressure, put forward by its Secretary of State, Cardinal Pacelli, to side with the military insurgents. Weeks after Gernika and the fall of Bilbao, Pacelli, as Pope Pius XII, would legitimize the Spanish military rebellion on July 1, 1937 with the encyclical "To the Bishops of the Whole World." The devout Catholic Agirre had to witness his pope blessing Franco and Hitler and Mussolini's destruction of Gernika. The very same day on which Franco's headquarters announced on April 1, 1939 that their victorious troops had achieved their objectives, Pope Pius XII sent a message of congratulation to the Caudillo.

Earlier that year, in January of 1936 Agirre had visited the Vatican with a delegation of his party. The Secretary of State Cardinal Pacelli refused to meet with them because they were not siding with the Spanish right. This is a fight between Christ and Lenin, they were told at the Vatican. The Basque nationalists, who had just attended mass and had communion in Saint Ignatius's room, were baffled that their religious commitment was being questioned. Agirre's subjectivity was Christian to the core yet his politics belonged to "red" Lenin. In a nutshell, his religious paradox and his breakthrough consisted in that being a true "Christian" required from him to be a "Leninist."

In tragic irony, Agirre's side and the fascist side were both fighting within a Christian symbolic universe presided over by the cross: the Nazis' Iron Cross, a symbol Hitler had rescued for his Luftwaffe war planes (the Knight's Cross of the Iron Cross was the award Hitler gave to Wolfram von Richthofen), the cross of the Spanish fascists and Carlists' *crusade*, as well as Agirre's and Aita Patxi's bloodied crucifix. It was the essential gap inside the same symbol, the *coincidentia oppositorum*—the apocalypse. Christian symbolism was no longer enough. Agirre had to side, beyond symbolism, with the *real* of Christian love and justice.

Agirre's breakthrough was no other than a partisan universality, in the manner Slavoj Žižek writes about *repeating Lenin:* "Lenin's wager—today, in our era of postmodern relativism, more actual than ever—is that universal truth and partisanship, the gesture of taking sides, are not only not mutually exclusive, but condition each other: in a concrete situation, its UNIVERSAL truth can only be articulated from a thoroughly PARTISAN position—truth is by definition one-sided."[6] Agirre embodied this partisan universality.

As Franco's army "liberated" Bilbao from Agirre's command, Areilza became the new mayor of the city. As new mayor, Areilza spoke harsh words that would define his legacy: "Bilbao is a city redeemed by blood. . . . Let it be clear: Bilbao conquered by arms. Nothing of pacts and posthumous thanks. The law of war, hard, virile, inexorable."[7] While Areilza was haranguing the public, the political commissars were executing their vanquished enemies. Could there be forgiveness? Areilza was talking of winners and losers, of heroic soldiers and sewer rats. It was the highly "educated" man who would become, as mayor of Bilbao, the man cheering for Franco's "liberation" and praising Hitler.

After the fall of Bilbao, Agirre's stance was different. He asked his followers to harbor no feelings of hatred or revenge against the victorious fascists. Christian life meant forgiveness. In time, even "victorious" Areilza distanced himself from the dictator and began to work to change the regime and, in his memoirs, he paid tribute to Agirre. While in the heat of the war Areilza's words about Agirre had been pitiless and unforgiving, in his autobiography Areilza praised him. Recognizing that "the nationalist error was an error of excessive love," Areilza recalled the moment when, after the fall of Bilbao, Agirre in public had warned, "Damned be whoever harbors in his heart a feeling of revenge." Areilza must have wished that as Bilbao's mayor he could have said the same. He visited and found Agirre's grave in Donibane Lohizune (Saint-Jean-de-Luz) "simple and moving," adding that such nobility "honors the memory of a man."[8] The vanquished man had won over the victorious one.

---

6. Slavoj Žižek, *Repeating Lenin* (Zagreb: Arkzin, 2001), 26.

7. Areilza, quoted in Iñaki Anasagasti and Josu Erkoreka, *Dos familias vascas: Areilza-Aznar* (Madrid: Foca, 2003), 146–48.

8. Areilza, quoted in Leizaola, *Conversaciones,* 138.

Crossroad 3. Gernika/Bilbao, Symbol/Iron

As if Spanish militarism and the Church's pro-fascist stance were
not enough, Agirre's defense of Gernika/Bilbao would put him
at the crossroads of the struggle between European fascism and
democracy as well. Bilbao's mineral reserves had strategic value.
"And there was another reason—the iron ore of the Basque provinces," observed the American ambassador in Spain, Claude
Bowers. "Franco needed this ore to trade for arms and ammuni-
tions; *and Nazi Germany needed it to prepare for its war against
European democracy.* The Basques were sending the greater part
to England, and the pledge of the rebels to divert it to Germany
had been given. Hitler had frankly announced in a public speech
that his soldiers were in Spain because Germany needed the iron
ore."[9] Gernika had been targeted "not only as a symbol of Basque
nationalism but because it was close enough to Bilbao to stand
as a warning to the people of that city of their fate if they did
not surrender."[10] Franco's main commander in the Army of the
North, General Mola, demanded the immediate surrender of
Bilbao under the threat that otherwise he would raze all Bizkaia
to the ground.

French historian Pierre Vilar pointed out the intimate bond
between Gernika and Bilbao:

> Why did the destruction of Gernika become, in turn, an
> *event-symbol* . . . .? It has been said at times that the world 'has
> known worse things,' but Gernika was the *first* to be destroyed,
> and by *German planes.* This fact had such implications that those
> who were responsible for it *denied* it, their supporters *believed*
> their denial and the spineless people *behaved as if they also
> believed it.* The effect of this denial may have saved Bilbao from
> the total destruction that had been announced by Mola.[11]

If Bilbao was the Basques' worldly city of commerce, industry,
and finance, Gernika with its Parliament and its Tree was the political city of the Basques' ancient law.

---

9. Claude Bowers, *My Mission to Spain: Watching the Rehearsal for World War
II* (New York: Simon and Schuster, 1954), 339.

10. Nicholas Rankin, *Telegram from Guernica: The Extraordinary Life of George
Steer, War Correspondent* (London: Faber and Faber, 2003), 117.

11. Pierre Vilar, *La guerra civil española* (Barcelona: Editorial Crítica, 1986),
81–82.

Agirre took his presidential oath in Gernika, but that very morning an event took place that defined Agirre's life. Following his wish, Agirre and all the authorities of the Basque Nationalist Party went to the Basilica of Begoña for a solemn and religiously intimate oath: "I swear in front of the Holy Host fidelity to the Catholic faith. . . I swear fidelity to my motherland Euskadi and to her service I surrender my life. . ."[12] Agirre's oath was sacramental in the strictest Catholic sense of the term. It was done in the presence of the Holy Host, kneeling over red velvet, under the motherly gaze of the Virgin. It was the sacrifice of the son for the Mother Virgin and the Mother Country. The die had been cast.

Agirre's experience of politics as sacrament was going to be betrayed by politics as democratic opportunism. The British government pursued a policy of neutrality relative to the turmoil in Spain. The Conservatives then in power had no appetite for a leftist Spanish Republican government, and under British pressure, the French Socialist government of Leon Blum and twenty-four other European governments accepted a pact of "nonintervention." Franklin Roosevelt did nothing to assist the Republic, while U.S. corporations like Ford, General Motors, Firestone, Texaco Oil, and other businesses helped Franco's fascists. Roosevelt later admitted that he had made "a grave mistake" and that soon afterward he had paid a price for it because the Western democracies' spineless response ended up emboldening Hitler. The word *Gernika* became taboo.[13] The only exception to the policy of nonintervention was the generosity and good will extended toward refugee children. It showed the contradictions of the humanitarian stance—let Franco and Hitler massacre them in Gernika/Bilbao, but we will feed the children if they manage to escape elsewhere. Orwell summed it up in a 1942 essay: "The outcome of the Spanish war was settled in London, Paris, Rome, Berlin—at any rate not in Spain. . . . The war was actually won for Franco by the Germans and Italians."[14]

"After all, the Basques were a small people," wrote Steer, "and they didn't have many guns or planes, and they did not receive any foreign aid. . . but they had, throughout this painful civil war, held

---

12. Leizaola, *Conversaciones*, 192.

13. Vilar, *La guerra civil,* 165

14. George Orwell, "Looking Back on the Spanish War," in *The Collected Essays, Journalism and Letters of George Orwell*, vol. 2, *My Country Right or Left 1940–1943*, ed. Sonia Orwell and Ian Angus (New York: Harcourt, Brace & World, 1968), 262–63.

high the lantern of humanity and civilization.[15] Steer could not hide his respect for Agirre's determination and humanity. "Martyr-dom of the Basques," Bowers entitled one of his chapters. He was another foreign observer with a "wholehearted sympathy"[16] for the Basques. The U.S. ambassador observes how the so-called "neu-tral" governments "meticulously . . . enforce[d] 'nonintervention' against the loyalists [Republicans] while turning a blind eye on the open flaunting of the Axis powers,"[17] including the French author-ities' seizure of planes headed for the defense of Bilbao when they landed in Pau for refueling. As a local newspaper put it the very day on which Gernika was to be bombarded, "Nonintervention is the most powerful cannon at the service of Franco."[18]

Crossroad 4. Nationalism/Internationalism. Particularism/Universalism

After being defeated in the war it was time for Agirre to go into exile and find help for his people from the international commu-nity—the only possible salvation for his nationalist cause. The fall of Bilbao pushed Agirre's government toward Santader. Agirre went to Villaverde de Trucios, "on a road packed with fugitives," he wrote, "and over which were flying, with the help of the moon, air-planes that, with their machine guns, produced many casualties."[19] George Steer, the journalist who had made international news with his "Telegram from Guernica," wrote about that night as well: "Here at least there was moonlight, a clear view along the gleaming ribbon road, the companionship of the softly flowing river and of many other mortals also fleeing west."[20] He wrote those lines with Agirre's pen that Steer had taken that very night in his last visit to the empty offices of the Basque government in the Hotel Carlton. Picasso's painting and Steer's pen would be critical for the interna-tional echo give to Gernika's massacre.

---

15. Steer, *The Tree of Gernika*, 365–66.
16. Bowers, *My Mission to Spain*, 340.
17. Ibid., 347.
18. The daily *La Tarde* of April 26, 1937, quoted in Gregorio Arrien, *Niños vascos evacuados a Gran Bretaña, 1937–1940* (Bilbao: Asociación de Niños Evacuados el 37, 1991), 32.
19. Quoted in Anasagasti and Erkoreka, *Dos familias vascas*, 129.
20. Steer, *The Tree of Gernika*, 331, 366-367.

After the Spanish Civil War the Basque government-in-exile moved its headquarters to Paris. During World War II Agirre was to experience a harrowing odyssey of escape with his family and a group of Basque exiles in Belgium. As caravans of refugees were marching along the roads toward France and Nazi planes were bombarding and firing at them from the air, Agirre noted: "This same air power had made the Basque roads during our war a mockery to civilization."[21] In fact, there was someone Agirre knew about who was actively involved from the air in "The Battle of France": he was von Richthofen, the destroyer of Gernika. Gernika and Belgium—it was all the same for the Nazi commander, and so it was for Agirre.

As he was eluding his Nazi and French and Spanish persecutors, Agirre was confronted with the collapse of European civilization. He saw the repetition of a continent in ruins and remembered the figure of Napoleon: "I recall Chateaubriand's writings of 1814, in which he announced the fall of the colossus through the constant accumulation of ruins. A nation where the Emperor entered was a ruined nation . . . Something similar is happening in what pertains to the ruin of the nations which Hitler is occupying."[22] Amid European ruins Agirre dreamed of America as "the promised land,"[23] as the "continent which . . . has attained a marvelous personality" and is the "country of salvation."[24] When he set foot in Brazil in late August, 1941, he wrote: "I felt like bending down and kissing it. Here was a free land, something I had not seen for a long time."[25] Agirre became staunchly pro-United States.

In Agirre's *From Gernika to New York, Passing through Berlin*, if Gernika was the origin of everything, New York was the final destination. New York, which had a Basque Center, had been chosen as the first U.S. "delegation" to which representatives of the Basque government were dispatched in August of 1938. Agirre arrived in New York with his wife and two children in December of 1941 and stayed there for the next four years writing and teaching at Columbia University. From New York Agirre traveled to Latin America to visit and work with Basque communities in Mexico, Guatemala, Panama, Columbia, Peru, Chile, Argentina, and Cuba. He was

---

21. Aguirre, *Escape via Berlin*, 29.
22. Ibid., 237.
23. Ibid., 294.
24. Ibid., 285
25. Ibid., 296.

received in every capital city with the honors of a head of state. His writings and speeches were focused on counteracting the anti-Basque propaganda, shoring up democracy against "Latin dictatorships," and promoting Christian democracy in Europe. Writers such as Jacques Maritain were among his closest advisors. Agirre was one of the forty-two European intellectuals who, in November 1942, signed the manifesto addressing the "world crisis" and setting forth the liberal the principles for a postwar Europe. He was active among the European Christian Democratic leaders who began regular meetings in New York in 1943.

"Liberty" was the cornerstone concept of Agirre's political thinking: "Only when one loses one's liberty does one become aware of the fact that it has no possible substitute."[26] Liberty was naturally tied to his nationalist program. But one should add immediately that his notion of liberty, and therefore of his nationalism, was premised on one avowed fundamental condition: *universality*. The "air of freedom" he would experience when he set foot in America was felt as "the strength and universality with which liberty endows even the smallest of men."[27] In the cargo ship that would take him and his family from Europe to the promised land of America he was accompanied by four high-ranking Polish Jews with whom Agirre discussed politics: "Will the universal ideas defended today be used for universal good? That is to say, will they be applied to all men and all nations equally, or will they be belittled an d reserved for the chosen few?"[28] His first proposition about liberty, underlined in Agirre's text, is: "*Liberty is a universal patrimony.*"[29] Agirre in fact draws a distinction between a nationality of an ethnic type that must be sacrificed for a nationality based on the principle of citizenship that can be rendered universal. Basque national identity, he argues, should be respected because it springs from the principle of universality (every nation has a right to freedom), not from any exclusive particularism.

For Agirre "America" included Latin America as well. The political vision of a world ruled by universalist principles requires for him "pan-Americanism." Agirre became a pioneer voice in

---

26. Ibid., 275.
27. Ibid., 303.
28. Ibid., 317.
29. Ibid., 321.

requesting that the Atlantic Charter, which should not "be based on anything but liberty," should also include Latin America, for otherwise, "It would lack that universality so important for the welfare of all in the present struggle, and it would be no guarantee of peace."[30]

Agirre's government-in-exile returned from New York to Paris by mid-1946. The Spanish economic situation worsened after World War II; Basque nationalist guerrilla groups, with the support of Agirre's government and led by Ajuriaguerra, began acts of sabotage against Franco's regime. Funds from a network of Basques communities were channeled for the cause. Agirre counted on an oral agreement negotiated in 1942 (known as the "Umbe Pact") between the Basques supplying espionage and combat troops in exchange for the Allies' intervention against Franco after the war. In 1947 the Basques launched a strike that lasted seven days; a larger strike that began in Barcelona and was seconded by 85 percent of the Basque work force took place in 1951. Agirre's cabinet even expelled the Communists from his cabinet to counter American objections. Agirre combined his pro-Basque activities with his dedication to the creation of a European federalist movement led by Konrad Adenauer and Alcide de Gasperi; the movement was officially formed in The Hague in May 1947 and Agirre was named to its Committee of Honor.

But the bitter political reality of principles and promises trumped by pragmatism would soon become apparent when, shortly after the 1951 strike, the United Stated reversed its position and sided with the dictator Franco. By 1953 the accord of the American bases in Spain in exchange for aid had been signed; this led to the international recognition of the Franco regime. France expelled Agirre's government from its building, which was now turned to Spain, and closed the clandestine radio station that broadcasted for Basques. This was democracy in action by the Western powers a few years after having defeated European fascism as Agirre had to discover to his dismay.

Crossroad 5: Gernika/Hiroshima. Agirre/Arrupe

At the end of his book/memoir Agirre quotes the Gettysburg address to make a profession of faith in the United States and issue

---

30. Ibid., 352.

a mandate: "Everything depends on you, America, more than on any one else. Because you are a new man, a symbolic fusion of all the races of the earth, all those who have fallen for the cause, all those who suffer and hope rely on you to carry to fulfillment their dreams of liberty."[31] Agirre collaborated actively with the Department of State and intelligence services by forming a Basque espionage network operating in Europe and Latin America. The ardent expectation from the Basque nationalists was that, after the loss of the war by the Axis powers, Franco's days were counted.

For Agirre the ideological struggle between fascism and democracy was nothing less than "a universal civil war" in which "a fight to the death between two diametrically opposed conceptions of life in which the spiritual destiny of all humanity will be determined."[32] His perspective on the leadership of the U.S. had nothing do to with empire, but rather on the fact that, "Providence has assigned a role of such universality to President Roosevelt," while at the same time promoting and reporting on "a universal feeling of faith in this man and what he stood for."[33] Still, there was little doubt of which was Agirre's ultimate aspiration: "Many people dream of the great synthesis which will bring us to the solution of the future. I dream of a return to the principles of the Sermon on the Mount and early Christianity."[34]

Prior to its support for Franco, Agirre failed to see the inaugural betrayal by the United States to his universalist politics—the nuclear destruction of Hiroshima and Nagasaki. It would take the eyes of the Bilbaino Jesuit Pedro Arrupe to see the enormity of the catastrophe that linked Gernika to Hiroshima. It was also this link that Mauriac saw in the face of his dead friend when he exclaimed "what a vision!" and remarked that the victory of the democracies at the end of great war "concealed, at the very heart of the West, another very hidden victory: the one of the professional armies and policemen."[35]

Agirre had experienced Gernika's horror as the prologue to the Holocaust and repeated again and again in every European city bombarded by the Nazis. But von Richthofen's words after destroying Gernika—it was "a complete technical success," the bombs

---

31. Ibid., 376.
32. Ibid., 304.
33. Ibid., 374–75.
34. Ibid., 327
35. Quoted in Ugalde, "José Antonio de Aguirre y Lecube," 58.

producing "marvelous effects"—would be replicated by Agirre's own savior, the United States, after "Little Boy" was dropped from the *Enola Gay* over Hiroshima—a bomb that most U.S. top military commanders opposed because they saw it as unnecessary to end the war. "This is the greatest thing in history,"[36] an excited President Truman had remarked in jubilation. The pilot who dropped the bomb, Paul Tibbets, said, "If Dante had been with us on the plane, he would have been terrified."[37] The success was such that it merited a repeat performance, and "Big Boy" was dropped three days later on Nagasaki—chosen instead of Kokura, the original target city, because of poor visibility there. The pilot reported, "Results clear and successful in all respects. Visible effects greater than any tests." When he was asked about any regrets, Truman replied, "not the slightest in the world," and when asked whether the decision had been difficult, he said, "Hell no, I made it like that,"[38] and he snapped his fingers. This was the same holocaust logic that Franco and Hitler had inaugurated in Gernika, now applied to a target many times larger: arbitrarily select a city, then sacrifice and obliterate it along with hundreds of thousands of people, and thus "send a message" to the enemy. Soon the scientists who made the bomb possible—Oppenheimer, Szilard, Einstein—were horrified by the monster they had created and begged the president not to use it, only to be met with scorn for having become cry-baby scientists. "We in America," wrote Lewis Mumford at the time, "are living among madmen. Madmen govern our affairs in the name of order and security."[39] This madness would extend to the Cold War and lead to the support of Franco's regime by the United States.

Agirre, the man of Gernika who must have felt that anything done to defeat Hitler was necessary and right, was now ideologically obliged to turn a blind eye to his own protector's atrocity. What was done to vanquish European fascism had to be right, even if it might entail answering hell with hell. It was Arrupe, then living in Hiroshima, who saw the historic novelty of the Event in all its horror. When the atomic bomb exploded, Arrupe was the

---

36. Harry Truman, *Memoirs by Harry S. Truman: 1945 Year of Decisions* (Old Saybrook, CT: Konecky Associates, 1999), 465.

37. Tibbets, quoted in Oliver Stone and Peter Kuznick, *The Untold History of the United States* (New York: Gallery Books, 2012), 167.

38. Truman, quoted in Stone and Kuznick, *The Untold Story,* 179.

39. Lewis Mumford, "Gentlemen: You Are Mad!," *Saturday Review of Literature,* March 2, 1946, 5.

master of novices in a Jesuit center at Nagatsuka, four miles from Hiroshima. Using the skills he had learned as a former medical student at the University of Madrid, and with help from the novices, he transformed the center into a clinic in which he attended to thousands of victims.

It was not only Arrupe who linked Hiroshima to Gernika. It was also connected in the experience of Robert Oppenheimer, the director of the Manhattan Project that would produce the atomic bomb at Los Alamos. One of the members of the Lincoln Brigade who died in the Spanish Civil War was Joe Dallet, whose widow, Kitty, would later marry Oppenheimer. To the surprise of many, the left-wing pacifist Oppenheimer became the ardent soldier and champion of the Cold War by his dogged determination to develop the bombs to be dropped over Hiroshima and Nagasaki. "From Spain to Los Alamos was a short step," wrote Freeman Dyson, a physicist who worked under Oppenheimer for twenty years. "Oppenheimer was as proud of his bombs as Joe Dallet had been proud of his guns. Oppenheimer became the good soldier that Kitty loved and admired."[40] Oppenheimer himself said that Gernika signaled the beginning of the atomic era.101a It was indeed a short step between Gernika and Hiroshima.

What Agirre saw in Gernika, Arrupe contemplated on August 6, 1945—the day of the Feast of the Transfiguration. He was thirty-seven. What he learned that day—the modern state's celebration of technologically sophisticated mass murder—changed him forever. In 1950, he traveled the world giving testimony of that day. His later revolutionary "re-foundation" of the Jesuit Order in the 1960s as its general head was the deferred action of the inner explosion that Arrupe experienced in Hiroshima.

Crossroad 6. Separatism/Federalism. Agirre/Prieto

Indalecio Prieto was the other "man of Gernika." When President Agirre swore the Basque Statute of Autonomy in Gernika, which implied the historic creation of Euskadi as an autonomous political entity, the Socialist Prieto supported it from Madrid's Government. He understood and loved Gernika and its historic significance, but from his own political perspective.

40. Freeman Dyson, "Oppenheimer: The Shape of Genius," *New York Review of Books*, August 15, 2013, 19.

Agirre and Prieto had represented the two dominant Basque political parties, Socialism and Nationalism, caught in a historic standoff to this day. Prieto was nationalism's nemesis in Bilbao. What most mattered for Prieto was his city, Bilbao. Although opposed to any talk of "independence," Prieto's ideology embraced a national affirmation of the Basque Country within a federal Spanish state. He served a militant nationalism of his own, based on the notion that Spain needed "to be saved among all of us." He argued against the monarchy that he despised and helped to exile. Like Agirre's fervent Basque nationalism, Prieto displayed "an ardent and patriotic regenerationist faith in Spain."[41] Agirre's support for Basque independence and Prieto's visceral opposition to it constitute, in a nutshell, the unbridgeable antagonism within Basque politics—one that, from Agirre's perspective, came down to the antagonism between Basque and Spanish nationalisms. Both men were from Bilbao, both accepted the legacy of Gernika, both recognized the existence of a Basque national entity—and yet each man's ultimate national frame implied the exclusion of the other's. It would be in exile that the two men would come to terms with the failure of their antagonism.

In the early 1940s, the Nationalist Agirre and his old antagonist/friend, the Socialist Prieto, would meet in New York's Jai Alai, Valentín Agirre's restaurant and port of entry for Basque refugees. Prieto had come there from Mexico for treatment of the degeneration of his cornea. Sometimes, in addition to Manu Sota and Jon Bilbao, the noted scholars Américo Castro and Fernando de los Ríos would join the party. Valentín Agirre would invite them for squid in its black ink and Marqués de Murrieta, the wine both Prieto and Agirre preferred. A recurrent theme in these evening meetings was the regeneration of Bilbao. Both men were planning a Basque public university in Bilbao, though it would have to wait decades until it materialized. One of their prewar projects had been the construction of a tunnel under Mount Artxanda to open the adjacent valley to future development. Prieto gave impetus to the idea, but it was Agirre's government that began work in 1936, after the war broke out. While Prieto served as minister of public works for the Spanish Republic in Madrid, in 1933 Prieto had developed, along with architect Ricardo Bastida, a series of urban

---

41. Prieto, Quoted in Alfonso Sáiz Valdivielso, *Crónica de un corazón* (Barcelona: Planeta, 1984), 143.

plans. There was only one problem—Prieto was an atheist socialist, Bastida a fervent Catholic. Religious faith being central to Bastida's life, he found a solution of sorts to their unlikely collaboration— Bastida gave the salary he received from Madrid to charity so that God would grant his friend religious faith.[42] When Prieto learned of his partner's action, he was moved to confess, "What a tragedy it is for me not to have religious faith."[43] Religion had also separated Prieto and Agirre. Yet the three Bilbainos, so apart in ideological terms, were bonded by friendship and civic responsibility. Gehry's and Guggenheim's late-century Bilbao was the deferred action of a plan designed seventy years earlier in Bilbao and New York by these three men's passion for their city.

After Prieto's cornea transplant failed in 1945, for days he was blind in the dark solitude of a New York hospital. In his imagination there was only one place to flee: Bilbao. "Every single night I think of Bilbao, of my Bilbao," he wrote. He was captive of a "Bilbao, city of iron, that forged chains of affection I could never break."[44] If Bilbao was the candle in the night of an exiled Prieto, his city of lights, politics was all darkness. "My failure is total," Prieto wrote in a November 1950 letter of resignation to the executive committee of his Socialist Party. Washington had decided to support Franco, and Prieto saw his party as the "victim of an illusion." As a socialist, he was embarrassed that of all the European countries that voted against Franco in the United Nations General Assembly, not one was socialist. Prieto suffered heart failure three times the following spring. Agirre held on to his pro-American dream until 1958, when finally he had to accept reality. He died of a heart attack in March 1960. Both were vanquished men, their hearts heavy and ready to explode, yet unwilling to bow to the betrayals of history.

When Prieto heard of his political antagonist Agirre's death, he wrote of "a wound I will never be able to close."[45] He eulogized Agirre's "innate goodness" and the "magical force" of his

---

42. See José Ramón Foraster Bastida, María Elisa de Bastida Díaz-Tejeiro, and Gorka Pérez de la Peña Oleaga, *Ricardo de Bastida: Arquitecto* (Bilbao: Colegio Oficial de Arquitectos Vasco-Navarro, 2002), 44.

43. Prieto, quoted in Alfonso Sáiz Valdivielso, "Prólogo," in Indalecio Prieto, *Pasado y futuro de Bilbao. Charlas en Méjico* (Bilbao: Ediciones El Sitio, 1980), ix.

44. Prieto, quoted in Sáiz Valdivielso, *Crónica*, 53.

45. Quoted in Leizaola, *Conversaciones*, 102.

"unshakable optimism." He praised Agirre's work as "inspired by the deepest personal conviction," and claimed that nobody in any party, including his own, combined Agirre's "exceptional qualities." But what is haunting is that Prieto started his eulogy by linking Agirre's death with his own son's, in a clear expression of a father/son relationship—"because José Antonio was a few weeks older than my son, dead—with the same illness!—twelve years ago. They shared the same draft, they served in the military during the same period, and they even played together in a reserve [soccer] team of the Athletic Club."[46] The loss of his son had left a grieving Prieto unable to function. Agirre, worried that Prieto might abandon politics altogether, had urged him not to give up. What Agirre could not have imagined was that his own death would be a reenactment of that filial one for Prieto. They were father and son, accepting the cross of history for the sake of their city and country. Prieto died two years later.

The exiled Prieto and Agirre, broken men drinking together in New York's Jai Alai restaurant, were stricken with the pathos of their singular political complicity. Half a century later, they remain a historic challenge to the Basque political deadlock still rumbling in Bilbao and Madrid. Despite his staunch nationalism, Agirre, considered by some as "a sort of *prietista avant la lettre*," displayed in exile extraordinary statesmanship—to the point that he was proposed to head the presidency of the Spanish Republican government-in-exile to carry out "the project of a co-federal [Spanish] State."[47] Without equivocation, he recognized that "today we know that the Spanish problem cannot be resolved without our collaboration. Ah! But neither can the Basque problem be solved without resolving at once the Spanish problem."[48] In 1944, when dealing with "The Iberian Problem," as with his "pan-Americanism," he applied he principle of universalism as his guiding view: "the future is pushing them [the Iberian nationalities] toward a confederation of Iberian peoples," he wrote, to then add: "This problem will be meaningless if it is not given a more universal focus, looking toward America on the one side, and on the other toward a closer understanding with Europe."[49] This co-dependency between

---

46. Quotes from Leizaola, *Conversaciones*, 110–11, 112, 102.
47. Ludger Mees, *El profeta pragmático: Aguirre, el primer lehendakari (1939–1960)* (Irun: Alberdania, 2006), 168, 151.
48. Aguirre, quoted in Mees, *El profeta*, 90.
49. Aguirre, ibid., 368.

the Basque and Spanish problems, so in contrast to his party-line Basque "separatism," caused even Agirre's closest collaborators to think he was betraying the cause.

How did Prieto and Agirre overcome their conflict? They had to accept that their antagonism could not admit a mediation—that, in sharp contrast to friendship or love, the enemy defines politics—while at the same time having to concede the *failure* of their antagonism. The only way each could be faithful to his own political truth and overcome its impasse was to include the other's perspective— they had to "bite the bullet" and see the validity of the other's truth. They saw the limits of their own oversimplifications when they divided their political space into two antagonistic fields, rather than situating one another in pluralist democratic space. Agirre and Prieto forged a new type of political relation in which previous oppositions were not dissolved in a plurality but articulated differently. Agirre and Prieto's recognition of their failures promised to transform the coordinates of what was politically possible.

A theoretical mapping of what Agirre and Prieto achieved can be articulated in terms of the changes they provoked in the hegemonic relations of their political system. The new articulation of political relations could at once, beyond the typical operation of populism, embrace what it opposes—that is, in Gramscian terms, a new hegemonic structure was needed able to create a different and more expansive system of equivalences that started by recognizing that the terms of their antagonisms were not fixed in past history or present political convenience. They took their antagonisms not as final limits but as frontiers through which they found a larger political field in which more autonomy meant simultaneously more hegemonic interaction. What defines antagonism is that "the presence of the 'Other' prevents me from being totally myself."[50] A crucial consequence of antagonism is that it provokes a misreading by which "the two antagonistic poles differ in the very way in which they define or perceive the difference that separates them."[51] A bipolar field gives rise to the "popular subject position" and is far different from a multipolar hegemonic field, ruled by the

50. Ernesto Laclau and Chantal Mouffe, *Hegemony and Socialist Strategy: Towards a Radical Democratic Politics* (London: Verso, 1985), 125.

51. Slavoj Žižek, "Da Capo senza Fine," in Judith Butler, Ernesto Laclau, and Slavoj Žižek, *Contingency, Hegemony, Universality: Cotemporary Dialogues on the Left* (London: Verso, 2000), 215.

"democratic subject position."[52] What Agirre and Prieto achieved was the transformation of their respective Basque and Spanish "popular" subject positions into truly "democratic" ones by erasing the nullifying presence and the mutual misreadings essential to the antagonistic Other. But we could say that they went even further in recognizing that democracy per se might not be enough to reconstitute a valid hegemonic project and that, besides de "democratic equivalence," what is needed is "the construction of a new 'common sense' which changes the identity of the different groups."[53] The current Basque political impasse calls for such "common sense" Prieto and Agirre displayed.

Crossroad 7. Reform/Revolution. Agirre/ETA

As these leaders died and ETA emerged as the new political power, the postwar generation had to confront all over again the unsolved political labyrinth regarding "the Basque problem." For the Basque resistance, an independent state with full sovereignty became the ultimate political desire. Hegel had claimed that the proper subject of historical narratives is the State, an abstraction made concrete in the conflict between desire and law. ETA's sacrifice has been the starkest proof of such an ultimate imperative. It had been easy to agree on the foundational idea behind ETA—"freedom"— yet its derivations into "independence," "sovereignty," or "nation-state" were far more contested. Influential authors such as Manuel Castells and Michael Keating wrote persuasively about the decline of the nation-state and about living in a "post-sovereign" era. European nation-states had delegated many of their basic historic competences to supra-state or sub-state institutions. Yet this "residual state," described in a series of reports in *El País* with the moon metaphor as "the waning state,"[54] is also the one that holds on to the fetish of its indissoluble sovereignty.

The day Agirre died, Julen Madariaga—who as a child had been evacuated from Bilbao following Gernika's destruction—was in a Bilbao prison charged with propaganda activities for ETA. He was released in time to cross the border clandestinely to attend Agirre's funeral. Agirre's remains had been flown from Paris to Donibane

---

52. Laclau and Mouffe, *Hegemony,* 131.
53. Laclau and Mouffe, Hegemony, 183.
54. *El País*, May 3, 2005.

Lohizune, and Madariaga kept a vigil at Agirre's corpse. He was there to receive the torch. "Aguirre dies and ETA is born," his biographer Batista wrote.[55] Madariaga had first met Agirre in the French Basque Country, where he had been sent to learn French and Agirre went for summer vacations. "José Antonio treated me like a son," Madariaga told me. The Madariagas were in fact close friends of the Agirres; Julen's uncle was married to Agirre's sister. The families lived on the same street, the Madariagas at 7 Sendexa, the Agirres at Number 15. They shared summers in Getxo until the Madariagas returned to Bilbao for the winter school months. The historic day when Agirre went from Bilbao to Gernika to be sworn in under its sacred oak as the first president of the new Basque government, Julen's father, Nicolás, was sitting next to him in the back of the chauffeured car. After the war Julen went to Chile's exile with his family. In 1947, Julen was finally sent back by his parents to his Basque "promised land" to attend a boarding school and later study law at the Jesuit University of Deusto. During the 1950s he would be one of the founders of Ekin and later ETA.

Agirre's fate was the political catechism in which the ETA generation was schooled. Nobody would question his democratic, Christian, and patriotic credentials, yet his defeat made a mockery of harboring any hopes of international support for overthrowing Franco's regime. Agirre's discussion of "the Iberian Problem" had ended in a dark prophecy: if the Peninsular peoples continued to be subject to dictatorship, he observed, "a new era of violence will result."[56] Just months before his death, Agirre learned of ETA's birth through a letter originating in the same office at 7 Sendexa Street in Bilbao where he had discussed Gernika's Statute with Julen's grandfather, the Republican Ramón de Madariaga, in the early 1930s. Even after Gernika had been destroyed by bombs, Agirre found reason for reassuring all who would listen that bombs and terror could not destroy the spirit of the Basque people. But before he died, the cruelest thought for Agirre was Gernika once again in flames, but this time with no Steer, Lauaxeta, or Picasso to show the world the difference between a true and a false crusade. It was Madariaga's turn to prove Agirre right or wrong. Both these Bilbaino men were adamantly nationalist yet,

---

55. Antoni Batista, *Madariaga. De las armas a la palabra* (Barcelona: RBA, 2007), 78.
56. Aguirre, ibid., 369.

beginning with religion, there was an abysmal gap between their worlds.

During the mid-1960s, at a moment of internal crisis in which Madariaga acted as the organization's leader, he proposed that Txabi Etxebarrieta should lead ETA's 1966 general assembly. Txabi's main ideological influence was his brother Jose Antonio, whose thinking is reflected in a text he wrote at the end of the 1960s. The brothers embraced an all-out armed struggle as the centerpiece of the new ETA. "We are for a radical and total change,"[57] Txabi declared, while opposing any type of reformism. The revolution demanded the country's complete national and social liberation. Pathetic reformists were not only the Agirres and Prietos of his parents' generation; so were the founders of ETA, such as Txillardegi (its main ideologue since the pre-ETA student group started in 1952) and his Socialist Group, whose program of mass action, working-class activism, and cultural struggle was voted down by ETA's Fifth Assembly as "petit bourgeois." "First is the attainment of a Basque national State,"[58] Etxebarrieta wrote. Agirre was criticized for working for the restoration of the Spanish democratic Republic and for upholding the legitimacy of a Spanish legality as the ground from which to seek Basque self-determination. He was blamed for his "naïve simple-mindedness"[59] in sacrificing an entire Basque generation for nothing, yet they could not see that they were putting ETA and the new generation onto the same path of reactive violence and martyrdom.

For the postwar generation, the fathers had lost the war against fascism. At the time of the transition, it was not uncommon to hear about the absence of an entire generation of Basque men from politics. Where had they been during Franco's forty years? The nationalist political father figure was embodied by the Basque Nationalist Party; they were the Agirres, Irujos, and Leizaolas, the war heroes so lauded by Steer, Bowers, Mauriac, and pro-Republicans worldwide. Yet for the new generation of young militants in the 1960s, these men were nothing but a bunch of Christian democrats, politically irrelevant in their Parisian exile—they were the impotent

---

57. Quoted in José María Lorenzo Espinosa, *Txabi Etxebarrieta: Armado de palabra y obra* (Tafalla: Txalaparta, 1994), 118.

58. Ibid., 116.

59. Jose Antonio Etxebarrieta, *Los vientos favorables. Euskal Herria 1839–1959*, ed. José María Lorenzo Espinosa and Mikel Zabala (Tafalla: Txlaparta, 1999), 125.

father who had sold his soul to bourgeois placidity. José Antonio Etxebarrieta, reflecting on the "impasse without exit" in which Agirre's generation had fallen in their gradualist and law-abiding approach to politics, characterized their struggle as a "crisis of adolescence"[60]—they had not even reached adulthood.

The Etxebarrieta brothers were partly right: Agirre believed he was the embodiment of Providence to save his people while was subject to the big Others not only of religion and his nationalist ideology, but also to the interests of America's Cold War politics. This made him, who was the most pragmatic of Basque politicians, deny the changes happening in the international arena. Agirre was for his generation the charismatic father whose authority rested on representing his people but who ended up as a stand-in for the interests of the United States or Europe. The man of integrity and unconditional surrender to the cause of his people could be seen by the new revolutionary generation as an impotent father, a substitute for powers external to his country.

But once again it would seem that Agirre would win over his opponents when Bildu, the political party that was carrying outs ETA's legacy after it deposed its arms, chose Laura Mintegi as its candidate for the Basque presidency. In an ideological reversal from the line traced for ETA by the Etxebarrieta brothers, Mintegi declared that "the style of politics" of former president Agirre was the new model for her coalition. After ETA, when the formation of a new political subjectivity became a primary task for my generation, Agirre was again the ultimate model.

A Paradigmatic Leader

Agirre has been described frequently as a "charismatic" leader. But if one examines the historical impasses he was faced with, he was above all the *paradigmatic* leader of Basque politics in a moment of his country's maximum danger. Exacerbated by Bilbao's industrial capitalism during the final part of the nineteenth century, modernity brought fundamental impasses and ruptures in Basque society and culture and politics. In Agirre's time it was no longer enough a nationalism anchored on the Sabinian notion of Basque race, nor was any longer valid a Christianity that would side with fascism. Modernity required a new articulation of hegemonic political

---

60. Ibid., 136.

relations with the surrounding states and European powers, as well as a new ideological horizon of universality. It required courage to face a powerful fascist army from a situation of great military disadvantage, as well as fortitude to endure with dignity a crushing defeat, while going into exile and mobilizing the support of the international community. A people traumatized by the tragedy of a Gernika razed to the ground, with the marks of a distinct language and culture engraved in its traditional identity, at the crossroads of all the ideological and political challenges faced by the turbulent European twentieth century—Agirre would paradigmatically embody all the impasses of his people and seek the possibility of breakthroughs in the best ideals of the Christian and Western legacies. That in a period of such radical transformations he was able to keep the loyalty of his people until the end is testament to his unique leadership.

Bibliography

Aguirre, José Antonio de. *Escape Via Berlin: Eluding Franco in Hitler's Europe.* 1944. Reprint, Reno: University of Nevada Press, 1991.

Anasagasti, Iñaki, and Josu Erkoreka. *Dos familias vascas: Areilza-Aznar.* Madrid: Foca, 2003.

Arrien, Gregorio. *Niños vascos evacuados a Gran Bretaña, 1937–1940.* Bilbao: Asociación de Niños Evacuados el 37, 1991.

Badiou, Alain. *The Century.* Translated by Alberto Toscano. Malden, MA: Polity Press, 2007.

Batista, Antoni. *Madariaga: De las armas a la palabra.* Barcelona: RBA, 2007.

Bowers, Claude. *My Mission to Spain: Watching the Rehearsal for World War II.* New York: Simon and Schuster, 1954.

Butler, Judith, Ernesto Laclau, and Slavoj Žižek. *Contingency, Hegemony, Universality: Cotemporary Dialogues on the Left.* London: Verso, 2000.

Dyson, Freeman. "Oppenheimer: The Shape of Genius." *New York Review of Books,* August 15, 2013, 18–19.

Etxebarrieta, Jose Antonio. *Los vientos favorables: Euskal Herria 1839-1959,* edited by José María Lorenzo Espinosa and Mikel Zabala. Tafalla: Txlaparta, 1999.

Foraster Bastida, José Ramón, María Elisa de Bastida Díaz-Tejeiro, and Gorka Pérez de la Peña Oleaga. *Ricardo de Bastida: Arquitecto.* Bilbao: Colegio Oficial de Arquitectos Vasco-Navarro, 2002.

Laclau, Ernesto, and Chantal Mouffe. *Hegemony and Socialist Strategy: Towards a Radical Democratic Politics.* London: Verso, 1985.

Leizaola, Jesús María. *Conversaciones sobre José Antonio Aguirre.* Bilbao: Idatz Ekintza, 1983.

Lorenzo Espinosa, José María. *Txabi Etxebarrieta: Armado de palabra y obra.* Tafalla: Txalaparta, 1994.

Mees, Ludger. *El profeta pragmático: Aguirre, el primer lehendakari (1939–1960).* Irun: Alberdania, 2006.

Mumford, Lewis. "Gentlemen: You are Mad!" *Saturday Review of Literature,* March 2, 1946, 5–6.

Orwell, George. "Looking Back on the Spanish War." In *The Collected Essays, Journalism and Letters of George Orwell.* Vol. 2, *My Country Right or Left 1940–1943,* edited by Sonia Orwell and Ian Angus. New York: Harcourt, Brace & World, 1968.

Rankin, Nicholas. *Telegram from Guernica: The Extraordinary Life of George Steer, War Correspondent.* London: Faber and Faber, 2003.

Sáiz Valdivielso, Alfonso. *Crónica de un corazón.* Barcelona: Planeta, 1984.

———. "Prólogo." In Indalecio Prieto, *Pasado y futuro de Bilbao. Charlas en Méjico.* Bilbao: Ediciones El Sitio, 1980.

Steer, George. *The Tree of Gernika.* 1938. Reprint, London: Faber and Faber, 2009.

Stone, Oliver, and Peter Kuznick. *The Untold History of the United States.* New York: Gallery Books, 2012.

Truman, Harry. *Memoirs by Harry S. Truman: 1945 Year of Decisions.* Old Saybrook, CT: Konecky Associates, 1999.

Ugalde, Martin de. "José Antonio de Aguirre y Lecube." In José Antonio de Aguirre y Lecube, *Obras Completas,* vol. 1. Donostia: Sendoa, 1981.

Vilar, Pierre. *La guerra civil española.* Barcelona: Editorial Crítica, 1986.

Žižek, Slavoj. *Repeating Lenin.* Zagreb: Arkzin, 2001.

Literature and Political Conflicts: The Basque Case

Mari Jose Olaziregi

Much has been written about the role that literature can play in a troubled political context, about its power to contribute nuances, to break taboos and reveal grey hues . . . all of them virtues that extoll its detabooing and performative power. The question is, I suppose, how to champion writing and reading when we are embroiled in a tragically violent context and the whirlwind of violent images that besieges us every day is incessant. Perhaps the difficult thing is not taking a stand against that violence, but, as Slavoj Žižek would say,[1] having the courage to try and figure out what the cause is. And that is where, in my opinion, literature can have a privileged function.

Not the singer, but the song, Hank Williams used to sing. That is where I would like to situate the start of this brief reflection on contemporary Basque literature about the conflicts and wars that have devastated us. I am interested in writers not on account of what they say, but for what they write, although saying this is, clearly, naïve in the current entertainment culture, in which writers must not only narrate, for example, violence, but also give their opinion about it, declare their position, even though in doing so they may go radically against what they have written. Jo Labanyi speaks in similar terms regarding Spanish novels about the civil war when she stresses the importance of the context in which that

---

* This article has been written as a part of the MHLI group IT 1047-16 project, financed by the Basque Government. Translated by Cameron Watson.

1. Slavoj Žižek, *Sobre la violencia. Seis reflexiones marginales* (Barcelona: Paidós, 2009), 18.

literature has been produced, consumed and explained.[2] Labanyi alludes to the social debates that have preceded Spanish works on the civil war, social debates framed, without any doubt, by significant media coverage. One could claim the same, certainly, for the socialization of what is termed the Basque conflict, a socialization that passes through (among other things) a media deployment that has clearly evolved toward more belligerent attitudes and that has been manifestly more and more conditioned by aspects like the terrible trajectory of ETA itself, the editorial line of the media outlet in question, or its place of publication. This is how recent research into the topic describes it:

> The treatment by the Basque press of the conflict evolved in response to the worsening activity of ETA. It became increasingly complicated to receive verified, open, corroborated, and critical information about the conflict. Editorial lines polarized toward extreme positions and "trench journalism" was the norm with the coming of the new century. . . . the attitude demonstrated by the Basque press in the post-ETA period (2011–2016) has been more constructive than that employed by the conservative press in Madrid, [which is] much more entrenched in old-fashioned positions.[3]

Although the objective of what follows is to reflect on the narrativization of the Basque conflict by Basque writers, I will not overlook the sociohistorical context in which this literature has been created, and the pressures/conditions that writers have faced in recent decades. This analysis will also incorporate the importance that novels about our historical memory, and especially the Spanish Civil War, has had in analyzing the causes of terrorism. In order to do this, I will organize the presentation in three clearly demarcated sections. I will start by contextualizing briefly the memory boom that we are also experiencing in the Basque context, before then moving on to outlining the evolution of Basque literature that addresses the topic and the debates that have generated such treatment. I will conclude my reflection with a very brief note on the gender politics that has followed the literary treatment of the conflict.

---

2. Jo Labanyi, "The Politics of Memory in Contemporary Spain," *Journal of Spanish Cultural Studies* 9, no. 2 (2008), 120.

3. Txema Ramírez de la Piscina, Imanol Murua Uria, and Patxo Idoiaga Arrospide, "Prensa y conflicto vasco (1975–2016): Recopilatorio de actitudes y vicisitudes," *Revista Latina de Comunicación Social* 71 (2016), 1029.

Conflict, What Conflict?

I should perhaps start by explaining the title of the article and asking myself what I mean by "Conflict, what conflict?" I would, almost certainly, be parodying any inhabitant of the Basque Autonomous Community, an inhabitant for whom, according to the latest survey published by the Basque Government Office for Sociological Research, dating from March 2016,[4] the ranking of the most important issues currently facing Euskadi is as follows, in descending order: the job market (83 percent), economic problems (15 percent), the political situation (politicians, political conflict) (12 percent), and housing (11 percent). It is evident that the results are similar across the different age spans addressed by the study (for example, 18–29 year-olds, 46–64 year-olds, and 30–45 year-olds). Meanwhile, as was to be expected, following the declaration of a ceasefire by ETA on October 20, 2011, the problem of ETA terrorism has been relegated to a secondary level when it comes to the concerns of Basque society. I would point out, lastly, that to date, ETA has staged its disarmament, but it has not dissolved.

We would have to add that in the Basque context, the term "Basque conflict" would refer to the story that left-wing Basque nationalism developed during the initial period of the armed group (the years 1958–1968). As the historian Leyre Arrieta explains,[5] they were the years in which the armed strategy was established, years in which the first victims were chosen, and a narrative was developed, encouraged too by publications like *Vasconia* (1963) by Federico Krutwig, about a legendary confrontation between Basques and Spaniards, a vision of a historical conflict that, according to this version, had existed since ancient times and would only conclude with independence and the creation of a socialist Basque state. This definition, widely contested, among others, by experts like Jesús Casquete, Gaizka Fernández Soldevilla, and Edurne Portella,[6] as well as by recent institutionalized discourses, has

---

4. See file:///Users/Marijo/Desktop/sociómetro%20vasco.pdf.

5. Leyre Arrieta, "ETA y la espiral de la violencia. Estrategias y víctimas," in *Imágenes de la memoria. Víctimas del dolor y la violencia terrorista*, ed. Pilar Rodríguez (Madrid: Biblioteca Nueva, 2015), 23.

6. Jesús Casquete, "Abertzale sí, ¿pero quién dijo de izquierdas?" *El viejo topo* 68 (2010), 15–19; Gaizka Fernández Soldevilla, "El nacionalismo vasco radical ante la transición española," *Historia contemporánea* 35 (2007), 818; Edurne Portela, *El eco de los disparos* (Barcelona: Galaxia Gutemberg, 2016), 19.

resulted in a censorship, a tabooing, I would say, of the term itself as opposed to terms like "consensus" or "negotiation," defended by a governmentally subsidized political economy and that argues for dismissing any terminology that might influence what pits us against or distances us from one another.

Even the political logic that sustains current Basque culture persists, in the same way that, according to Luisa Elena Delgado, that which dominates Spanish culture does,[7] consensus and normality. For her part, the anthropologist Jacquline Urla has analyzed the evolution of linguistic policy and planning in Euskadi, concluding that arguments that spoke in the terms of "linguistic conflict" have evolved into "total *quality language revival*," in which antagonistic discourses about Euskara (the Basque language) have been overcome and a plan of action established to restore and broaden the consensus surrounding Euskara.[8] Whatever the case, the use I will make here of the word "conflict" will refer to the common meaning this has in English, that is, to a struggle, problem, or armed confrontation.

Memory Studies about Conflict in the Basque Context

Much has been said about the memory boom within the humanities in recent decades;[9] about the impact that discourses and studies about memory in the 1980s in Europe and the United States have had, and about the globalization of memory of the Holocaust by the late 1990s.[10] Obsessed with memory, there has even been talk of marketing nostalgia, of the need to transform peoples and landscapes into museums, of the growth in autobiographies and postmodern historical novels, and of a museification of a world that seeks full total memory.[11] In the Basque case, the last three decades have witnessed a blossoming of memory. Not just on an

---

7. Luisa Elena Delgado, *La Nación Singular. Fantasías de la normalidad democrática española (1996–2011)* (Madrid: Siglo XXI, 2014), chaps. 1 and 3.

8. Jacqueline Urla, "Total Quality Language Revival," in *Language in Late Capitalism: Pride and Profit*, ed. Alexandre Duchene and Monica Heller (London and New York: Routledge, 2012), 73–92.

9. Jan-Werner Müller, *Memory and Power in Post-War Europe: Studies in the Presence of the Past* (Cambridge: Cambridge University Press, 2002), 13.

10. Andreas Huyssen, *Present Pasts: Urban Palimpsests and the Politics of Memory* (Stanford: Stanford University Press, 2003), 13–14.

11. Ibid., 14.

institutional level, where, from the Basque government General Secretary's Office for Peace and Coexistence, projects related to the civil war and ETA terrorism have been picked up and established; projects like the preparation of a Memory Map, proposals such as *Eskolabakegune*, which includes the Adi-Adian program in which victims and perpetrators of terrorism present their testimony in schools,[12] and so on. Moreover, city ouncils, like that of Donostia-San Sebastián, have created human rights departments, in which tributes to, the visibility of, and recognition of the victims of the Franco regime and terrorism have an unquestionable prominence.[13] For their part, sites of memory of the civil war in Euskadi, like Gernika, have embraced interesting projects like the town's Peace Museum in Gernika,[14] to cite just one example.

For its part, too, the Basque literary institution has come up with critical discourses and analyses about our most recent historical memory: doctoral theses;[15] projects undertaken by established research groups on historical memory;[16] and publications financed by universities or published in the academic field.[17] Other recent

---

12. See http://www.euskadi.eus/victimas-proyectos/web01-s1lehbak/es/.

13. See https://www.donostia.eus/taxo.nsf/fwNweb?ReadForm&idioma=cas&id=A513328&doc=Area.

14. See http://www.museodelapaz.org/.

15. See for example Izaro Arroita, "Ramon Saizarbitoriaren nobelagintza Memoria Ikasketen ikuspegitik," PhD Diss., University of the Basque Country, 2015.

16. MHLI: Memoria Histórica en las Literaturas Ibéricas (http://www.mhli.net/).

17. For example, Egaña and Zelaieta, 2006; Mari Jose Olaziregi, "Basque Narrative about the Spanish Civil War and Its Contribution to the Deconstruction of Collective Political Memory," in *War, Exile, Justice, and Everyday Life, 1936–1946*, ed. Sandra Ott (Reno: Center for Basque Studies, University of Nevada, Reno, 2011), 117–32 and "Cartografía de la memoria en la literatura vasca actual," in *Conflictos de la Memoria/ Memoria de los conflictos. Modelos narrativos de la memoria intergeneracional en España e Italia*, ed. Leonardo Cecchini and Hans Lauge Lansen, Col. Études Romanes 62 (Copenhaghen: Museum Tusculanum Press, University of Copenhagen, 2015), 219–30; Jon Kortazar, ed. "La Guerra Civil en la literatura vasca," special issue, *Cuadernos de Alzate* 45 (2011); Jon Kortazar and Amaia Serrano, eds., *Gatazken lorratzak. Euskal arazoen islak narratiban 1936tik gaurdaino* (Donostia: Utriusque Vasconiae, 2012); Izaro Aroita and Lourdes Otaegi, eds., *Oroimenaren lekuak eta lekukoak. Gerra Zibilaren errepresentazio artistikoak vs. Kontaera historiko politikoa* (Bilbao: Universidad del País Vasco-Euskal Herriko Unibertsitatea, 2015).

publications, meanwhile, although not the products of Basque publishing houses or academic institutions, have also turned to the study of or reflection on narrative representations of the different Basque conflicts.[18] It is a question of studies in which the key concepts of Memory Studies, like collective memory, sites of memory, cultural memory, communicative memory, the postmemory generation, and the perpetrator/victimization/victim triad have been applied time and time again in order to analyze a Basque literature on memory widely canonized via the most prestigious awards in our literary field: the Euskadi Prizes. In fact, one could argue that, since 2000, there has always been a work in some form or genre (fiction, essay, children's and young adult literature) related to memory that has won a prize, both in Basque and in Spanish. Thanks to this commitment toward the past, Basque literature has also been transformed into a literature of resistance, to use a term coined by Barbara Harlow and that Sharon Roseman applies to the study of memory in the Galician context.[19] This seeks to reveal the differences between, on the one hand, a memory we may classify as *institutional/official* and driven, for example, by the winners of the Spanish Civil War, or even by governmental institutions that take humanitarian encouragement in a *cosmopolitan memory*;[20] and on the other, a national memory, often antagonistic and mythifying,[21] which seeks to uncover contradictions in the standardizing global historiographical story.

Basque narrative, especially that written in Basque, was slow in tackling representation of the civil war and Basque terrorism. As regards the former, hardly any novels were published during

---

18. Daniela Bister, *La construcción literaria de la víctima. Guerra Civil y Franquismo en la novela castellana, catalana y vasca* (Frankfurt: Peter Lang, 2015); Pilar Rodríguez, ed., *Imágenes de la memoria*; Edurne Portela, *El eco de los disparos* (Barcelona: Galaxia Gutemberg, 2016).

19. Sharon Roseman, "Celebrating Silenced Words: The 'Reimagining' of a Feminist Nation in Late-Twentieth-Century Galicia," *Feminist Studies* 23, no.1 (1997), 43.

20. Daniel Levy and Natan Sznaider, "Memory Unbound: The Holocaust and the Formation of Cosmopolitan Memory," *European Journal of Social Theory* 5, no. 1 (2002), 87–106.

21. Cf. the notion of "antagonistic memory" in Astrid Erll, *Memory in Culture* (New York: Palgrave Macmillan, 2001) and Joep Leerssen, "Monument and Trauma: Varieties of Remembering," in *History and Memory in Modern Ireland*, ed. Ian McBride (Cambridge: Cambridge University Press, 2001), 204–22.

the war itself, and even exiled authors like Jon Andoni Irazusta avoided relating the wartime tragedy in publications like *Joanixio* (1946), the first novel published in the postwar era. Nor did the entrance into modernity in the 1960s and the subsequent experimental phase that followed in Basque narrative until the mid-1970s encourage historical or realist novels about the conflict;[22] and as a consequence, the most significant representative of Basque academic critique, Professor Jesús María Lasagabaster, had no hesitation in pointing out, in 1990, that Basque literature continued to turn its back on reality.[23]

In effect, Lasagabaster was referring not to the limited representation that the Spanish Civil War had in our narrative, but to the scarce presence that the tumultuous Basque reality of the time, sadly marked by the activity of the terrorist group ETA (1959–), had in Basque literature. The terrorist group was at its deadliest in the 1980s, with massacres such as the notorious Hipercor bombing in 1987, which left twenty-one people dead. Right at that very time, the panorama of the Basque novel was dominated by dark rural themes and fantasy short stories clearly under Latin American influence that served to *deconstruct* the bastion of the Basque *costumbrista* novel, that is, the rural world, idealized by very traditional Basque nationalism and based on the Catholic faith, race, and the defense of regional rights. The violence that inundated these fictions, as in the case of *Hamaseigarrenean aidanez* (It happened on the sixteenth, 1983) by Anjel Lertxundi, could also be read as a metaphor of the violence that was rooted in Basque society.

The Basque Novel about ETA Terrorism

The major emergence of the topic of ETA terrorism in Basque- language novels and short stories began in the 1990s with the publication of novels like *Gizona bere bakardadean* (1993; in English, *The Lone Man*, 1996) and *Zeru horiek* (1995; *The Lone Woman*, 1999) by Bernardo Atxaga and the novel *Hamaika pauso* (Innumerable steps, 1995) by Ramon Saizarbitoria. The narrative strategies used by Atxaga in his two works transformed them into psychological

---

22. Olaziregi, "Basque Narrative about the Spanish Civil War."
23. See Jesús María Lasagabaster, ed., *Contemporary Basque Fiction*, trans. Michael E. Morris (Reno: University of Nevada Press, 1990), 22.

novels permeated by a high emotional content. These would include, among other things, the reduction of spatial-temporal elements to a limited number of days and places, the preeminence of heterotopic spaces of crisis or digression (the hotel or the prison), the obsessive repetition of metaphors, images, or dreams (the dream of the frozen sea in *The Lone Man* or the utopian arcadia that Irene, the protagonist of *The Lone Woman*, dreams about), and the use of intertexts that underscore the disillusion of former revolutionary ideas, such as texts by Rosa Luxemburg or Adriana Kollontai in the case of *The Lone Man* and the selection of "cursed" poets in the case of *The Lone Woman*. The protagonists of both novels share a destiny of uprooting and solitude. I would, finally, point out that Atxaga was inspired by real-life graffiti that alluded to an ETA "traitor" in order to outline the story of Irene.[24] Basque readers who picked up the novel cannot have failed to see behind Irene, the protagonist, the shadow of a former ETA member, María Dolores González Katarain or "Yoyes," who was assassinated by ETA in front of her son in 1986. I will return to her later.

One could say that the blossoming in the 1990s of addressing ETA in the Basque novel coincided with a similar tendency in English-language novels.[25] However, there are certain particularities that clearly distance the former insofar that, while it also demonstrates a notable diversity of approaches and typologies, it seems that it does not evince, at least until very recently, such a strong tendency to focus on events narrated from the victim's point of view as is the case of its English-language counterpart. Instead, the Basque novel has focused more on the perspective of the perpetrator, the terrorist. If, as Francis Blessington argues,[26] all novels that tackle terrorism seek to understand and test why someone chooses terror, what the terrorist mindset is, that has been the goal of the nearly seventy novels in the Basque language that have addressed the topic. In that sense, one could say, following the argument of anthropologists Joseba Zulaika and William A. Douglass,[27] that this approach has sought, above all, to

---

24. *El Dominical*, April 21, 1996.

25. Robert Appelbaum and Alexis Paknadel, "Terrorism and the Novel, 1970–2001," *Poetics Today* 29, no. 3 (2008), 395.

26. Francis Blessington, "Politics and the Terrorist Novel," *Sewanee Review* 116, no. 1 (2007): 117.

27. Joseba Zulaika and William A. Douglass, *Terror and Taboo: The Follies, Fables, and Faces of Terrorism* (New York: Routledge, 1996).

de-taboo terrorism of its fetishist and ritualized elements. For her part, Edurne Portela has pointed out the importance of analyzing the representation of the perpetrator, since "we need to consider and analyze critically what the role is played in our imagination by those perpetrators who, at the end of the day, form a part of our social configuration."[28]

But speaking about literature, about literature in the Basque language that has tackled the conflict and affirming categorically that it has not focused on victims is, I believe, oversimplifying the semantic and symbolic capacity of all literary texts; the nuances, what is implied, especially when they address the complexity of topics we are alluding to here. In fact, recent studies on the literary construction of the victim in Iberian novels, like that of Daniela Bister,[29] confirm such an argument. Bister contends, as regards the identity of victims and their representation in novels in Iberian settings that address the recovery of the historical memory of the civil war and the Franco years, that:

> In the literary field, there are no longer any attributions of uni-dimensional roles, that is, of victims and perpetrators, which demonstrates that literature thematicizes more in the detail and in a more differentiated way the problem of victim identities. In literary texts people are presented whose roles and identities are unclear: Are they victims? Are they perpetrators? Are they victim and perpetrator at the same time? Political discourse avoids such reflections and seems less critical and advanced than literary discourse.[30]

Bister analyzes Basque publications like *Gorde nazazu lurpean* (2000; *Guárdame bajo tierra*, 2002) by Ramon Saizarbitoria, *Soinujolearen semea* (2003; *The Accordionist's Son*, 2007) by Bernardo Atxaga, and *Antzararen bidea* (2008; *El camino de la Oca*, 2008) by Jokin Muñoz, and she often uses the concept "intermediate zone,"[31] in a similar way to that of Primo Levi's "grey zone," to refer to victimizations between the poles of victim and perpetrator. This concept would dismantle the rigid victim/perpetrator concept and capture the inquiring, reflexive will that a good book searches for.

---

28. Portela, *El eco de los disparos*, 126.
29. Bister, *La construcción literaria de la víctima*.
30. Ibid., 17.
31. Ibid., 65.

Indeed, there are formal and thematic similarities in the three aforementioned volumes. As regards the last two, I would point out the preeminence therein as well as in other novels on the conflict of metafictional structure and the reflection on writing.[32] As regards thematic similarities, I would highlight that in all of them the civil war appears as from the perspective of the losing side, and two of them especially—the novels of Atxaga and Muñoz—relate the radicalization of Basque politics to the Franco repression that came after the war.[33] Sites of memory like Gernika in the case of Atxaga's novel or the Erribera region of Navarre in the case of Muñoz's novel are used for attributes that Pierre Nora points out regarding these matters, that is, in so far as they bring together a deposited memory that seeks to promote social consensus in the national context.[34] Yet, at the same time, both sites of memory incite a dual memory, that of the civil war and that of ETA terrorism, in their attempt to offer a reflection on the causes and development of violence in the Basque Country. While personalities like Joseba and Agustin in *The Accordionist's Son* contend before the remembrance of the victims of the bombing of Gernika that, "we cannot hold up our heads until we've made them pay for that," (297),[35] Muñoz associates the image of socialist activists being shot in the back of the head in Erribera in 1936 by Francoists with that of a socialist activist being shot in the head by ETA in 2003. The Navarrese author turns to the idea that violence has been perpetuated and inherited from generation to generation among the perpetrators: "I would bet that more than one grandchild of the Requetés [Navarrese Carlist militiamen who sided with Franco in the civil war] from that time is

---

32. Mari Jose Olaziregi and Mikel Ayerbe, "El conflicto de la escritura y la re-scritura de la identidad: análisis de la narrativa de escritoras vascas que abordan el conflicto vasco," in *Identidad, género y nuevas subjetividades en las literaturas hispánicas*, ed. Katarzyna Moszczynska-Dúrst, Karolina Kumor, Ana Garrido Gonzalez, and Aranzazu Calderon Puerta (Warsaw: Instituto de Estudios Ibéricos de la Universidad de Varsovia, 2016), 45–66.

33. Olaziregi, "Cartografía de la memoria en la literatura vasca actual," 224–27.

34. Pierre Nora, *Realms of Memory: Rethinking the French Past*, vol. 1, *Conflicts and Divisions*, ed. and with foreword by Lawrence D. Kritzman, trans. Arthur Goldhammer (New York: Columbia University Press, 1997), 2210.

35. Mari Jose Olaziregi, "Los lugares de la memoria en la narrativa de Bernardo Atxaga," in *Bernardo Atxaga*, ed. Irene Andrés-Suárez and Antonio Rivas (Madrid: Universidad de Neuchâtel-Arcolibros, 2011),

all Basque Country this and Basque Country that. It is in their blood."[36]

Conflict and Generational Transmission: Ramon Saizarbitoria's Novel

For his part, the solid literary trajectory of Ramon Saizarbitoria is marked by a willingness to analyze our troubled reality and the myths that sustain it. In the first Basque novel on the conflict, *Ehun metro* (1976; *100 Meter*, 1985), Saizarbitoria described the politi-co-cultural repression of the Basque Country during the Franco period. Set in 1974, and through emblematic sites of memory in Donostia-San Sebastián like Constitution Square—named July 18 Square during the Franco uprising and in later years—the novel denounces a Basque collective identity suppressed and rejected by Franco; moreover, through intertextual allusions and well-known poems by Jaques Prevert, it explores the sense and use of the armed struggle, the horror of spilt blood.[37]

The novel *Hamaika pauso* focused on the last executions by the Franco regime, specifically that of ETA member Angel Otaegi, who was shot next to Juan Paredes Manot "Txiki" and three members of the FRAP (Frente Revolucionario Antifascista y Patriota, Revolutionary Antifascist Patriotic Front), on September 27, 1975. Saizarbitoria gave us a complex novel that included a secondary narrative level that thematicized the writing of a homonymous novel by the protagonist Iñaki Abaitua. It is a true literary palimpsest, a novel about metamemory[38] that, as stated in the reiterated quote attributed to Claude Simon (namely, "memory is a broken plate"), wrote about/constructed the memory of a Basque generation that during the period spanning 1973 to 1984 had gone from clandestine resistance to the Franco regime to the radicalization of the growth of terrorism. In order to do so, the novel incorporated techniques such as the repetition of scenes and elements that acted like true *corps conducteurs* in the style of the Nouveau Roman, and sketched out a bloody political itinerary whose ending for its

---

36. Muñoz, 2008, 164.
37. Olaziregi, "Basque Narrative about the Spanish Civil War."
38. See Ofelia Ferrán, *Working Thorough Memory: Writing and Remembrance in Contemporary Spanish Narrative* (Lewisburg, PA: Bucknell University Press, 2007).

protagonists, Iñaki Abaitua and Daniel Zabalegui, is tragic death. The repeated phrase "I don't know where all this is leading us" (157) in the mouths of activists, as well as the use of the Angel Otaegi trial, pointed to the leitmotiv that gave life to the novel: death as a final destination not just for the protagonists and its tragic victims, but for the Basque Country as a whole.

It is, precisely, that legacy of blood and death that Saizarbitoria's later novels address and critique: *Bihotz bi, gerrako kronikak* (1996; *Amor y guerra*, 1999), the already alluded to *Gorde nazazu lurpean* (2000), and *Martutene* (2012; English version, 2016). If the dignity of the losers, which the *gudaris* (Basque nationalist soldiers) demonstrated during the civil war, is a legacy that Saizarbitoria pays an emotional tribute to in the novel *Bihotz bi, gerrako kronikak* or in narrations like *The Lost War of the Old Gudari*,[39] in which the Donostia-San Sebastián writer narrated the feeling of loss that devastated a generation of gudaris who lost the war, the same is not true when it comes to the legacy of decades of terrorism in Basque society. In effect, Saizarbitoria clearly contrasts the legacy and noble humanist values of the gudaris and their Basque nationalist leaders during the war (Manuel Irujo, Juan Ajuriaguerra, and so on) with the so-called gudaris of ETA, from whom Saizarbitoria's characters distance themselves (*Los pasos incontables*, 399–400); and they suffer on discovering that sacred symbols like the *ikurriña* (Basque flag) have lost the symbolic value they once had for the old gudaris (*Guárdame bajo tierra*, 28). The progressive appropriation of concepts and symbols of traditional Basque nationalism by the radical Basque nationalism that Saizarbitoria's literature denounces is a fact that has been demonstrated by historians like Jesús Casquete, who has analyzed this appropriation through an analysis of symbols and sites of memory like the so-called Gudari Eguna, the Day of the Basque Soldier.[40]

Whatever the case, it is in *Martutene* (2012) where Saizarbitoria states most explicitly his rejection of transmitting ETA's legacy. It is, as stated by one critic in reference to the English-language edition,[41] a total novel that demands of readers attentive and reflexive reading, a "slow Reading" (sic). It is a "moral" book in the sense

---

39. See Olaziregi, "Basque Narrative about the Spanish Civil War."

40. Jesús Casquete, "Gudari Eguna," in *Diccionario ilustrado de símbolos del nacionalismo vasco*, coord. Santiago de Pablo et al. (Madrid: Tecnos, 2013), 430–43.

41. Mike Provata-Carlone "A Loftier Reality" (2016), at http://bookanista.com/loftier (accessed April 29, 2017).

of Kundera,[42] in so far as it seeks to discover or clarify a previously unknown truth; and in this complex novel in which truth has to do with a reality and a cartography marked by the consequences of decades of terrorism. The itineraries of the characters in the novel are marked by cities, streets, bars, and so on; marked by the memory of victims like Blanco, Mújica, and so forth; or by those threatened by the group who see their everyday lives terrorized by the threat of a possible attack. It is the novel in which the explicit description of the critique of terrorism in the mouths of characters like Julia, the translator, is absolutely irrefutable. This is a character who states she is glad that some ETA members have been arrested (*Martutene*, 2032–34),[43] who contends that she is shocked by the empathy her mother shows toward ETA prisoners and not their victims (2034–35), and who is ashamed by how long terrorism has been going on and the collective cowardliness hindering its defeat; an unreserved critique of a reality and a legacy that Julia, moreover, refuses to transmit to her son. In effect, Julia, the ex-partner of an ETA member with whom she had a son, Zigor, refuses to show him that letter that her father wrote to him and asked her to pass on. In the face of that legacy, she prefers the verses of J. Miguel Ullán in order to verbalize what the memory is she wishes to transmit to future generations: "tell them/that the only race is chance, that the only homeland is pain" (295).

Victims

As well as those mentioned, we could also note some recently published novels that have represented the conflict with different objectives. These include, for example, novels that speak about the need to raise awareness in the face of the brutality, such as *Zorion perfektua* (2002; *Perfect Happiness*, 2007) by Anjel Lertxundi; or those that suggest the need to air our dirty laundry like *Etxeko hautsa* (2011; *Los trapos sucios*, 2011), also by Lertxundi. Other works have gone further and have attempted to condemn the supposed guilt or equidistance of Basque society in the face of the conflict, such as the novel *Mea Culpa* (2011) by Uxue Apaolaza, among others. There are abundant and diverse themes but what stands out, obviously, is the need to analyze and analyze ourselves,

---

42. Kundera (1987), 16.
43. References are to pages in the electronic version of the book in Basque.

to judge attitudes and roles, to reflect both morally and ethically, and to contribute, by means of the cultural memory that literature creates, to shaping a collective memory that includes the suffering and recognition of the pain caused and contributes to resolving the conflict and to coexistence. I would say that the Basque novel is contributing to breaking the re-mythologizing of the terrorist, thereby answering the different types of fictional representation that the media or political powers have carried out for decades.

The same could be said with regard to short fiction, a genre in which recent anthologies like, for example, *Haginetako mina* (Toothache, 2008) edited by Mikel Soto, and *Our Wars: Short Fiction on Basque Conflicts* (2012) edited by Mikel Ayerbe, show the diversity of authors and approaches that the representation of the conflict has had in the field. This is a field in which, moreover, writers like Iban Zaldua have published essays such as *Ese idioma raro y poderoso* (2012; published in English as *This Strange and Powerful Language*, 2016), awarded the Euskadi Prize in 2013, about the attitudes and initiatives that Basque writers, especially those who write in the Basque language, have embraced in recent decades.

In any event, as Maurice Halbwachs states,[44] literature contributes to the construction of collective memory and this, like all memories, is changing and conditioned by social contexts. Without any doubt, the raison d'être of the significance that victims have acquired in recent decades, both at the Spanish state and international level, is to be found in events like the debates that surrounded the Law oh Historical Memory in 2007, in the emergence of transitional justice following the truth and reconciliation commissions in countries like Argentina (1983–84) and Chile (1990–91) and in the creation in 1998 of the International Court of Justice, which allowed for the international prosecution of dictators and criminals. In this way, victims who had been silenced and made to feel invisible for decades gradually acquired a global prominence that had been unknown to that time. One could argue much the same as regards the recognition that the victims of ETA terrorism have gained in recent years. It is a collective that was forgotten for too long, and that scarcely produced any social mobilization to condemn its situation for decades.[45] It even took some years before

---

44. Maurice Halbwachs, *On Collective Memory*, ed., trans., and with intro. by Lewis A. Coser (Chicago: University of Chicago Press, 1992), 191–235.

45. Rodríguez, ed., *Imágenes de la memoria*, 7–8.

associations like AVT, Asociación de Víctimas del Terrorismo (the Association of Victims of Terrorism, 1981–), had any visibility at all. An important contribution to this change was also made by pacifist groups that silently condemned the attacks, such as the coordinating body Gesto por la Paz de Euskal Herria (A Gesture for Peace in the Basque Country), created in 1986 following the fusion of several smaller organizations. Other groups, such as Bakea Orain (Peace Now) and Denon Artean (Among All of Us), worked along the same lines. According to experts, in recent years we have witnessed a clear politicizing of victims, especially in the aftermath of the attacks perpetrated by Islamist radicals on March 11, 2004 in Madrid.[46] Later reports and publications have only confirmed the importance of the defense, study, and reparation that victims have received in recent years; an importance that, as noted above, has been shaped institutionally in initiatives that both the Basque and central governments have undertaken in recent years.

Basque film and literature have also addressed the increasing importance of victims. In the case of film, as Santiago de Pablo contends, there has been a clear evolution from "a certain benevolence or understanding in the face of terrorism, which tended to be seen as a legacy of the Franco era" toward "more ethically committed viewpoints, [that] have focused on ETA's victims."[47] Since 2000, then, victims have been more unquestionably more prominent in Basque film. Feature films like *La casa de mi padre* (2008) by Gorka Merchán, *Zorion perfektua* (2009) by Jabi Elortegi, based on a novel of the same name by Lertxundi, and *Lasa y Zabala* (2014) by Pablo Malo are an example of what I am referring to. But it was a documentary, *La pelota vasca. La piel contra la piedra* (2003) by Julio Medem, which surpassed all others in the impact and controversy it provoked. That is how Joxean Fernandez,[48] Director of the Basque Film Archive, puts it at the same time as he demonstrates and analyzes the awful consequences of all this for Medem himself. For Fernandez the political climate of the time weighed too heavily

46. Arrieta, "ETA y la espiral de la violencia," 45.

47. Santiago de Pablo, *The Basque Nation On-Screen: Cinema, Nationalism, and Political Violence* (Reno: Center for Basque Studies University of Nevada, Reno, 2012), 414.

48. Joxean Fernnadez, "Razones y contextos de cuatro polémicas en el cine documental vasco," in "Basque Studies Monograph," ed. Mari Jose Olaziregi and Juan Arana Cobos, special issue, *Bulletin of Hispanic Studies* 93, no. 10 (2016), 1098.

on how the film was received. The expert Carlos Roldán Larreta expresses this in similar terms:

Condemning state violence—tortures, GAL [groups set up secretly by the Spanish government that carried out a "dirty war" against ETA in the 1980s], etc.—and its impunity, even though there is also a clear rejection of ETA's crimes, ended up costing him dearly. The day someone holding high political office apologizes for state violence and its impunity—as Ibarretxe did with regard to the silence of Basque society in the face of ETA—a giant step will have been taken in this country. The current dynamic, unfortunately, is to harass the artist who condemns that violence. Julio Medem is a good example. The lynch mob campaign he suffered with *La pelota vasca* and the pressure from the Partido Popular and its supporters to impede screening this documentary should have had no place in a democratic country.[49]

Twist (2013), by Harkaitz Cano, is a novel that, besides presenting a metafictional structure, focuses precisely on some of the victims alluded to in the previous paragraph: namely, victims of the dirty war like Lasa and Zabala. The novel is gaining international renown insofar that, as well as Spanish, it has been translated into Bulgarian and translations are being done into Serbian and English. One could say that it is a novel resembling fantasy poetics, and which turns to ghostly apparitions in order to narrate the condemnation of that crime committed in the past. That spectral presence, that tortured body that wakes up and appears all of a sudden, symbolizes resistance in the face of an unpunished crime. As Jacques Derrida states in *Spectres of Marx* (1993):

It is necessary to speak *of the* ghost, indeed *to the* ghost and *with* it, from the moment that no ethics, no politics, whether revolutionary or not, seems possible and thinkable and *just* that does not recognize in its principle the respect for those others who are no longer or for those others who are not yet *there*, presently living.[50]

The ghost, therefore, reveals to us a macabre crime committed in the past. Intertextual references to the disappeared in the

---

49. Carlos Roldán Larreta, "Imágenes de odio, sangre y muerte: las víctimas de la violencia política ante las cámaras de los cineastas vascos," in *Imágenes de la memoria*, ed. Rodríguez, 69.

50. Jacques Derrida, *Specters of Marx: The State of the Debt, the Work of Mourning, and the New International*, trans. Peggy Kamuf (New York: Routledge, 1993), 13.

Southern Cone during the dictatorships of the 1970s and 1980s transform Cano's novel into a good example of transnational memory, which alludes to those people who, according to Argentinian law 24.321, are neither alive nor dead: "Isn't it beautiful to be alive? But you're not alive exactly, you're dead and awake. It's not the same thing" (*Twist*, 33). A novel, in sum, in which:

> rewriting acquires special importance not just because of the question of plagiarism or recreation, but also because Lazkano will be entrusted with adapting the translation of Chekhov's work *Platonov*, which in a metafictional way deals with subjects addressed in *Twist* and whose text is clearly and extensively set out towards the end of the novel.[51]

Furthermore, we could state that Cano's novel reflects on the capacity of literature to narrate the horror. "Can on sublimate torture through art? Can one overcome terror through art?" (*Twist*, 375), are the questions that the narrator of the work asks. The answer, at the end of the novel: while literature may not seem to do so sufficiently, writing can cure and redeem us (*Twist*, 493).

Silences

It was in 2007 when, in an act held before three hundred victims of ETA, the *lehendakari* (Basque president) Juan José Ibarretxe apologized "for the silence of Basque society."[52] This was a silence that had already been broken by public manifestos, like that titled "of the 33" in May 1980,[53] or by that of "Isiltasuna ez da aterpe" (Silence is no refuge), which 140 of us from the world of Basque culture in the Basque language signed on September 21, 2000. This was social condemnation of too many years of brutality, a

---

51. Mikel Ayerbe, "Work in conflict: (Meta)literatura y escritura en novelas que abordan el conflict vasco," in *Eridenen du zerzaz kontenta: Sailkideen omenaldia Henrike Knörr Irakasleari (1947–2008)*, ed. María José Ezeizabarrena and Ricardo Gomez (Bilbao: Universidad del País Vasco-Euskal Herriko Unibertsitatea, 2015), 108.
52. Isabel C. Martínez. "Ibarretxe pide perdón ante 300 víctimas de ETA por el silencio de la sociedad vasca." El País April 23, 2007, http://elpais.com/diario/2007/04/23/espana/1177279204_850215.html (Accessed May 9, 2017).
53. Antonio González, "Treinta y tres personalidades vascas vinculadas a la cultura contra la violencia de ETA" (1980), at http://elpais.com/diario/1980/05/28/espana/328312806_850215.html.

condemnation with which a considerable number of Basque-language writers were involved.

It was also the condemnation of silence on the part of Basque society during years of the conflict that inspired the book of short stories *Bizia lo* (2003, *Letargo*) by Jokin Muñoz. Here, the Navarrese author describes in the five short stories that make up the volume a Basque society in which ETA violence and the political conflict are present from childhood, even in everyday children's games (see the short story titled "Xantilli"). Other short stories, like "Isiluneak" (Silences), describe the tense situation of some parents waiting to hear news of the death of their son on handling a bomb. Thanks to the alternation of the narrative focus from one parent to another, we can overcome the silence that paralyzes both protagonists, anxiously awaiting a telephone call or some TV news images to confirm their fears. Meanwhile, another Basque author recognized for his long career as a short storyteller, Iban Zaldua, has also repeatedly addressed the topic of the conflict in books like *Gezurrak, gezurrak, gezurrak* (2000, *Mentiras, Mentiras, Mentiras*) and *Traizioak* (2001, *Traiciones*). Using a direct, ironic style that favors metaliterary games, Borges-style, or fantasy embedded in everyday life à la Cortázar, Zaldua has managed to suggest a reflection on the contradictions and dramas during years of living with the conflict. A good example of what I am talking about is to be found in the short story *Bibliografia*, in which the aloof objective narration of the itinerary of a book reaches its pivotal moment when referring to the victim of a terrorist attack, Alicia Fernández de Larrea, the librarian who registered the book. Even accepting that reality and art can bring together interpretations made from opposing ideological positions like those of the characters in the short story (the alleged terrorist, the police officer, the prisoner, the prison officer, and so on, all of them referred to in codes, initials, or first names), what cannot be interpreted is the tragedy of the death of innocent victims.

Gender Politics

In the above lines I have commented on the themes and narrative strategies used by contemporary Basque writers who have represented the conflict in the Basque language. I would like to ask myself now about the similarities and/or differences that may exist, both thematically and formally, between men and women writers. For example, in their novels do women writers demonstrate their wish to take on the role of writers about the conflict by means of metafictional structures? Is the recovery of historical memory as evident in the narrative of women writers? It is true that narratives on the Basque conflict written by women do not fictionalize their protagonists as "writers" about the conflict, but instead include characters who maintain an epistolary relationship with a textual receiver that does not transcend the private intimate sphere, the nucleus of friendships, or the family of the protagonist. Put another way, men's novels demonstrate fictional structures that would denote the active role that the Basque male writer seeks to have in the face of the conflict, while women's narratives narrate the Basque conflict from structures approximating different autobiographical styles. In effect, the latest novels written by women about our recent historical memory are mediated through homodiegetic or autodiegetic narrators, as in the novels *Aulki jokoa* (Game of chairs, 2009) by Uxue Alberdi, *Hobe isilik* (Better quiet, 2013) by Garbiñe Ubeda, and *Txartel bat (des)herrira* (A ticket to exile, 2013) by Garazi Goia. All of them tell stories set in the Spanish Civil War or in the postwar era, exploring aspects such as the sexualization of the repression on the part of the National side (the Francoists) and misogynist stereotypes, paternity conflicts, the exile of thousands of children during the war and their alienation on British soil, and so on. Meanwhile, novels like *Nerea eta biok* (1994; *Nerea and I*, 2005) by Laura Mintegi and *Koaderno Gorria* (1998; *The Red Notebook*, 2008) by Arantxa Urretabizkaia make use of the epistolary genre to narrate stories about the conflict. The former recounts the four-year epistolary relationship between Isabel, a university professor, and Nerea, an ETA prisoner in a Paris prison.[54] Themes like political commitment, lesbian relationships, maternity, and so on are tackled in these letters that allow Isabel to get to know herself and discover complications and affections that she did not realize existed between women. But moreover, as Linda White points out in the prologue to the English-language version of the novel, the story reflects on the limitations and censures that women face in Basque society.[55] In sum, one could say that the novel points

---

54. Olaziregi and Ayerbe, "El conflicto de la escritura y la rescritura de la identidad," 56–57.

55. Linda White, "Introduction," in Laura Mintegi, *Nerea and I*, trans. Linda White (Berlin: Peter Lang, 2005), 82.

toward a political commitment that flees patriarchal heteronormative stereotypes and that, moreover, allows female complicities into a world, that of ETA, whose military structure has prioritized the masculinizing ethic and in which traditionally, "men are the gudariak (warriors) and initiators of the radical discourse, women are the strong and supportive wives and mothers."[56] As Carrie Hamilton demonstrates,[57] it was not just ETA's own development that influenced that role assignment, but also the images that were repeatedly shown in the media; images of mothers and widows of ETA members and their victims that idealized the strength of these women in the face of suffering; images, in short, of their maternal sacrifice.[58]

María Dolores González Catarain, *Yoyes*, was one of the few women who managed to reach a leadership position in ETA. Her leaving the group, exile, and later return to the Basque Country was unacceptable for ETA and she was assassinated on September 10, 1986, in front of her three-year-old son. The abundance of critical studies that have analyzed and interpreted her life,[59] as well as different narratives, both written and film, which have been inspired by her (such as Helena Taberna's movie *Yoyes* and Atxaga's *The Lone Woman*) show just how important she was. One could also say that *The Red Notebook* by Arantxa Urretabizkaia, insofar as it explores the relationship between motherhood and political activism, was inspired by the life of Yoyes. Set out on two narrative levels, the first of these includes the extensive letter that the protagonist, the Mother, sends to her children, from whom she has heard nothing since, seven years previously, their father fled with them to Venezuela. This letter is written in a red notebook, a detail that conditions the paratext of the novel. The second narrative

---

56. Cameron Watson, "The Tragedy of Yoyes," in Amatxi, Amuma, Amona: Writings in Honor of Basque Women, ed. Linda White and Cameron Watson (Reno: Center for Basque Studies, University of Nevada, Reno, 2003), 151.
57. Carrie Hamilton, *Women and ETA: The Gender Politics of Radical Basque Nationalism* (Manchester: Manchester University Press, 2007), chap. 4.
58. Ibid., 102.
59. For example, Begoña Aretxaga, "The Death of Yoyes: Cultural Discourses of Gender and Politics in the Basque Country," *Critical Matrix: The Princeton Journal of Women, Gender, and Culture* 1 (1988), 1–10; Watson, "The Tragedy of Yoyes"; Joseba Zulaika, *ETAren hautsa* (Irun: Alberdania, 2006); Cristina Ortiz Ceberio, "Paradigmas éticos-políticos en los diarios Yoyes desde su ventana," in *Imágenes de la memoria*, ed. Rodríguez.

level narrates the journey of the woman lawyer "L" to Venezuela, where she must hand over the notebook to the children. In a very intense lyrical prose, then, Urretabizkaia suggests a reflection on motherhood and commitment, a critique, through the voice of that mother whose children were kidnapped, of role stereotyping at the heart of radical Basque nationalism. Being a mother and an activist were incompatible for Yoyes, and as Begoña Aretxaga sees it, the fact that Yoyes opted for motherhood is key to understanding her assassination: "A mother by definition cannot be a hero or traitor in the cultural context of radical nationalism; she is beyond these categories. Yoyes collapsed gender differentiations at a moment when ETA (m) needed them more than ever."[60] Subverting the symbolic order of the organization meant, for Yoyes, accepting her wish to be a mother, to escape the "male-activist" role that the organization had assigned her: "I do not want to become the woman who, because men consider in some way 'macho', is accepted,"[61] she wrote in her diary.

Likewise, some short stories written by women also use the epistolary genre to mediate the plot. On could cite, for example, short stories like "Gehienez bost hilabete" (Five months at most, 2005) by Arantxa Iturbe or "Politika Albisteak" (Political news, 2004) by Eider Rodriguez, a short story that also includes a reflection on motherhood and commitment. Here, the epistolary relationship is narrated between her alienated protagonist, Idoia, and her ex-boyfriend, an ETA member. Idoia feels that time is passing her by, that she is literally decaying from within, and that the function for which she was raised, namely that of producing "offspring that may give continuity to the struggle" (sic), will not be fulfilled. This is a short story that, in sum, describes like few others the claustrophobia and decadence of a political reality whose most invisible and silent dimension is to be found on the domestic terrain of the women who inhabit it, women that no longer produce life or dreams, but who are trapped in a role (that of self-sacrificing mothers and girlfriends) and in a language (in the media, military language) whose phallocentrism and patriarchalism end up crushing them.

---

60. Aretxaga, "The Death of Yoyes," 8.
61. Quoted by Ortiz Ceberio, "Paradigmas éticos-políticos en los diarios Yoyes desde su ventana," 148.

By Way of Conclusion

As a quick conclusion, I would say that Basque men and women writers first embarked on narrating and representing the most dramatic and globally known political conflict in the Basque setting, namely, the terrorism of ETA, some time ago. Transformed into a narrator who narrates and reflects on that troubled reality, the desire and obligation to relate/understand what has taken place determines the reflexive metafictional tone of texts that seek an ethical and moral debate around questions such as legitimacy, justice, and blame. But what is more, the interpretation offered here from the prism of gender, an interpretation that has revealed disparate narrative subjects and forms into order to shape this debate, will have to discern whether the dynamics of memory that are being produced in our narrative will perpetuate or not the role divisions on which the patriarchal logic is based.

Bibliography

Apaolaza, Uxue (2011). *Mea Culpa*. Donostia: Elkar, 2011.

Appelbaum, Robert, and Alexis Paknadel. "Terrorism and the Novel, 1970–2001." *Poetics Today* 29, no. 3 (2008): 387–436.

Aretxaga, Begoña. "The Death of Yoyes: Cultural Discourses of Gender and Politics in the Basque Country." *Critical Matrix: The Princeton Journal of Women, Gender, and Culture* 1 (1988): 1–10.

Arrieta, Leyre. "ETA y la espiral de la violencia. Estrategias y víctimas." In *Imágenes de la memoria. Víctimas del dolor y la violencia terrorista*, edited by Pilar Rodríguez. Madrid: Biblioteca Nueva, 2015.

Arroita, Izaro. *Ramon Saizarbitoriaren nobelagintza Memoria Ikasketen ikuspegitik*. PhD Diss, University of the Basque Country, 2015.

Arroita, Izaro, an Lourdes Otaegi, eds. *Oroimenaren lekuak eta lekukoak. Gerra Zibilaren errepresentazio artistikoak vs. Kontaera historiko politikoa*. Bilbao: Universidad del País Vasco-Euskal Herriko Unibertsitatea, 2015.

Atxaga, Bernardo. *Gizona bere bakardadean*. Iruñea: Pamiela, 1993. English: *The Lone Man*. Translated by Margaret Jull Costa. London: Harvill, 1996.

———. *Zeru horiek*. Donostia, Erein, 1995. English: *The Lone Woman*. Translated by Margaret Jull Costa. London: Harvill, 1999.

————. *Soinujolearen semea*. Iruñea: Pamiela, 2003. Spanish: *El hijo del acordeonista*. Tranlasted by Asun Garikano and Bernardo Atxaga. Madrid: Alfaguara, 2004. English: *The Accordionist's Son*. Translated by Margaret Jull Costa. London: Harvill, 2007.

Ayerbe, Mikel, ed. *Our Wars: Short Fiction on Basque Conflicts*. Reno: Center for Basque Studies, University of Nevada, Reno, 2012.

————. "Work in conflict: (Meta)literatura y escritura en novelas que abordan el conflicto vasco." In *Eridenen du zerzaz kontenta: Sailkideen omenaldia Henrike Knörr Irakasleari (1947–2008)*, edited by María José Ezeizabarrena and Ricardo Gomez. Bilbao: Universidad del País Vasco-Euskal Herriko Unibertsitatea, 2015.

Bister, Daniela. *La construcción literaria de la víctima. Guerra Civil y Franquismo en la novela castellana, catalana y vasca*. Frankfurt: Peter Lang, 2015.

Blessington, Francis. "Politics and the Terrorist Novel." *Sewanee Review* 116, no. 1 (2007): 116–24.

Cano, Harkaitz. *Twist*. Zarautz: Susa, 2013. Spanish: *Twist*. Translated by Gerardo Markuleta. Barcelona: Seix Barral, 2013.

Casquete, Jesús. "Abertzale sí, ¿pero quién dijo de izquierdas?" *El viejo topo* 68 (2010): 15–19.

————. "Gudari Eguna." In *Diccionario ilustrado de símbolos del nacionalismo vasco*, coordinated by Santiago de Pablo et al. Madrid: Tecnos, 2013.

De Pablo, Santiago. *The Basque Nation On-Screen: Cinema, Nationalism, and Political Violence*. Reno: Center for Basque Studies, University of Nevada, Reno, 2012.

Delgado, Luisa Elena. *La Nación Singular. Fantasías de la normalidad democrática española (1996–2011)*. Madrid: Siglo XXI, 2014.

Derrida, Jacques. *Specters of Marx: The State of the Debt, the Work of Mourning, and the New International*. Translated by Peggy Kamuf. New York: Routledge, 1994.

Ibon Egaña and Edu Zelaieta. *Maldetan sagarrak. Euskal gatazka euskal literaturan*. Iruñea: Udako Euskal Unibertsitatea, 2006.

Erll, Astrid. *Memory in Culture*. New York: Palgrave Macmillan, 2001.

Fernandez, Joxean. "Razones y contextos de cuatro polémicas en el cine documetal vasco". In "Basque Studies Monograph," edited by Mari Jose Olaziregi and Juan Arana Cobos, special issue, *Bulletin of Hispanic Studies* 93, no. 10 (2016): 1081–1102.

Fernández Soldevilla, Gaizka. "El nacionalismo vasco radical ante la transición española." *Historia contemporánea* 35 (2007): 817–44.

Ferrán, Ofelia. *Working Thorough Memory: Writing and Remembrance in Contemporary Spanish Narrative.* Lewisburg, PA: Bucknell University Press, 2007.

Goia, Garazi. *Txartel bat (des)herrira.* Donostia: Elkar, 2013.

Gonzalez, Antonio. "Treinta y tres personalidades vascas vinculadas a la cultura contra la violencia de ETA" (1980), at http://elpais.com/diario/1980/05/28/espana/328312806_850215.html.

Halbwachs, Maurice. *On Collective Memory.* Edited, translated, and with an introduction by Lewis A. Coser. Chicago: University of Chicago Press, 1992.

Hamilton, Carrie. *Women and ETA: The Gender Politics of Radical Basque Nationalism.* Manchester: Manchester University Press, 2007.

Huyssen, Andreas. *Present Pasts: Urban Palimpsests and the Politics of Memory.* Stanford: Stanford University Press, 2003.

Iturbe, Arantxa. "Gehienez bost hilabete." In *Adiskide maitea.* Tafalla: Txalaparta, 2005.

Kortzar, Jon, ed. "La Guerra Civil en la literatura vasca," special issue, *Cuadernos de Alzate* 45 (2011).

Kortazar, Jon, and Amaia Serrano, eds. *Gatazken lorratzak. Euskal arazoen islak narratiban 1936tik gaurdaino.* Donostia: Utriusque Vasconiae, 2012.

Kundera, Milan. *El arte de la novella.* Barcelona: Tusquets, 1987.

Labanyi, Jo. "The Politics of Memory in Contemporary Spain", *Journal of Spanish Cultural Studies* 9, no. 2 (2008): 119–25.

Lasagabaster, Jesús María. ed. *Contemporary Basque Fiction: An Anthology.* Translated by Michael E. Morris. Reno: University of Nevada Press, 1990.

Leerssen, Joep. "Monument and Trauma: varieties of remembering." In *History and Memory in Modern Ireland*, edited by Ian McBride. Cambridge: Cambridge University Press, 2001.

Lertxundi, Anjel. *Hamaseigarrenean aidanez.* Donostia: Erein, 1983.

———. *Zorion perfektua.* Irun: Alberdania, 2002. English: *Perfect Happiness.* Translated by Amaia Gabantxo. Reno: Center for Basque Studies, University of Nevada, Reno, 2007.

————. *Etxeko Hautsa.* Irun: Alberdania, 2011. Spanish: *Los trapos sucios.* Translated by Jorge Gimenez. Irun: Alberdania, 2012.

Levy, Daniel, and Natan Sznaider. "Memory Unbound: The Holocaust and the Formation of Cosmopolitan Memory." *European Journal of Social Theory* 5, no. 1 (2002): 87–106.

Mintegi, Laura. *Nerea eta biok.* Zarautz: Susa, 1994. English: *Nerea and I*, translated by Linda White. New York: Peter Lang, 2005.

Müller, Jan-Werner, ed. *Memory and Power in Post-War Europe: Studies in the Presence of the Past.* Cambridge: Cambridge University Press, 2002.

Muñoz, Jokin. *Bizia lo.* Irun: Alberdania, 2003. Spanish: *Letargo*, translated by Jorge Giménez. Irun: Alberdania, 2005.

————. *Antzararen bidea.* Irun: Alberdania. Spanish: *El camino de la Oca*, translated by Jorge Giménez. Irun: Alberdania, 2007.

Nora, Pierre. *Realms of Memory: Rethinking the French Past*, vol. 1, *Conflicts and Divisions*, edited and with a foreword by Lawrence D. Kritzman. Translated by Arthur Goldhammer. New York: Columbia University Press, 1997.

Olaziregi, Mari Jose. "Basque Narrative about the Spanish Civil War and Its Contribution to the Deconstruction of Collective Political Memory." In *War, Exile, Justice and Everyday Life, 1936–1946*, edited by Sandra Ott. Reno: Center for Basque Studies, University of Nevada, Reno, 2011.

————. "Los lugares de la memoria en la narrativa de Bernardo Atxaga." In *Bernardo Atxaga*, edited by Irene Andrés-Suárez and Antonio Rivas. Madrid: Universidad de Neuchâtel-Arcolibros, 2011.

————. "Cartografía de la memoria en la literatura vasca actual." In *Conflictos de la Memoria/ Memoria de los conflictos. Modelos narrativos de la memoria intergeneracional en España e Italia*, edited by Leonardo Cecchini and Hans Lauge Lansen. Collection Études Romanes 62. Copenhaghen: Museum Tusculanum Press, University of Copenhagen, 2015.

Olaziregi, Mari Jose, and Mikel Ayerbe. "El conflicto de la escritura y la rescritura de la identidad: análisis de la narrativa de escritoras vascas que abordan el conflicto vasco." In *Identidad, género y nuevas subjetividades en las literaturas hispánicas*, edited by Katarzyna Moszczynska-Dúrst, Karolina Kumor, Ana Garrido Gonzalez, and Aranzazu Calderon Puerta (Warsaw: Instituto de Estudios Ibéricos de la Universidad de Varsovia, 2016).

Ortiz Ceberio, Cristina. "Paradigmas éticos-políticos en los diarios Yoyes desde su ventana." In *Imágenes de la memoria. Víctimas del dolor y la violencia terrorista*, edited by Pilar Rodríguez. Madrid: Biblioteca Nueva, 2015.

Portela, Edurne. *El eco de los disparos*. Barcelona: Galaxia Gutemberg, 2016.

Provata-Carlone, Mike (2016). "A loftier reality" (2016), at http://bookanista.com/loftier (Accessed April 29, 2017).

Ramírez de la Piscina, Txema, Imanol Murua Uria, and Patxo Idoiaga Arrospide. "Prensa y conflicto vasco (1975–2016): Recopilatorio de actitudes y vicisitudes." *Revista Latina de Comunicación Social* 71 (2016): 1007–1035. At http://www.revistalatinacs.org/071/paper/1132/52es.html DOI: 10.4185/RLCS-2016-1132.

Rodriguez, Eider. "Politika albisteak." In *Eta handik gutxira gaur*. Zarautz: Susa, 2004. English: "Politics Today." In *Our Wars: Short Fiction on Basque Conflicts*, edited by Mikel Ayerbe Sudupe. Center for Basque Studies, University of Nevada, Reno, 2012.

Rodríguez, Pilar, ed. *Imágenes de la memoria. Víctimas del dolor y la violencia terrorista*. Madrid: Biblioteca Nueva, 2015.

Roldán, Carlos. "Imágenes de odio, sangre y muerte: las víctimas de la violencia política ante las cámaras de los cineastas vascos." In *Imágenes de la memoria. Víctimas del dolor y la violencia terrorista*, edited by Pilar Rodríguez. Madrid: Biblioteca Nueva, 2015.

Roseman, Sharon. "Celebrating Silenced Words: The 'Reimagining' of a Feminist Nation in Late-Twentieth Century Galicia." *Feminist Studies* 23, no.1 (1997): 43–71.

Saizarbitoria, Ramon. *Ehun metro*. Donostia: Kriselu, 1976. English: *100 meter*. Translated by Gloria Castresana. Reno: Basque American Foundation, 1985.

———. *Hamaika pauso*. Donostia: Erein, 1995. Spanish: *Los pasos incontables*, translated by Jon Juaristi. Madrid: Espasa Calpe, 1996.

———. *Gorde nazazu lurpean*. Donostia: Erein, 2000. Spanish: *Guárdame bajo tierra*. Translated by the Fundación Eguia Careaga. Madrid: Alfaguara, 2002.

———. *Martutene*. Donostia: Erein, 2013. English: *Martutene*, translated by Aritz Branton. Madrid: Hispabooks, 2016.

Soto, Mikel. *Haginetako mina*. Tafalla: Txaparta, 2008.

Ubed, Garbiñe. *Hobe isilik*. Donostia: Elkar, 2013.

Urla, Jacqueline. "Total Quality Language Revival." In *Language in Late Capitalism: Pride and Profit*, edited by Alexandre Duchene and Monica Heller. London and New York: Routledge, 2012.

Urretabizkaia, Arantxa. *Koaderno gorria*. Donostia: Erein, 1998. English: *The Red Notebook*, translated by Kristin Addis. Reno: Center for Basque Studies, University of Nevada, Reno, 2008.

Watson, Cameron. "The Tragedy of Yoyes." In *Amatxi, Amuma, Amona: Writings in Honor of Basque Women*, edited by Linda White and Cameron Watson. Reno: Center for Basque Studies-University of Nevada, Reno, 2003.

White, Linda. "Introduction." In Laura Mintegi, Nerea and I. Translated by Linda White. Berlin: Peter Lang, 2005.

Žižek, Slavoj. *Sobre la violencia. Seis reflexiones marginales.* Barcelona: Paidós, 2009. English: *Violence: Six Sideways Reflections*. London: Profile, 2008.

Zaldua, Iban. *Gezurrak, gezurrak, gezurrak*. Donostia: Erein, 2000. Spanish: *Mentiras, mentiras, mentiras*. Madrid: Lengua de Trapo, 2005.

———. *Traizioak*. Donostia: Erein, 2001.

———. *Ese idioma raro y poderoso*. Madrid: Lengua de Trapo, 2012. English: *This Strange and Powerful Language*. Translated by Mariann Vaczi. Center for Basque Studies, University of Nevada, Reno, 2016.

Zulaika, Joseba. *ETAren hautsa*. Irun: Alberdania, 2006. Spanish: *Polvo de ETA*, translated by Gerardo Markuleta. Irun: Alberdania, 2007.

Zulaika, Joseba, and William A. Douglass. *Terror and Taboo: the Follies, Fables, and Faces of Terrorism*. New York: Routledge, 1996.

13

The Growth of the International Legacy of Lehendakari Jose A. Agirre's Government through Academic Cooperation

Andrea Bartoli and Borislava Manojlovic

The Lehendakari Jose A. Agirre wrote in his diary of his arrival in New York on November 6, 1941 and his teaching at Columbia University in the middle of World War II. In February 1942, a few months after his arrival, he started teaching. Through his courses, Agirre was able to present to the students the riches of a complex political itinerary that led to the defeat of the republican forces in the Spanish Civil War and the beginning of a long journey of resistance and recovery that would lead many years later to the current scenario that sees the Basque Country with a new lehendakari democratically elected after a series of very decisive steps.

The title of this symposium *1936-2016. The International Legacy of Lehendakari Jose A. Agirre's Government* seems to imply that there is indeed some sort of continuity between the experiences of 1936 and the current patterns eighty years later. This chapter argues that the connection between the experience of Lehendakari Agirre and today's developments in the Basque Country lays in the value system that generated his political claims in the first place and inspires the experimental approaches of the Agirre Lehendakaria Center for Social and Political Studies (ALC).

The ALC center was the product of a dedicated, collaborative investment of cultural, political, and economic actors interested in the generativity of the Basque case. Juan José Ibarretxe Markuartu had written the study titled *The Basque Case: A Comprehensive Model for Sustainable Human Development* published in 2012. It is clear in this text that shared values played a critical role in the successful transformation of the Basque Country after the end of the

Franco regime (Ibarretxe 2015). In many respects, the understanding of the Basque case can only start from the references to the way Agirre and the Basque people at large handled the transition after 1936: culturally and politically. While the violent repression forced Agirre and many others into exile and the population was forced to assimilate even more into a Spain to be termed *una, grande y libre* (one, great, and free), they simply continued to be Basque, to resist the assimilation through a series of small daily acts of resistance like speaking and teaching Basque but also through bold cultural statements such as Picasso's painting *Guernica* (Kopper 2014). A painting is a painting, right? And yet that particular painting linked an experience of the past with the longing of the future not only for the Basques but for humanity itself. The painting found its home in the United Nations headquarters in New York, which ensured a continual connection between this city and the Basque Country.

The past, both in the case of the bombing of Gernika and the Agirre government, is actually always open to reinterpretation, to an understanding that defies the contours of previously established meaning. It can be argued that the artistic response to the aerial bombing by the Germans did not go very far, that its impact was very limited, and that the hard structures of military power actually won the day. The almost daily aerial bombing of cities in Syria is just a reminder of the coercive power of military investments. Yet there is the strength of an understanding shared by many that humans should actually not bomb others and that airplanes would be better used for peaceful purposes rather than killing and destroying.

So if the debate over Gernika, its history, and the responses that surrounded it is now relevant in the defining of violent conflicts, the politics of an autonomous entity claiming self-determination has become relevant not only regionally and continentally but worldwide. What is the meaning of an event? Who is attributing this meaning? When is meaning acquired?

The Agirre Lehendakaria Center aims at engaging the world with the Basque Country in new ways, at the nexus of culture and emergent history. It seeks, at the same time, meaning in the past and foresees the unfolding of the future; possible development as anticipated by what has been already accomplished. The ALC does this through an interesting blend of action and research joining universities across the Atlantic and engaging institutional entities around the world that have expressed interest in collaborating (ALC n.d.).

In his book *De Guernica a Nueva York pasando por Berlín*, Agirre notes how Gernika is the cradle of Basque democracy but also how the very existence and language of the Basques are a mystery (Agirre 2004). For him, as for many other Basques, this shared identity requires careful attention, especially through the active defense of freedom. The Bourbons might have interrupted the formal recognition of the *fueros*, the old laws from time immemorial (Jauregui 1986), but the Basques have not forgotten their commitment to liberty and shared dignity.

Agirre aimed at living an authentic life, deeply immersed into the search for values shared in a vibrant cultural context. It is very clear in his texts that he sees himself as a Basque, sees his work as a politician serving the Basques, and expressed his commitments frequently in terms of defending freedom, acquiring freedom, and respecting freedom. There is little doubt that he saw his role as *lehendakari* as a service to the Basque nation and its aspirations. It was not an imperial project. It was not an exploitive project. It was a highly collaborative political project conceived as a way to defend the rights and prerogatives of a people. His service aimed at representing politically the needs, dreams, and aspirations of a people.

In doing his service, Agirre assumed a cultural identity expressed both linguistically (Basques are those who speak Euskera) and ethnically (Basques are the children of Basques). The nation, culturally constructed, precedes the political formation (Anderson 1991). Culture comes before political representation. This insight is important in appreciating today's work of the ALC. On the one hand, there is a recent development that must be presented around the world as a model of sustainability. On the other hand, it is imperative to understand the cultural framework that created the conditions for the recent development in the first place. So the work that is emerging in the ALC is intriguingly iterative. On one hand there is an effort to "export" the successes not in the form of mere replication but rather as a creative process that can identify and encourage emerging scenarios in other areas of the world. From Croatia to South Africa, from Latin America to the United States, the ALC has engaged with a number of partners to seek areas of development (ALC n.d.). What is interesting in these interventions is the claim that self-government is the key to Basque success and that the formal recognition of such structures (perceived by some as limited and limiting) through the Statue of Gernika is essential to understanding this success. Human development is defined by the ALC as "socially committed" and economic progress is defined as "balanced" (the balance coming from its commitment to social and environmental concerns.) So the contours that emerge are of a peculiar relationship between the people (the Basques, those who speak Basque, were born into a Basque family, or live in the Basque Country), the society that they form, and the government. This relationship is defined as culture and precedes the political dimension of government. Values such as a solidarity, transparency, and honesty are conditions that precede the emergence of "good governance." In a blog entry on "Institutional Integrity" posted on the ALC website, Rafael Jiménez Asensio writes: "The ethics of public institutions can hardly be safeguarded with a citizenry that does not also preserve those values" (ALC n.d.). The institutions are as good as the people, as committed as the people, as effective as the people. So the ALC finds itself in a very promising line of work: contributing to the understanding of Basque specificity by discovering its relevance for all. Uniqueness and universality are both inherent to the human condition. Agirre took seriously the challenge of his own time and the ALC is trying to build on that legacy through new interpretations.

One area in which this commitment to uniqueness and universality is particularly telling is language. "The Agirre Lehendakaria Center is developing a new line of work, inside its intervention projects, based on the recovery of minoritized languages in several regions and countries (ALC n.d.). The main goal of this is collaborating with cultural and academic institutions in order to share the Basque experience in the recovery of the Euskera, taking the Basque linguistic promotion plans as a reference. ALC will also work in the future for the recovery of the Quechua language in South America." In 2017, the Agirre Center works in Peru on the Quechua language; in Mexico on the Mixe language; and the Uchinaguchi, Kunigami, and Miyako languages in the Okinawan islands.

This investment in language is remarkable because what is shared is obviously not language per se, but the methodology used to preserve, standardize, and revitalize language through consistent and growing use both in everyday conversations and in the official, institutional arena. Language is the first vehicle of cultural formation, institutional stability, and societal health. There is a strong correlation between language and the emergence of a polity. Language allows for meaning to be expressed, for symbols to be identified, and for procedures to be explained. Language is foundational for the society and allows for the generativity of what is coming, for the connection of the past with the future. Without the capacity to make meaning there is no possibility of social, political, and economic development. All transactions must be performed through an exchange of meaning. As Bernard Lonergan observes that, "all humans move from immediacy to a world mediated by meaning and motivated by values." He continues by saying,

objectivity was the fruit of authentic subjectivity, and authentic subjectivity was the result of raising and answering all relevant questions for intelligence, for reflection, and for deliberation. Insofar as one is inauthentic, there is needed an about-turn, a conversion—indeed, a threefold conversion: an *intellectual conversion* by which without reserves one enters the world mediated by meaning; a *moral conversion* by which one comes to live in a world motivated by values; and a *religious conversion* when one accepts God's gift of his love bestowed through the Holy Spirit. (1980, 31–37)

Our contention is that the Agirre Center comes together as a platform for collective exploration of what it means to be Basque in the twenty-first century and that this exploration is led by Juan José Ibarretxe Markuartu. The way this leadership is expressed is very interesting for an observer—like the authors—who is also a member of the process. First of all, there is no fear of experimenting. The ALC did not exist a few years ago. There was no real model, certainly not in the Basque Country, but even elsewhere it is not easy to find an entity with a similar ambition. The ALC is also a mix of academic, public, and private actors. Interestingly, an informal cap on funding was determined to avoid the hegemony of the "owner": the ALC is truly "owned" by many and has the ambition to be "owned" by the Basque people. In many ways it can be said the ALC is run through a fiduciary relationship with the people of the Basque Country as a whole. While its members come from different political persuasions, the ALC is clearly not an expression of one political party. Rather it is a space in which it has been possible to imagine the Basque Country that is emerging. In this, there is a parallel with the experience of Agirre himself. Agirre experienced firsthand the challenge of representing the interests and aspiration of the Basque people in the context of a very reduced political space. There was no doubt that the Basques existed. The question was: what was the best political representation of the existing community? Agirre's response was twofold: cultural and diplomatic. The first response was cultural in the sense that having lost the strengths of a state, the very identity of the Basques needed to be preserved (and in many ways reaffirmed). Agirre at Columbia University was not only a political exile: he was Basque. He was not interested in progress generically: he was devoted to the cause of the Basques specifically. The representation of the Basques culturally was a first fundamental step in creating the conditions for a possible future reestablishment of more favorable political institutions. The second strategy was diplomatic and required a certain degree of innovation because diplomacy presupposes a state. Agirre used his former role prudently to maintain, strengthen, and nourish relationships outside and inside Spain and the Basque Country that addressed the fundamental issue of self-identification and self-representation. Before posing the question of "determination," there is the need to preserve the contour of what the identity is in the first place. To "explain," to "represent" the interests and needs of the Basques to outside actors, strengthen the identity of the people, and their political trajectory.

Agirre subjectively understood that the political project had to be founded on values and mediated via a culture that would strengthen at the same time the identity of the Basques and their connectivity with the world outside Spain. This is why he became a significant point of reference for many. Probably due in large measure to the leadership of Juan José Ibarretxe Markuartu, the ALC has had the capacity to serve the specific identity as well as to create the connections with the outside world. What is interesting is that the instrument—in the case of the ALC—is academic, cultural, and not political per se. Yet, it is an institution that cannot avoid the very political role of gathering, connecting, supporting, encouraging. The ALC constantly engages Basque interlocutors as well as international ones in an effort to contribute to the emergence of the Basque Country in the twenty-first century through culture and diplomacy. It does so because the last century witnessed the growth of entities able to perform diplomatic functions. From the International Committee of the Red Cross to the Carter Center, from the Community of Sant'Egidio to thousands of NGOs around the world, many have contributed to the evolution of the international system without being the formal representatives of a state. The plasticity of the international system almost requires the diplomatic creativity that Agirre himself had to experiment with in his lifetime. The ALC does not operate outside the democratic institutional setting created after the death of Franco. Rather, it expands its reach making it clear that the achievements of the past will take full effect and will be preserved only if they are fully understood and shared with humanity as a whole.

Bibliography

Agirre, José A. 2004. *De Guernica a Nueva York pasando por Berlín.* Ediciones AKAL.

ALC. n.d. Agirre Lehendakaria Center for Social and Political Studies. Accessed 2017. http://agirrecenter.eus/en/honi-buruz/.

Anderson, Benedict. 1991. *Imagined Communities: Reflections on the Origin and Spread of Nationalism.* London and New York: Verso.

Ibarretxe, Juan José. 2015. *The Basque Case: A Comprehensive Model for Sustainable Human Development.* Colección de Estudios Internacionales.

Jauregui, Gurutz. 1986. "National Identity and Political Violence in the Basque Country." *European Journal of Political Research* 14 (5–6): 587–605.

Kopper, Akos. 2014. "Why Guernica Became a Globally Used Icon of Political Protest? Analysis of Its Visual Rhetoric and Capacity to Link Distinct Events of Protests into a Grand Narrative." *International Journal of Politics, Culture, and Society* 27 (4): 443–57.

Lonergan, Bernard. 1980. "Reality, Myth, Symbol." *Myth, Symbol and Reality.* Alan M. Olson, ed. pp. 31-37. Notre Dame, IN: University of Notre Dame Press.

14

Reflections on a Grandfather I Never Met: How Did I Get To Know You? What Did I Inherit from You?

Amaia Agirre

Three years ago, before the death of my father, Lehendakari Ibarretxe came home to talk to us about the Agirre Lehendakaria Center project. It had been a long time since I had heard someone talk that way about the so-called "Basque case" and my heart skipped a beat. It was not the first time I had listened to those ideas.

Today, I have been asked to talk about a grandfather I never met. It is not going to be easy, as he is one of the most significant political leaders of the twentieth century in the Basque Country, because of his ideas, his charisma, and his *savoir-faire*. So I will do it with the utmost respect.

He died very young, but I have been lucky enough to get to know him through his writings and through the family. In a sense, I feel very fortunate.

As I mentioned earlier, he was admired and appreciated in the Basque Country. This is evident in the names of streets, squares, and bridges and in many sculptures… And not only that. Since my childhood I have seen many different people approach us to tell us stories and anecdotes they had experienced with him. Always with respect and a deep emotion.

In the family, the grandfather was always present as well. His ideas and values have been transmitted to us in a very deep way.

So I have come today to present grandfather Agirre, the first Lehendakari (president) of the Basque government, through seven ideas that sum up his legacy, supported by extracts from his own writings and diaries:

The Importance of the Family

"Teaching. If education is the inescapable duty of the family, teaching is one of the elements of that function. That right came before and is higher than the State. . . . the State is artifice. It depends solely on will, but there is something that does not die, that came beforehand, that remains today and will remain tomorrow, whether the state is that way or any other way, i.e., the natural entities that make up society; and first of all is the family."

Disguised as a Panamanian landowner with fake glasses and a thick mustache (which he had never worn, nor would he ever wear again), hidden in a convent in Brussels, Agirre lived apart from his family. His strategy was to get papers and permits in Berlin, the center of Nazism, to be able to leave Europe.

"From the moment I had a permit to enter Germany in my possession, my optimism grew and I had full confidence in myself." (He had outsmarted the Gestapo). And as I had been separated from my family for a long time, I decided to go and see them. I was going to embark on a new adventure, more dangerous than all the ones I had experienced till then, and I felt a great desire to say goodbye to my wife, my children, my mother, my brothers..."

The Basque Language

The Basque language has always been very important in our family because language helps to shape our personality, our interpersonal relationships, and is part of the way we conceive the world and is an essential component in constructing our identity.

Because of the war, many members of the family went into exile and they narrowly managed to maintain the Basque language. One could say that the generation born in 1971 was the first to become literate in Basque.

Keeping this in mind, other languages, such as French or English, have always been spoken at home, as each brother was literate in a different language. Basque, however, has always occupied a special, privileged place. Everyone knew that it was a treasure that should not be lost.

In this sense Lehendakari Agirre said:

> Thanks to Basque patriotism, the Basque language has resisted the action of centuries and today begins the way to revival. . . .

> Love for our language will show the strength of patriotism and patriotism will definitely push our people to the necessary success of our language. The two loves are complementary. If one of them fails, our people would not be known through the most vigorous and tangible exponent of its strong personality.

Returning to the twentieth century, after the dictatorship, the first Basque government took a great decision, to make a commitment to the Basque language and to the education. With much sacrifice, our native language was again studied and freely spoken. Today, 90 percent of the younger generations know Basque.

The Political Leadership

In addition to being a family man, Agirre was a political leader. As I mentioned before, he was the first Lehendakari of the Basque government.

In his complete works, he says:

> I am a member of the Basque Nationalist Party. The party has as motto comprised of two terms Jaungoikoa and Lege Zaharra (God and The Old Law). Insofar as the first word refers to God, we understand that our party is confessional [or so it was until the Iruña National Assembly in March 1977] and, in this ridiculous right-wing/left-wing phraseology, we have a clearly defined position . . . If "right-wing" means to be opposed to the legitimate progress of democracy against absolute powers, if that is being right-wing, then we are left-wing. If right-wing is understood to be the consubstantiality of religion with any regime and no absolute independence of church and civil powers in their respective areas, then we also are left-wing. And if right-wing is understood to be, in the social order, the opposition to the legitimate progress of the proletariat, even reaching the absolute transformation of the current regime, if that is understood to be right-wing, then we are also left-wing. However, if left means going against the family, against the sacred principles of the Catholic Church, whose standards we profess, then in that phraseology, which I believe to be ridiculous, we are right-wing. I speak to you with sincerity. And now, let us examine the second term, The Old Law. Today, more than ever, at the political level we aspire to full sovereignty of the Basque Country.

Social Consciousness

"I would argue that financial gain is neither fair nor lawful except after every basic need of honest men has been looked after."

In 1935 they submitted a bill in the Madrid Parliament to be implemented across Spain for the creation of a family wage, with wage increases for workers when they married and as they had children. General rules were set out for the creation of the relevant clearing offices. The second part of the bill laid down the general rules for the distribution of profits taking into account worker participation. Obviously the project was rejected. In fact they did not even allow it to be debated.

Many people would say that these proposals were not realistic but he spoke from his own experience, as these initiatives had been implemented in the family business (Chocolates Chobil) with very good results. It should be mentioned that, sixty years later, social wages became a reality in the Basque Country.

Sense of Freedom

Freedom is a word that is constantly repeated in the writings of Lehendakari Agirre; freedom of men and of the peoples of the world. In his traditional Christmas message, the Lehendakari said,

> The Basque people have a centuries-old tradition of freedom and our own political education, which is not just of today. Our tradition will serve as a basis for the march towards the future. We do not need foreign materials of any kind. We have had everything right here at home for centuries. Democracy without demagogy—remember our general meetings. Strong power without dictatorial erring—remember our Government of the Lordship. Social justice, subordinated to the principle of the common good—remember our Ley Foral (constitution). Aristocratic equality of citizens. We want equality in welfare. We do not want it in extreme poverty.

The Sense of History and Country

When death surprised him on March 22, 1960, Lehendakari Agirre was engaged in writing a "History of the Basque Country." He was a scholar of the Basque fuero because he knew that the knowledge of their own history helps people develop a national conscience and also provides the political leader with a perspective on what is happening in the present and a certain degree of future forecast.

Thus he said at the Madrid Parliament:

> "I am loyal to the history of my parents. I defend something that we enjoyed because it was ours and which a cunning betrayal of the monarchy snatched away from us in 1839, against all the charters of our homeland and of humanity."

And further on, he declared in front of the Spanish Parliament:

> "I accept that some may say that they do not want the Charter. I even accept that some may say that for Spain to live, the Basque Country must dies. What I cannot accept is for anyone to say that the Charter in our country was not freedom, was not sovereignty, was not independence, was not homeland, because that is a historical falsehood."

The European Sense

Agirre's European sense is well-known. He took part in the construction of Europe working within Christian Democracy, working together with the well-known "fathers of Europe," the Frenchman Robert Schuman (father of the European Coal and Steel Community), the Italian Gasperi, the Belgian Van Zeeland, and the German Adenauer.

In a speech to the diplomatic corps in Paris in 1949 he advocated:

> "The creation within the European federal organization of a special section that would permanently look after the interests and protection of nationalities without their own state, where they would have direct and permanent representation."

Sixty-seven years later we are still demanding it...

A Deep, Christian Sense of Dialogue and Humor

To properly understand Lehendakari Agirre, we have to take into account his profound sense of Christianity, his sense of dialogue, and his sense of humor; a common trait of the Agirre Zabala family.

Agirre was always accompanied by his deep Catholic faith. For him, Jesus Christ's Sermon on the Mount is the true liberation of man. We can even say that while he was hiding in Berlin, he made a great spiritual and philosophical journey. He went from being a man hailed by the crowds to absolute solitude, depending only on his person. Through his diary, we can see the books he read on his adventure; authors such as Plutarch, Cicero, Mauriac, Blaise Pascal, and many others.

My father always said that his faith along with his sense of humor helped him enormously to manage through that adventure and all the disappointments he suffered throughout his life. As Freud said, "humor is the highest manifestation of the individual's mechanisms of adaptation."

In his book *Escape Via Berlin: Eluding Franco in Hitler's Europe*, he narrates what happened on May 13, 1941 when the Venezuelan Ambassador told him that:

> "The War widow (Grandmother Mari, his wife disguise of Venezuelan widow) arrives tomorrow with your children (my father and my aunt). . . . my eyes rose to thank the good Lord who looks after men..." Dr. Despradel (Ambassador of Venezuela) had lent me a translation of the Sacred Scriptures and the Gospels. It is my daily essential reading."

Lehendakari Agirre was a very passionate man, a humanist, with clearly marked values, ideas and goals (freedom and respect for individuals and peoples, for democracy...). He did not live to see the results. Every Christmas he said "next Christmas we will spend at home" but this did not happen.

He was a man who listened, who tried to reach agreements, because he did not believe in violence. He believed in respect for one's adversaries, for individuals, for their ideas...

Today, in the twenty-first century, if we look at his story, it seems like the story of a man who suffered so much and failed, who watched his people die, exile, and never return and whose great allies turned their backs on him to support the Franco dictatorship.

But I do not see it like that because many of the ideas in which he believed have become a reality today. And in the Basque Country and at the ALC, we continue working on them.

About the Contributors

Amaia Agirre holds a degree from the University of the Basque County and professional certificate in mental health from the Deusto University. In addition, she received research credentials in clinical psychology from the University of the Basque Country. She has wide experience in conflict resolution and is certified by Université René Descartes, the Boutique de Droit de Lyon, the Association for Conflict Resolution in the United States, the Centro de Resolución de Conflictos APSIDE in Madrid and Gernika Gogoratuz. She has directed GEUZ, the University of the Basque Country's conflict resolution studies center. She has also designed conflict resolution and mediation projects at HIZKETAN, Bilbao, and coordinated social projects in the Congregación Salesiana, Bilbao and as a clinical psychologist the University Hospital in Genova, Switzerland. Since 2015, Amaia has combined her work with the Agirre Center with the councillorship of the city government of Getxo, Bizkaia.

Leyre Arrieta Alberdi holds a PhD in Modern History. She is an Associate Professor at the University of Deusto, Bilbao and Donostia-San Sebastián, and has been head of the Communication Department of the faculty of Social and Human Sciences and the University of Deusto Communication degree since 2009. She has lectured in subjects ranging from World History II, Modern History, Modern Social Thought, History of Scientific and Philosophical Thought, Today's World and Interpretative Frameworks for Today's World to Challenges and Dilemmas of Society Today

I. She has worked on individual and team research projects involving areas such as Basque nationalism, exile and integration within Europe, as well as the history of Basque nationalist radio. Her most noteworthy publications are: *Radio Euskadi, la voz de la libertad* (1998, with José Antonio Rodríguez Ranz), *Diputación y Modernización: Gipuzkoa 1940–1975* (2003, with Miren Barandiaran Contreras), *Ekinez egina: La política educativa a través de sus textos* (2005), *Estación Europa: La política europeísta del PNV en el exilio (1945–1977)* (2007), *La historia de Radio Euskadi (Guerra, Resistencia, Exilio, Democracia)* (2009), *Fondo Gobierno de Euzkadi: Historia y contenido* (2011) and, with others, *Diccionario ilustrado de símbolos del nacionalismo vasco* (2012).

Miren Arzalluz read History (BA) at the University of Deusto and Comparative Politics (MSc) at the London School of Economics before specializing in the history of dress and fashion at the Courtauld Institute of Art (MA). She has been curator and head of collections at the Cristóbal Balenciaga Foundation between 2007 and 2013. In 2011 she published her book Cristóbal Balenciaga. The making of a Master (1895-1936) (V&A Publications), and she continues her research on 20th century fashion as a PhD candidate at the University of Deusto. She is currently director at the Etxepare Basque Institute.

Andrea Bartoli is the Dean of the School of Diplomacy and International Relations at Seton Hall University. He works primarily on peacemaking and genocide prevention. Dr. Bartoli has been involved in many conflict resolution activities as a member of the Community of Sant'Egidio. Among his publications is *Negotiating Peace: The Role of Non-Governmental Organizations* (2013); he co-edited *Peacemaking: From Practice to Theory* (2011) and is one of the authors of *Attracted to Conflict* (2013). He lives in New York City.

Julián Casanova is Professor of Contemporary History at the University of Zaragoza and Visiting Professsor at the Central European University of Budapest. His publications include *La historia social y los historiadores* (1991); *Anarchism, the Republic and Civil War in Spain: 1931–1939* (2005); *La Iglesia de Franco* (2001, 2005); *The Spanish Republic and Civil War* (2010); *A Short History of the Spanish Civil War* (2012); *Europa contra Europa, 1914–1945* (2011); and, with Carlos Gil Andrés, *Twentieth Century Spain: A History* (2012). His most recent book is *La venganza de los siervos. Russia 1917* (2017). Professor Casanova has been Visiting

Professor in several universities in England, the United States, and South America, among them Queen Mary College (London), Harvard University, University of Notre Dame, New School for Social Research (New York), and FLACSO (Quito). He is member of the Editorial Committe of the journal *Historia Social* and member of the Advisory Board of *The International Journal of Iberian Studies* and *Cuadernos de Historia de España*.

Xabier Irujo is the director of the Center for Basque Studies at the University of Nevada, Reno, where he is professor of genocide studies. The author was the first guest research scholar of the Manuel Irujo Chair at the University of Liverpool and regularly teaches courses on genocide and cultural genocide at Boise State University and the University of California, Santa Barbara. He holds three master's degrees in linguistics, history and philosophy, has two PhDs in history and philosophy. Irujo has lectured in various American and European universities and has mentored several graduate students. Member of the editorial board of four academic presses, Irujo has authored more than ten books and a number of articles in specialized journals and has received awards and distinctions at national and international level. His recent books include *Gernika 1937: The Market Day Massacre* (Nevada University Press, 2015) and *Legal History of the Basque Language* (HAEE, Bilbao, 2015).

Borislava Manojlovic is the Director of Research and Adjunct Professor at the School of Diplomacy and International Relations, Seton Hall University. She is an expert in conflict analysis and resolution, atrocities prevention, dealing with the past and education in post-conflict settings. She worked on minorities and reconciliation related issues with the United Nations and the Organization for Security and Cooperation in Europe in both Croatia and Kosovo for more than seven years. As the Director of Research, she led and implemented numerous research projects that focus on peacebuilding, education, governance and gender. Her most recent book *Education for Sustainable Peace and Conflict Resilient Communities* was published in 2017.

Ludger Mees performed undergraduate studies of History and Social Sciences at the Universities of Münster and Bielefeld (Germany); PhD in History at the University of Bielefeld (1988); 1989-91: Assistant Professor at the University of Bielefeld; since 1991 Professor for Contemporary History at the University of the Basque

Country (Bilbao, Spain); since 2004: full professor (catedrático); between 2004 and 2009 Vice-Chancellor of the University of the Basque Country. Author, co-author or editor of 15 books and about 80 articles and book chapters dealing with topics like nationalism, social movements, historiography and agrarian history.

Ingo Niebel is a historian and freelance journalist living and working in Germany. He received his PhD on the Basque Government during the Spanish Civil War (1936–1937) from the University of Cologne (Germany) in 2012. Since 1996, he is a member of Eusko Ikaskuntza, the Society of Basque Studies. He has published several books and articles in German and Spanish about the Basque Country, its past and present. He is finishing now his research on the Basque president Agirre's escape through the German Reich. Intelligence, including historical cryptology and specially the German secret services and police system, are another of his fields of investigation. Currently he is researching the life of Kurt Lischka, the third man of the SS and Sipo/SD hierarchy in occupied France (1940–1943) and who in 1980 was sentenced to jail for being responsible of the mass deportation of Jews from France to the German extermination camps in Eastern Europe.

Mari Jose Olaziregi holds a PhD in Basque literature. She is an Associate Professor at the University of the Basque Country (Vitoria-Gasteiz, Spain), and between 2007- 2009 she was an Assistant Professor at the Center for Basque Studies (University of Nevada, Reno). She been Guest Professor at the University of Konstanz, Germany (2010), the Bernardo Atxaga Chair at the Graduate Center of the City University of New York (2014-2015) and the Koldo Mitxelena Visiting Professor at the University of Chicago (2016). She holds a MA on the Promotion of Reading Habits from the Ramon Llull University (Barcelona), and a MA in Studies in Fiction at the University of East Anglia (UK). She specializes in Contemporary Basque and Iberian literature, Memory Studies, and Gender Studies. Olaziregi is the author of seven books on Basque literature, 60 book-chapters, 10 edited books, and 70 articles in international journals. Among them, *Euskal eleberriaren historia* (History of the Basque Novel, 2001), *Writers in Between Languages: Minority Literatures in the Global Scene* (2009), and *Basque Literary History* (2012). Dr. Olaziregi is a correspondent member of the Royal Academy of the Basque Language, Euskaltzaindia, and between 2010 and 2016 the Director for the Promotion and

Diffusion of the Basque Language at the Etxepare Basque Institute (Basque Government). Since 2013, she coordinates the "Historical Memory in the Iberian Literatures" Consolidated Research Group at the University of the Basque Country.

Hilari Raguer i Suñer was born in Madrid 1928. He got a Master's degree in law in Barcelona in 1950 and a degree in political science and in social psychology in Paris in 1962. He got his PhD in Barcelona in 1975 with a thesis on the Catalan Christian Democratic Party and the Civil War. He is specialized in the Catholic Church during the Spanish civil war. He has authored many articles in specialized journals and several books, among them *The Gunpowder and Incense: The Church and the Civil War*, 1936–1939 (2001; 2nd revised edition, 2008; English edition, 2007).

Nicholas Rankin grew up in Kenya, was educated in England, and worked for BBC World Service radio for 20 years. He is the author of *Telegram from Guernica* (2003)/*Crónica desde Guernica* (2006), the biography of G. L. Steer, who wrote the classic history of the Basques in the Spanish civil war, *The Tree of Gernika*. His other books for Faber are *Dead Man's Chest, Churchill's Wizards,* and *Ian Fleming's Commandos*, translated into Spanish, Arabic and Polish respectively. He has just completed a new book, *Defending the Rock: How Gibraltar Defeated Hitler*, and is planning to write about the Basque contribution to the Second World War.

Joan Villarroya Font holds a PhD in History from the University of Barcelona. His thesis was "Violència y represión en la retaguardia catalana (1936–1939)" (1988). He is a full professor (Catedrático) in Modern History at the UB, he currently teaches undergraduate and graduate courses in Modern and Modern World History. His most recent research project has been an analysis of the Civil War in Catalonia, published in atlas form, *Atles de la Guerra Civil espanyola*. He is the author of numerous articles published in national and international journals and has also been the author and editor of various books, especially regarding the Civil War in Catalonia and Valencia.

Angel Viñas is a Spanish economist, historian and diplomat, known for his studies on the Spanish Civil War and Francoism. Doctor in Economic Sciences, he studied in Madrid, at the University of Hamburg, in the University of Glasgow and the Free University of Berlin, where he witnessed the construction of the Berlin Wall.

From 1971 to 1982 he was professor of applied economics at various universities (Valencia, Alcala de Henares and UNED) and at the Diplomatic Academy of Madrid. In 1982 he was appointed professor of applied economics at the Complutense University. In 1983/1987, he served as executive advisor to the Spanish Ministers of Foreign Affairs Fernando Morán and Francisco Fernandez Ordoñez. In Brussels he was General Director of the European Commission for Asia and Latin America and later on for multilateral relations and security policy and human rights and assistance to democratization. He was also Ambassador of the European Union to the United Nations in NewYork. Author of some thirty books on the Spanish Civil War and the Franco regime, individually or in collaboration. In 2010 he was awarded the Grand Cross of the Civil Merit for his research in the field of history. Currently he is professor emeritus at the Complutense University of Madrid. He was made doctor honoris causa by the University of Alicante in early 2017.

Joseba Zulaika is a researcher at the Center for Basque Studies, University of Nevada, Reno. He received an undergraduate degree in philosophy at the University of Deusto, an M.A. in Social Anthropology at the Memorial University of Newfoundland, Canada, and a Ph.D. in Cultural Anthropology from Princeton University. During the course of his studies, Dr. Zulaika has conducted fieldwork and published ethnographies of deep-sea fishermen, farmers, soldiers, terrorists, hunters, and artists, including *Terranova: The Ethos and Luck of Deep-Sea Fishermen*; *Basque Violence: Metaphor and Sacrament*; *Ehiztariaren erotika*; *Chivos y soldados: La mili como ritual de iniciacion*; *Bertsolariaren jokoa eta jolasa*; *Del Cromañón al Carnaval: Los vascos como museo antropológico*. He has published extensively on terrorism and counterterrorism, including *Terror and Taboo: The Follies, Fables and Faces of Terrorism* (with William Douglass); *Terrorism: The Self-Fulfilling Prophecy*, as well as numerous articles on the culture of violence and terrorism. His latest work has concentrated on the urban and political renewal of the city of Bilbao; among his publications are: *Cronica de una seduccion: El museo Guggenheim Bilbao*; *Guggenheim Bilbao Museoa: Museums, Architecture and City Renewal*; *Learning from the Bilbao Guggenheim* (with Anna Guasch); *That Old Bilbao Moon: The Passion and Resurrection of a City*. He is currently researching drone warfare in the context of Nevada's history.